James Abbott

Prometheus' Daughter

A Poem

James Abbott

Prometheus' Daughter
A Poem

ISBN/EAN: 9783744776196

Printed in Europe, USA, Canada, Australia, Japan

Cover: Foto ©Thomas Meinert / pixelio.de

More available books at **www.hansebooks.com**

PROMETHEUS' DAUGHTER.

A Poem.

BY

COLONEL JAMES ABBOTT,
H. M. BENGAL ARTILLERY,
AUTHOR OF "NARRATIVE OF A JOURNEY FROM HERAUT TO KHIVA."

LONDON:
SMITH, ELDER AND CO., 65, CORNHILL.
M.DCCC.LXI.

TO HER

WHO, FROM THE DAWN OF REASON UNTIL NOW, HAS BEEN

THE MODEL FROM WHICH I HAVE BORROWED EVERY ATTEMPT TO PORTRAY

THE PURITY, DIGNITY, AND TENDER DEVOTION OF

THE FEMALE CHARACTER:

To my Sister

I DEDICATE A WORK

WHICH, IF IT HAVE ANY MERIT, HAS DERIVED IT FROM THOSE IMPRESSIONS

OF

HER EXCELLENCE,

WHICH HAVE FORMED THE CHIEF CHARM OF MY BEING.

CONTENTS.

CANTO		PAGE
Preface	- - - - - - - -	vii
Introduction	- - - - - - -	1
I.—The Exiles	- - - - - - - - -	5
II.—The Minstrel	- - - - - - - -	23
III.—The Pilgrimage	- - - - - - -	53
IV.—The Vigil	- - - - - - - - -	67
V.—The Quest	- - - - - - - - -	93
VI.—The Defiance	- - - - - - -	127
VII.—The Dethroned	- - - - - - -	165
VIII.—The Avenger :—To Pontus	- - - - - -	189
IX.—The Snare	- - - - - - - -	233
X.—The Eve of Battle	- - - - - -	271
XI.—The Succour—Part I.	- - - - - -	295
Part II.	- - - - - -	307
XII.—The Battle—Part I.	- - - - -	329
Part II.	- - - - - -	348
Conclusion	- - - - - - - -	377
Notes	- - - - - - - - -	379

PREFACE.

THE half-fabulous tradition of Prometheus has afforded subject for the drama to the Greek tragedian Æschylus and to the poet Shelley; the poem of the latter being a beautiful completion of the bold outline of the Greek.

No resemblance to either, whether in plot or character, will be found in the following work. But, as the Author has presumed to read differently from those two great names the tradition or allegory of Prometheus, a reason for the deviation may be expected of him.

The sufferings of Prometheus, as narrated by Æschylus, afforded the Greeks their noblest idea of moral sublimity. The spectacle of a mighty being deliberately choosing to suffer the most terrible of tortures for 30,000 years, rather than betray a secret which would confirm the tyranny of Jupiter over Gods and Men, is undoubtedly sublime. But that sublimity is more effectively rendered in a score of words than in a volume. And probably there are few readers of Æschylus, or of Shelley, who will not allow that our sympathy with the great victim would have been greater had his complaints been less. The dignity of silent sorrow is expressed in few words; and the expansion of that single idea into a drama robs it of its greatest power over the heart.

My purpose, however, is not to criticize, but to explain my motives for deviating from the assumption of two great authorities. To the human mind there can be but *one object,*—absolutely good, absolutely great, absolutely glorious. Other beings can be so only by comparison. When, therefore, Prometheus is made better and wiser than the greatest of the Gods; when the existence of that God is made to depend upon the breath of Prometheus' nostrils, we do not so much perceive Prometheus to be elevated as that the Godhead is degraded: for Prometheus is confessedly a finite being.

To sympathize with any being, we must understand his nature so thoroughly as to be able to enter, as it were, into his breast. The human can sympathize with the human—can even descend to sympathize in a less degree with the inferior creation. But when a man is called on to sympathize with a being so incomprehensible as Prometheus—who is, in fact, the Godhead in his beneficent attribute of Divine Providence—he finds it impossible to fit his own nature into the shapeless and boundless mould before him. His reason is shocked to find the higher attributes of God—his love, his mercy, truth, justice, and knowledge—in subjection to attributes which, disjoined from these, take the character of brute force, yet appertain to the so-named King of Gods. The kingship of the latter conflicts with our high estimate of the former; and the subjection of the former desecrates the high pretentions of the latter; and thus the two divine natures cancel one another.

It has always seemed to me that the story of Prometheus was susceptible of its sublimest interpretation by regarding him as a mortal King, impressed with a sense of the misery and moral degradation of his people, resulting from a false and perverted worship; and standing forth, alone and unsupported, against a corrupt and all-powerful priesthood,—whom he challenges to prove their vaunted infallibility in the selection of a victim for sacrifice. They accept the challenge and the test. The result disproves their own asserted infallibility, and with it, the divinity of their Jupiter.

Incensed at this, Jupiter (*i.e.* his Priests) withhold fire from the Earth: religious rites, perhaps. The nation is excommunicated. Prometheus, by the aid of Minerva (Wisdom) climbs the heavens, and conveys to man the Divine Fire (of Truth) from the source of life and light, typified by the Chariot of the Sun. Jupiter (*i.e.* the Priesthood) seize and chain him to a rock of the Caucasus.

Whatever may be the capacity of Angels to appreciate the sufferings of an order of beings higher than Man, it is certain that, to human contemplation, no spectacle can exceed in sublimity that of a mortal king deliberately enduring, for the love of his people, and to rescue them from moral degradation, the utmost torture which human malice could invent. This fills up the measure of our capacity to admire, and rivets all our sympathies.

The Greeks, indeed, being familiar with the superhuman attributes of Prometheus, would ill have endured that he should be lowered to the standard of humanity. But a modern public are under no such restraint, and would (it is believed) give their sympathies more readily to a mortal than to a demigod.

PROMETHEUS' DAUGHTER.

INTRODUCTION.

Know'st thou how Day declines, where mountains rise
To greet with rugged brows his farewell ray?
Know'st thou how Night descends from Alpine skies
O'er Alpine thrones to hold majestic sway?
Know'st thou, how, pausing on their downward way,
Th' ethereal coursers curb their steps of fire,
Champ the bright bit, in lingering, long delay,
And backward gaze with memory's fond desire,
Ere in the golden West their glorious course expire?

Oh! there *be* lands, whose boast is in the dower
Of Nature's lavish and o'erteeming breast,
Lands of the Field, the Orchard, and the Bower,
Of Ceres cherish'd, of Pomona blest:
Where, by the gentle violence opprest
Of the Day's Lord to store and garner, flow
The riches Man first priz'd and first possess'd,
Ere from Earth's bowels wrung those ores did glow,
Fruitful, alas! of crime, dull care, and carking woe!

On fertile plains the Day-star glides away,
And Evening heralds soul-subduing Night:
But here, the rival thrones of Night and Day
Together wage th' intense tho' silent fight:
For while thine eye drinks deep the roseate light
Of some high summit, in the dell below
Darkness hath wing'd her mystery-burden'd flight,
And rules supreme her sombre realm of woe
Down in the deep, deep glen, where cedar forests grow.

And in mid-air a dreamy twilight floats,
Where the twin realms harmonious blend together.
Darkness and Light, with all their mimic motes
In contest soft contending each with other.
And the mock'd eye seeks vainly to discover
Where meet the limits of their neighbour reign,
And on the ear sweet sounds are wafted over
From thickets where in rival notes complain
The birds of Night and Day, of blithe and solemn strain.

Such, when serene the mountain shadows grow
From base to summit. But, when Daylight dies
Mid the loud crash of tempests, would'st thou know
What might majestic their wild rage supplies
To Beauty, form'd alike to harmonize
With Heavens all peace and their chaotic jar?
Then follow me; for even now do rise
Moans on the breeze, betokening from afar
The Powers of Woe abroad, Death and the scythe-arm'd
  Car.

PROMETHEUS' DAUGHTER.

Canto I.

THE EXILES.

"Sweet Mother, haste thee to the lattice. Mark
How whelm'd the East with storm-clouds dense and
  dark.
Still gleams the Sun: his parting glance repay
With smiles, Lake, mead, soft basking in his ray.
The waving oaks that in his glory stood
Sombre and threat'ning as some midnight flood,
Now, as he quits the world he fill'd with light,
Veil all their sternness in the farewell rite,

And take, return the warm, impassion'd hue
Diffus'd o'er Heaven, as glows his last adieu :
Whilst o'er yon Eastern pile of mountains rude
Night pours the terrors of her solitude.

" Long as engag'd in training up the Vine,
And golden jasmine, and fair eglantine,
That shade the sunbeams from my elfin bower,
I've watch'd the gloom increasing, hour by hour ;
And as the hues of amethyst decay
O'er mountains swath'd in ether, far away,
And as the purple of the sunset sky
Declines apace, yon summit looms more nigh ;
And old Traditions heaviest woe portend
From the near frown of snow-clad Demawend."

" Child of my joyless age, my widow'd breast,
Thou young Aurora of Life's dire unrest,
What be the portents of an evening sky
To her, whose sunset gleams in years gone by,
Whose very night, unlighted, save of one
Sweet Star of Hope, so tremulous and lone,

Declines apace, foreshadowing with its gloom
The direr Night and thraldom of the Tomb?
Thou my sweet bosom-flower, sprung up ere yet
The soil empoison'd, or the curse deep set
Of barrenness for all save that which grows
From hopeless prospects and remember'd woes :—
Thou my sweet flower! Oh, yes! to view that form
Of life and light in contrast with the storm
Brooding o'er yonder heights ; to watch thee nigh,
Hope in thy smile, young promise in thine eye ;
Whilst the far realm to which those young hopes tend
Glooms like the wrack o'er snow-girt Demawend ;—
Oh, yes! to this dim eye it still is given
To view, not all unmov'd, the signs of Heaven,
To pray the bolt its vengeance may fulfil
On this scath'd trunk, and leave my flower of Promise,
    still."

" Nay, sweetest Mother, first, best guardian, nay,
Thy fears recall, thy fond vows yet unsay.
If life have trouble in its mingled flow,
The hand that mixed can temper every woe.

For me its cup all blessedness hath been,
Peace, health, and hope, light griefs and hours serene:
A Heaven most kind, o'ershadowing me above,
On Earth, a Mother's arms, a Mother's beauteous love.
On thee the storm hath lour'd: on thy sad path
Unsparing rag'd Affliction's fiery wrath:
But, sweetest Evenings bless the storm-clear'd sky,
And peace gains beauty from each woe gone by,
And those black shadows in thy path attest
How bright on high the sunshine of thy rest."

" Indra, my sweet enthusiast, yet awhile
Beam o'er my soul that pure and guileless smile!
For, basking in its ray, I drown life's care,
And catch Hope's wreck, regurging from despair.
Oh! were all hearts prophetic as thine own
Of such fair promise for the hour to come:
Were not Experience but a name the more
For inward death to sympathies whose lore
Was fram'd for world less perishably fair:
Were Truth less frail and falsehood less sincere,

We yet might drag along Life's carking chain,
Nor curse the future, which brings round again
The record drear of toils without an aim;
The tale of woes whose very sameness cloys,
And thin, dim wrecks of mutilated joys,
A Future, only diverse from the Past,
In that its vista's swallowed up, at last,
By the sheer precipice o'er whose dread brow
Hang gloom and terror and mysterious woe,
The shrieking things abhorr'd of Nature most,
And far beneath that soul-affrighting coast,
To which, unskill'd, we names of gloom bequeath,
As Ades, Léthé, Nullity or Death.

"Death! Ah, that name hath terror in its tone.
What! must the hope which scarce hath buoy'd us on
O'er each most sad vicissitude bygone,
With all its promise unfulfill'd, be o'er
And set in gloom profound, to rise no more?
Drear as Life still hath been and sad as be
Our cold dim prospects of Futurity,

'Twere easier far its countless ills to brave,
Than brook the heart-loath'd mystery of the Grave:
To cease at once from sympathies, inwove
By Sorrow's self all closely with our love,
To go, we know not whither, be, we know
Nor what, nor how; it may be, far below
The meanest thing, that trails its form along
And ends existence with the setting sun:
Piecemeal dispers'd on Earth, air, fire or wind
The frame corporeal and the mystic mind:
Pain to such nullity were simple bliss,
And Life's worst bondage freedom, weigh'd with this.

" But mark, how denser pil'd and nearer grown,
Yon mighty heap of watery gloom rolls on,
Like some dark pall with mournful mystery rife,
To cloak Death's dismal triumph over life.
While still, above each deep'ning shade of gloom,
Which Earth and Heaven's commingling bounds assume,
His brow upheaves th' empyreal vault to rend,
With snows age-crown'd, majestic Demawend.

Low at his feet, where crouching mountains bow
The dwindled form and pride-despoilëd brow,
Low at his base and round his footstool sweep
Floods, like old Ocean's, swelling blue and deep:
But not a wave shall toss its angry spray,
And not a cloud shall climb the upward way,
And scarce a sigh of all the wrathful blast,
In yon black dungeon pent and prison'd fast,
Shall with its idle breath the peace molest
Or break the stillness of his awful crest.

" Child of an ancient Race, sublime and lone,
O'er Man uprais'd, like yon cloud-girdled throne,
Ah! why hath Fate, to Might material kind,
Still wreak'd her fury on the matchless Mind?
Thy first great Sire, who brav'd the Thunderer's might
To snatch from Heaven Truth's soul-reviving Light,
For love to Man reap'd perfidy and hate:—
All hearts have quail'd o'er great Prometheus' fate.
He fell: and from his phœnix dust did spring
A long proud Line, of Prophet, Chief, and King;

Each with *his* spirit's glowing seal imprest,
Truth's zeal, Man's love inspiring each large breast;
Each to like doom decreed:—an infant lone
Last heir,—and exil'd from Prometheus' throne.
Here, refuge from Man's hate the princely child
Found mid Hyrcania's rocks and mountains wild;
Bequeathing for the boon his matchless Line,
To build mid barbarous hosts a fane divine.

" Hence sprang thy matchless Sire. My Indra, how
Describe his stately mien, his princely brow,
Those attributes sublime, which mark the mind
Form'd by its majesty to awe mankind.
Against a nation in that nation's cause
He stirr'd his might, dragg'd forth her tarnish'd laws
To open day; despoil'd the worshipp'd fire
Of honours vain; taught mortals to aspire
To worship worthy of the wise and free,
The great First-Cause, th' essential Deity.
Indra, thou know'st his fate. 'Twas such a day
As this: the Summer sun's declining ray

Stream'd o'er an ocean of dark clouds, afar
Pil'd o'er yon Eastern heights :—th' infuriate war
Of elemental Powers drew slowly on,
And Demawend's vast mass upheav'd and lone
Stood like wave-girdled pinnacle of snow.
Ne'er since that Eve so near hath gloom'd his brow,
So vast hath seem'd his tempest-skirted form:
That was the Eve when thou, sweet child, wert born;
Born mid thy father's blood, thy mother's woes.
And this—ay! this so semblant eve will close
The fourth sweet lustre of my child's career,
And a like term of widowhood to her,
Whom Man, more cruel than relentless Death,
Bereav'd of peace, yet left the curse of breath.
'Twas such an eve as this——"

                            " Forbear, forbear,
Sweet Friend.   That dismal record will impair
Thy shatter'd strength.   In characters of fire
Lives each dread record of her matchless Sire
Upon his daughter's grateful soul imprest.
He fell, but not ignobly: his large breast

O'erteemed with fires divine that never die.
He was a martyr for the Truth, and high
As Truth can lift Man's tarnish'd soul, he rose,
And seal'd his birthright in the very woes,
Devis'd of thankless Man."

" 'Twas even so
He spake and look'd. The glory of his brow
Thine own hath caught. Ah! could he see thee now!
Far from me, Love, for ever, ever far
Be it thy meek and beauteous faith to mar
With the dark doubts by mental woe imprest
And dread experience on this widow'd breast.
It were a bliss I dare not hope, to dwell
On some bright future, where the word ' farewell '
Is a forgotten sound :—where we might claim
All that high promise, coupled with Love's name,
In which we fondly, trustingly invest
The wealth, the peace, the sunshine of the breast.
But where is Truth? All things around us fade;
E'en Love and Friendship side by side are laid
In a few fleeting hours: all seek *one* bourne,
With tidings of its nature none return:

Mid signs of Death innumerous, where may be
The path the clew to immortality?"

" Where!—Oh! I've trac'd it in the breeze that flies
Laden with incense of a thousand sighs;
In every stream bright-gushing from the rock;
In every thunder's hoarse conflictive shock,
In the fork'd lightning, quivering as it plays,
The Moon's pale beam, the Sun's life-kindling rays,
In the Morn's music and the Eve's still sigh;
And in that heart-pause of intensity,
When Night hath banish'd each distracting sound,
The World shut out and drawn her curtain round
My soul, my conscience and that awful eye,
Which scans the records of Eternity.

" Ah! scorn not, Mother dear, that Realm refin'd
By Reason sway'd, the Empire of the Mind.
Think not, our aspirations pure and high
To Virtue, goodness, immortality,
Can ever (more than senseless matter) prove
Curb'd in duration,(1) or compell'd to move

In sphere unworthy their exalted aim.
Think not—oh! scorn to think, that when this flame
Leaps from its urn, to leave it dark and lone,
A lifeless wreck, its essence bright hath flown
Back to the prison of some baser clod,
Deflected from the path it erst had trod
Tow'rd the pure presence of its source and God."

She ceas'd, then meekly on her knees sank down
With eye uprais'd and tresses backward thrown,
And lip that quiver'd with the struggling fire
Of chasten'd rapture's most sublim'd desire.
" Spirit of Truth," she said, and every word
Distinct amid the stilly pause was heard
Of the vex'd elements, tho' deep and low
From the heart's inmost fane it seemed to flow.
" Spirit of Truth, whose seal we find imprest
On Heaven's starred vault, Earth's fair and genial breast,
In flowery mead and memory-haunted grove,
The Day-star's glory and Eve's star of Love,
Springs gushing bliss, still Autumn's sheeny gold,
And hoarse-voic'd Winter, cloud and thunder-roll'd,

And (than eternal Nature mightier still)
In each sublime and mystery-hidden thrill
Of inward consciousness, each strong desire
To pierce beyond the visible World, and higher
E'en than the highest soar, t' attain to Thee,
Wellspring of Truth and Love and Purity;
Here at thy feet, and meekly to thy shrine,
We bring the offering, worthiest thee and thine,
Thine own best gifts, the thoughts that fain would rise,
The hopes that root their anchors in the skies,
Th' intense desire, more potent far than death,
To burst the chains of ignorance and breathe
Truth's pure, inspiring atmosphere, and be
Freemen, by Truth, Eternal Truth, set free.

" Alas! we gaze around us, all in vain;
Earth, wrapt in error, loves the sensual chain:
Night robes the Earth in her funereal pall,
And eyes, long us'd to darkness, vainly call
That, good, which our best sympathies within
Abhorring, own is vanity and sin.

Whither, ah! whither shall we turn? To thee?
And wilt thou, Spirit of dread Purity
Thron'd in ineffable perfection, deign
Thine ear in pity to a Worm's sad plain—
Or stoop one thought tow'rd those whose feeble prayers
Are drown'd in music of ten thousand spheres,
And shouts of mighty, bright angelic throngs,
And answering raptures of material tongues
Swarming through Nature's realm? Ah! rather, say,
Hast thou, in boundless plenitude of sway,
Created aught beyond thine own control,
And cast the wondrous structure of the soul
Like dew, upon the desert to expire,
Merg'd in its sands or withered by its fire,
A fruitless, useless waste? Or hast thou wrought
One utmost point of Space, from which thy thought
Is bounded by remoteness; or, which Thou
Found'st worthy to create, yet deem'st too low
To claim thy sovereign care? Our hearts reply,
Accurst the doubt, attaching the Most High
Of error, feebleness, inconstancy!

" Then, where is truth ?   Once more to thee we turn.
Hast thou delight to see thy creatures mourn
And pine for that thou hold'st in boundless bliss ?
What! shall a Worm impugn of littleness
Heav'n's Majesty supreme ?   Yet, this our Earth
Continues still, as at primordial birth,
Sighing for truth, with not one gracious ray
To streak its void, its darkness roll away.

" Spirit of Truth!   And is it thus ?   Hast thou
Ne'er sent a message of thy love below ?
Ne'er felt the pleading of thine own great might,
Thine own large goodness, to vouchsafe the light
Thou causest us to pine for ?   Can there be
In unparticipated wealth, that free
Unbounded bliss our hearts ascribe to thee ?

" Then, were good, evil.   Then, were darkness, light.
Then Chaos' self were order.   Then, this bright
And beauteous Earth were but an humbling blot
On the great hand which formed it, yet forgot
His own strange nature; causing it to spring
A deep reproach to him, its architect and king.

"It is not thus. Oh! by thy thunders say
It is not, cannot be. E'en tho' thou slay
Deny us not; for rather would we fall
By thy great hand, than brook th' ignoble thrall
Of that our souls despise. If Truth's pure light
Must needs destroy these mortal frames, too bright
For their gross fabric,—spare, oh! spare them not.
Launch down thine awful bolt, e'en on this spot,
And, whatsoe'er the grosser wreck may be,
Let thy large goodness set our spirits free.

"But, if thou rather lov'st to work thy will
Benign and righteous, by the peaceful rill
Than the hoarse torrent: if the fruitful shower
And gentle dew be tokens of thy power,
And ruin thy strange work: oh! then distil
Into our hearts the truth we pine for, still;
Or if that truth has been to Earth sent down
Make its blest precepts evermore our own."

She ceas'd. Down glanc'd as 'twere in answer dire
O'er her fair brow Heaven's fork'd, destroying fire,

Lit up that forehead with surnatural light,
All too effulgent for her Mother's sight;
Who in the fancied wreck before her spread
Bow'd, shuddering, to the Earth her careworn head.
But, harmless o'er Prometheus' child did play
Promethean fire with consecrating ray,
Touch'd the tiar her fairy brow that bound,
And fus'd the ores in golden showers around;
But spar'd the delicate cheek, the fearless eye,
Pouring its own pure flood of light on high,
The tresses sacred to the soul of night,
The forehead glistering in its snowy height.
Yes! forth Prometheus' fearless daughter came
From searching test of fire's intensest flame.
Her beauty, breathing of the hand divine,
Her soul, aspiring to its source sublime,
Offer'd no base alloy t' incense the ray,
Beneath whose touch Earth's purest ores decay.

END OF CANTO I.

Canto II.

THE MINSTREL.

Days of the shadowy Past, dim years and lone,
Whose knell uprises from the dark abyss,
Where have your dun, far-glooming pinions flown
With all the Night and Sunshine, woe and bliss
Of our vain World; its pomp and littleness?
The Mighty of old Times ye've swept away;
Yea! the dread Shades, once visitant of this
Our dwindled World, may here no longer stray,
Nor on our moonlit lawns disport the frolic Fay.

What have ye left us for the treasures, merg'd
In those black caverns, buried out of sight;
For souls of fire, whose daring genius urg'd
E'en to the gates of Heaven their eagle flight?
For him, who robb'd Sol's chariot of the light
And brav'd the Thunderer in his people's cause?
For him, whose justice triumph'd o'er thy might,
Paternal love, and rebaptiz'd the laws
In blood, the dearest, Woe from Man's crush'd bosom draws?

A dwindled world—a race of little men,
Gigantic prejudice, and coward crime;
The sceptic snarling in his secret den,
The bigot stabbing in the broad sunshine;
The foul seducer and the heartless mime;—
These have ye left, for those ye've downward drawn;
The flash gin-palace, for the marble shrine,
And for the fairy dance on midnight lawn,
Her step, Man's victim pale, heartbroken and forlorn.

What have ye left us, for the faith approv'd,
The leal, warm heart, the hospitable board?
The rude old hall our Fathers' Fathers lov'd,
The manly spirit and the stainless sword?
What fate perverse invests an insect word
With immortality, to deeds denied?
That thou canst but the Poet's song accord,
For all thou'st whelm'd beneath thy plombless tide—
For all our World's best wealth, its glory, boast and
    pride?

Who would abide on this dispeopled Land,
Its honour tarnish'd and its might decay'd?
Nor pant to join that old, illustrious Band,
Beneath thy banner, awful Power, array'd?
To meet the Sage of Academus' shade,
Each stainless Martyr to his Faith and Race,
Th' angelic soul, of Heaven that breath'd and made
An Eden bloom on Earth's sin-blighted face,
And link'd us to the skies, with pure, ineffable grace?

Oh! bear me hence, ye billows that roll on
Your gloomy channel to the vasty Deep!
Bear me to realms that own no tarnish'd sun
Beyond Earth's cavern'd cell and dungeon keep.
Waft, whirl me onward, downward o'er the steep,
Where billows of the Past have hurl'd their spray,
To where the Mighty of all Times from sleep
Have ris'n to greet the Beauteous, Wise, and Gay,
And of the dower of Eld, but Woe hath known decay.

Night glooms without: but in Prometheus' Hall
The cresset lamp lights up the old rude wall,
Casting long, wavering shadows, crost in path
By countershades, projected from the hearth:
As crackling high those cheerful flames aspire,
And Man owns friendship with destroying fire.
That ruddy flame might well the gloom allay
Of the rude Hall that feels its genial ray;
But how dispel the still encroaching night
Shrouding their hearts, lone watchers of its light?

" What holds his step? Alas ! what led him forth
To brave the Night gloom and the tempest wroth ?
Indra my child ? Ah me ! that blinding flash,
That peal, as Heaven and Earth in one dire crash
Were wreck'd together ! Fearful is the night,
And what avail firm heart and nerve of might
When age-pil'd rocks the Whirlwind's fury own,
And e'en the Monarch of the Woods is thrown
From his primæval base."
      The Maid replied
With words of cheer, whose faltering notes belied
Th' assum'd composure she would fain instil:
" Wild is the night, the rude gale rises still,
And the fork'd lightning's flash incessant plays
Scatt'ring the gloom with dire yet friendly rays:
But Dion kens each sign the welkin shows
Of brooding storm ; and never tempest rose
With more of portent to forenounce its path
And warn the wanderer of impending wrath.
I heard the mighty Mountain's distant groan, (2)
I heard the woodland Spirit's plaintive moan,

I saw the Tarn in silvery waves upbreak,
When not one Aspen's mobile leaf might quake,
Whilst (grown so near his mass) each rift was kenn'd
Scarring the awful front of Demawend:
These Dion could not miss, nor scan in vain:
He, doubtless, shelters with some friendly swain.
Fear not for him, whom Heaven reserves a place
Mid chiefs and heroes of our ancient Race."

The grace of eloquence was in her eye,
The fervor, kindled in the soul, by high
And holy confidence: yet as she spoke
At times the faltering of frail nature broke
The current of her voice, and on her cheek
The deadly pallor and the hectic streak
Emotion's conflict with the spirit speak.

Deeper, meanwhile and deadlier in its ire
The Tempest pour'd its mingled flood and fire:

Howl'd the Night-blast and hoarsely peal'd on high
In awful bursts the chorus of the sky.
While at each flash that lonely cresset's glare
Pal'd into dimness: then, with sickly flare
Resum'd, th' effulgence past, its languid reign,
Dim as the twilight of some battle-plain,
Where Man's fell passions from their drear abode
Hell's thin ghosts muster to their feast of blood.
Still, at each gust of that all-powerful blast
Trembled the walls, of massive fabric cast,
And wildly shook, as 'twere to giant's hand,
That door of strength like screen of willow wand;
And still young Indra to the portal pass'd
Listing each shrill note of the fitful blast,
And half believ'd, amid the jarring war
Of the vex'd elements, the shriek to hear
Or wail of human woe; and scarce might quell
Her own wild cry of anguish, as they fell:
Yet, veiling in calm mien her soul's alarms,
Return'd to fill her widow'd Mother's arms,
And felt the terrors of her heart surcease
In anxious ministry to others' peace.

'Twas now the midnight time; and there is power
(Who hath not own'd it?) in the midnight hour.
E'en when the sun hath left a cloudless sky,
And all Night's golden host keep watch on high,
'Tis not, alone, that slumber then hath prest
Her solemn signet o'er Creation's rest,
And that our fancies take the mournful tone
Of things that walk the noiseless World alone;
But that a slumb'rous torpor hath o'erta'en
The healthful guardians of the teeming brain,
And dark and restless Spirits freedom win,
To range at large the gloomier world within.
'Tis thus, that judging Nature's happier cause
By the stern verdict of his bosom's laws,
Man peoples Earth with many a fearful throng
Of phantom shapes that to the soul belong,
Inverting Nature's order, till are hurl'd
The Mind's dark outcasts on the natural world.

'Twas, when the loudest peal did bellowing swell
Throughout that spacious hall, and down each dell,

And round each mountain skirt the echoes woke,
That sunder'd, sudden as by thunder-stroke,
Wide, with terrific shock, the portal flew;
And while those lonely Watchers backward drew,
And each to other in amazement clung,—
And while the rude gale in its fury swung,
Howling thro' that drear Hall, and in its might
Flar'd, wan'd, and leaping high, expir'd the light
Of the pale lamp,—a shadowy form 'gan glide
Into the darken'd chamber, stride by stride,
To where they shrinking stood: when, as each heart
Flutter'd and paus'd in awe's unwonted start,
The Lightning's flash lit up a well-known form:
'Twas Dion's self, sore batter'd by the storm,
Silent, absorpt, as by some potent charm.
Joy chas'd from Indra's heart her wild alarm.
" Safe, safe—oh, safe, at last! Sweet Mother, see
How dear to Heaven the Widow's sorrows be,
How dear the Orphan's tears!"
                       And running on
With passion's inconsistency she wrung

Her slender hands, and wept by turns and smil'd,
And question upon question ceaseless pil'd—
Till, struck by that she read on Dion's brow,
She sudden check'd her joy's exuberant flow,
And paus'd inquiringly, half chill'd with dread.
" Mother, my more than Mother," calmly said
The storm-drench'd Wand'rer, " not alone I come,
A stranger craves the shelter of our home,
O'erta'en like me. Awhile, without we stood,
My voice drown'd, doubtless, by the thunder flood,
Till wide the portal flew."

" What! rests there, still,
One lone storm-beaten Wand'rer of the hill,
Expos'd the while to this so fearful blast?"
Swift from his side Prometheus' Daughter pass'd
Mid the wild storm: and soon with lofty stride
The Stranger cross'd their threshold at her side.

Tall as the giant Sons of Earth his form,
It rose, like granite Mount, by many a storm
From dateless ages lash'd, each thund'rous shock
Denuding more the scath'd and rifted rock:

Till, reft each line of grace, thro' Heaven uphurl'd
The mighty Skeleton o'crawes a World.
He seem'd of ancient days. Not that the snow
Of age hung hoar o'er that majestic brow,
But that his mien and bearing did display
The legend old of some far-distant day.
He was all-diverse from Man's minish'd Race;
And 'twas enough, at that lone hour, to trace
The sweeping lines of his majestic height,
Breathing of power defac'd and ruin'd might,
To lead the fancy back o'er ages gone,
And deeds by men of higher lineage done,
To times all-hallow'd by the lapse of years,
Whose page hath fir'd our hearts, or triumph'd o'er our
 tears.

In ample folds his cloak of sable hung
Around that mighty form, and lightly strung
A minstrel harp beneath his arm he bore,
Whose silver wires the rude gale murmur'd o'er
In melancholy descant. And his brow,
Furrow'd so deep with lines of thought or woe,

A golden circlet bound. Her own the Maid
Half deem'd it, as her hand instinctive stray'd
In search of that had bound her forehead fair,
Awestruck and startled not to grasp it there.*

Awhile beside that peerless maid he stood;
His own vast frame and sinewy bulk endued
With twofold might contrasted with her form:
So, when the night-clouds muster for the storm,
Glooms o'er the fairy skiff, with rifted keep
And shattered hull, some tyrant of the Deep.
Awhile he paus'd: his stately stride resum'd,
And as the dark folds of his drapery gloom'd
In the uncertain light, his noiseless tread
And form unearthly stirr'd a secret dread
In either bosom: an unsanction'd chill,
That jarr'd the nerves with momentary thrill,
Nor yielded place entirely to the sway
E'en of that voice the spirit-tides obey—
The calm high tone of Reason, side by side
With meek-ey'd Faith and Virtue's blameless pride.

---

* See p. 21, line 8, Canto I.

The board is spread: with gesture, voice, and smile
They seek their lone guest's sadness to beguile,
And press their homely fare. But if, perchance,
His eye responds one instant to their glance,
'Tis but with stately gesture to decline
The cates unhonour'd, the untasted wine,—
While, self-absorb'd, droops low his shadowy brow
As brooding o'er unutterable Woe.

" Stranger," the Maiden said, and as she spoke,
And her rich silvery voice the silence broke,
She started at the murmur: " Stranger, say,
Lies it in our poor gift to wile away
By deed or sympathy the gloom-cloud spread
O'er thy care-burden'd mind? If with the Dead
Thy hopes and vows lie buried, brief the hour
Ere the cold grave shall cease its envious power
To sever hearts that love. Or if it be
That thou dost seek the feeble sympathy
Of human souls, the law that bids us give
The homeless shelter binds us to relieve

The burden of his cares, and balm impart
To staunch the death-wounds of the writhing heart.
But if thy sorrow hide in that deep mine
Where never ray of mortal lamp might shine ;
If from thyself, thy conscience thou dost flee,
And, seeking refuge, find'st but misery :
We, who like thee have borne the wearying load,
Would point or lead thy footsteps to thy God.
He gave us rest."

    She ceas'd, for she had broke
The spell of darkness : In his eye there woke
A lambent flame of soft and hallow'd light
That beam'd benign on her, and seem'd t' invite
Her heart's full tenderness. 'Twas even so
Her own great Sire, if lingering still below,
Perchance had beam'd, had gaz'd upon his child :
Yet he, mid his dread sufferings might have smil'd
Rich in a parent's love : and this lone brow,
So scarr'd with care, so furrow'd deep with woe,
Seem'd ne'er such passing luxury to have known.
—But hark ! he wakes his wild harp's wizard tone,

And his full breast outpours the flood of song
To whelm and waft the hearer's heart along.
His voice rose like some spirit of the Deep
Who sings the waves and warring winds to sleep:
A voice of other days, a buried sound,
Call'd into Life from Memory's funeral ground:
A melancholy descant, whose high sway
Hope, fear, love, passion, madness' self obey:
E'en the rude storm grew hush'd as it did swell,
And bellowing thunders moan'd their last farewell.

Song.

Proudly above the rock-pil'd mount he stood:
Beneath him spread, with inlet, cape and bay;
Old Pontus roll'd afar his sombre flood,
And calm repos'd in conscious power of sway.
Is it the murmur of his young waves' play,
Each coursing other to the mountain shore?
No! 'tis a voice which deeper tides obey,
The hum of human life, as densely pour
The multitudinous waves of Being, o'er and o'er.

For at his feet expectant nations throng,
Summon'd to view and weigh with temperate eye
Light's strife with Night, the war of Right with Wrong—
A mortal king Jove's majesty defy.
There stand his white-stol'd priests: their looks bely
The fainting of their hearts, as call'd to prove
Their gift infallible, or haply die
The scorn of men below and gods above:
How may dead phantoms aid? What help from thun-
    dering Jove!

" Proceed ye priests of Jove." The altars smoke,
The victims bleed, the incense clouds arise;
The prostrate priests their deity invoke,
The rocks, the glens, revert their frantic cries.
The entrails they consult; yon azure skies,
Which calmly witness their un'vailing care,
Are search'd from East to West for auguries,
Each winged wanderer of the pathless air,
Summon'd to aid their choice and guide their judgment fair.

"And now bring forth the test. Ye ancient Seers,
Let your great Master here his offering claim,
And be his choice the proof, or that he wears
No heavenly crown, or that his mighty name
Hath been malign'd by me. And thus shall shame
Henceforth light only on the guilty brow.
So shall Jove's foil'd divinity proclaim
Your faith unsound, or e'en Prometheus bow
Before your countless Joves low as he scorns them
  now."

Deeply the Conclave paus'd, that test survey'd,
With anxious eye would fain explore it thro'.
On that dread stake their fame, their power was laid—
Existence' self, perchance, the breath they drew,
The very life-blood eddying warmly through
Their daunted hearts: and worse than all to be
The vulgar scorn of the infuriate crew,
So long the dull slaves of their tyranny.
Oh! of scorn's venom'd breath how oft the scornful die!

The lot is cast, the die is thrown. "Now see,
My fellow citizens, how wise the choice
Of Jove the Thund'rer. Worship him with me,
And in his novel rites with me rejoice.
Behold the offal which his own dread voice
Selects to grace th' inviolable shrine.
Long have ye thought to pamper him with joys
Of the gross sense. Jove most delights to dine
On carrion, Dogs despise, Immortals deem divine.

" O ye with Reason's glorious gift endow'd,
Of mien erect and brow that fronts the skies,
Have ye in sooth so long, so blindly bow'd
To type of all on Earth ye most despise?
Is aught but goodness noble in your eyes?
If crime or lust as attributes belong
To an almighty Father, Earth supplies
Full many, mighty in pursuit of wrong,
Who babes in virtue crawl with grovelling brows along."

He ceas'd: and at his words, from far and near,
Around, beneath, loud shouts of triumph rise.
The woods, the rocks, reverb that mighty cheer,
Which rising, circling, settles in the skies.
Through all his coasts old Pontus multiplies
The glorious plaudit. 'Tis a Nation sends
Her mighty shout afar; and Earth replies;
And Heaven itself a note accordant lends,
As to the Dome serene Truth's jubilee ascends.

Another shout. But ah! how different this!
It rather seem'd Humanity's dread ban,
Or some dire curse deep mutter'd from th' Abyss
Where Things immortal writhe in deathless pain.
Like a chill blight it fell, nor rose again,
For Echo loath'd th' abhorr'd and guilty sound,
And Heaven ejected from its pure domain
Those demon notes, and the blue Euxine found
No answer to their din throughout his tranquil bound.

'Twas the fell curse of vengeance: "Tear them down,
On their own altars rend the paltering throng,
And from each victim's entrails be it known
Why Truth has suffer'd contumely and wrong."
Frantic they rush in one mad crowd along
To wreak the curse each readier tongue had found:
And all had perish'd, but that instant rung
His voice, so deep and awful in its sound,
And with resistless spell their frantic progress bound.

"Peace!"—and the tumult ceas'd. That single word,
Which far and near earth, air, and ocean gave,
(So seem'd to each,) hath quell'd the dire accord
Of vengeful spirits, stilling every wave
Of wroth in trancement settled as the grave:
Each paus'd, and wonder'd that he paus'd, yet sought
No effort to shake off the spell nor brave
That strange ascendance which a sound has wrought
O'er each reluctant pulse, each feeling, power and thought.

All stood, all gaz'd in expectation deep
On stern Prometheus, as alone he stood
High o'er the rest, like some rock-anchor'd steep
Mid the wave-myriads of the briny Flood.
The scorn, which curl'd his lip and fix'd the blood
In one swart flush upon his else pale cheek,
Subsided calm beneath the graver mood
Of thought sublime and sympathies that speak
Heart-stirring language there, in many a soften'd streak.

" Men, Brethren, would ye stain a holy cause
With dastard murder? Ye have quell'd indeed
A faith, perverting justice', mercy's laws:
Would ye, dread Até should to Jove succeed?
Hate, discord, murder, your accursed creed?
Truth leads Hope, Peace and Mercy, in her train.
One God our Father, Love our sacred need.
What wretch with blood our spotless league would stain,
Our high and holy cause with hellish rites profane?

" Where'er degrees be found of Good or Great,
   There needs must be a Greatest and a Best.
   Man, first of all the visible create,
   Nor made himself, nor skills with life t' invest
   The veriest insect, which the glowing West
   Lulls to eternal sleep.   Man, then, is not
   Or best, or greatest; higher soars our quest.
   There is a God, who Heaven and Earth begot.
To search, fulfil his laws, our highest, happiest lot.

" Him by his works we judge,—harmonious all:
   The law which fram'd and guides the spheres is one.
   Earth rose from Chaos' murk and deadly thrall,
   By the blest music of the Morn-Star won
   To being;—basking in the new-born Sun.
   Her pulse rich tides of harmony still move.
   Concord's blest laws Man violates, alone
   Of Things on Earth beneath, in Heaven above,
For Harmony's essential soul, God's law divine, is Love.

" But see, he comes, the King whose Empire pure
All hearts of flesh, all spirit wills obey.
Lo! where the gates of light wide-spread appear,
The mighty valves of everlasting day.
Lift up your heads, ye gates, and ye who lay
In Discord's bondage, lift the drooping brow;
Heaven sheds the peaceful splendours of its ray,
And every knee and every heart shall bow,
And Heaven with Earth shall meet and blend in Love's
    harmonious flow."

He ceas'd: the waves were still'd. No longer rave
The frantic bloodhounds of the general breast:
Peace, harmony, like her whom Ocean's wave
Bore in her beauty from his dark unrest,
Pervade that mighty tide of Life. They feast
On great Prometheus the unsated eye:
Till a low murmur from their hearts releas'd,
" Friend, Father of our Race," like winds that sigh
O'er surf-strown shores, did swell, rise, falter, fade and die.

The Minstrel paus'd: a silence deep and long
Took place of that most wild and thrilling song.
For, winds at rest, and thunders hush'd afar,
No sound of life or strife the ear might jar,
Save when the glancing drops with plashy sound
Fell from the sated roof those walls around,
With mournful, drear monotony that brought
No break to stillness, no relief from thought:
As, wrapt in wonder of their Minstrel Guest,
His audience seiz'd each varying mood exprest
By those awe-kindling features: till each tone
Of passion, thence transferr'd, became their own:
Till as he gaz'd, they gaz'd, or sigh'd, they sigh'd,
Breath'd as he breath'd, or as he paus'd replied
By a like pause, that had well nigh exprest
Th' instinctive throbs of each excited breast.
Again, his hand the silent chords awoke,
His voice of power that settled stillness broke,
And thrilling wildly as the harp-notes rung
'Twas thus, his strain renew'd, the Minstrel sung.

Song—*continued.*

" Where is the great Prometheus ?   Not where rise
   You incense-clouds around Saturnius' shrine.
   Orphans their father seek : a Nation's sighs
   Are for the Chief of that illustrious Line
   By them esteem'd scarce lower than divine,
   Whence the High Stewards of their rights still spring :
   Th' Opprest and Friendless at *his* loss repine
   Whom Truth inspir'd : the Land bewails her king.
Shout high ye priests of Jove, let the blue welkin ring.

" Seek ye your king, vain Men !   Seek first the wing,
   Of soaring eagle to ascend yon height,
   Where the great Master of Deceit doth fling
   O'er rugged rocks his frame of giant might,
   And toss th' unquiet limbs in torturous plight,
   Seeking the rest he never more shall know :
   While still the hovering bird of Jove in sight
   Stoops o'er his prey and slakes the fiery glow
That lights his cruel eye in the red torrent's flow."

So spake th' insidious priests. A cloud of gloom
Hangs o'er Prometheus' fate, who never more
Walk'd in the ranks of Men. The envious tomb
Of Error sepulchred the flame he bore
From Heaven to darken'd Earth. On Error's shore
Time since hath roll'd full many an Age away :
Yet, still when round Elborus' forehead hoar
The Tempest lours and the vext Euxine's spray
Meets with the clouds above, and glancing Meteors play,—

The awestruck peasant views that mighty form, (3)
Scarr'd by a thousand years of torturous woe,
And marks the Eagle shrouded in the storm
Stoop o'er his victim to repeat the blow;
And mid the gale's dull moaning, lists the low
Deep plaint, by more than mortal suffering wrung,
Where the great Victim wipes his careworn brow,
And, dauntless, braves a fate he will not shun,
Spurning the proffer'd truce would chain his free-born
 tongue.

Again the harp-notes paus'd; and with them fell
The minstrel-song that with resistless spell
Had chain'd each list'ning ear; and rising slow,
Without or word of speech or sign of brow—
As some dark cloud upheaves from Ocean's breast
Its vasty bulk and gloom-infolden crest,—
Stalk'd thro' the twilight Hall their minstrel guest;
And, as he pass'd and his long shade did fall
O'er half the midnight silence of the hall,
His giant height, his robe of raven dye,
And mien reserv'd of gloom and mystery,
View'd at that solemn hour, strange awe impress'd,
And wild surmise on each excited breast.

Morn dawns. Arrang'd their hospitable hoard,
Their stranger guest seeks not the lowly board,
His chamber vacant proves, his couch unprest:
No vestige trace they of their recent guest,—
Save that the wizard harp he sway'd so well
Remains, conjecture's wildering maze to swell.

Howe'er departed, whatsoe'er his birth,
A phantom shape, or lone sad child of Earth,
No more by those lone Watchers of the Hill
His form of mystery or his wizard skill
Thenceforth was known. The hamlet search'd around
No clew to aid their anxious quest was found:
One aged sire his hoar head shook to hear
Their tale, and spake of woes impending near,
And of an awful form from ages past
Haunting that mountain skirt, what time the blast
Swept with unwonted violence to rend
The treasur'd snow-wreaths from proud Demawend:
Whose harp-notes heard, when sobs the Night storm low,
Are still to Man dread harbingers of woe.
More that grey Seer had said: but Death's arrest
That instant still'd the pulses of his breast;
And backward lapsing on his couch, with eye
Fixt in its glassy lustre on the sky,
And finger pointing to that mountain height,
O'er which hung, glooming in the dim twilight,
One spectral cloud, his spirit pass'd away!
Aw'd and dismay'd his hearers left the clay

So late instinct with life; and speeding home
Gaz'd back in dread upon that summit lone,—
Where tower'd, like Titan limn'd against the sky,
Motionless, pois'd in Heaven's immensity,
That spectral cloud:—Their hearts were chill'd, their breath
Disturb'd not Night's lone conference with Death.

END OF CANTO II.

Canto III.

THE PILGRIMAGE.

'Tis Morn's first struggle with the thrall of Night,
Darkness' last sob, the birth of jocund Light.
Freshness is in the air, and o'er the flowers
Tears mid their tranquil slumbers have been shed;
And tho' no breeze is stirring in the bowers
Nature hath broke her covenant with the Dead.
The Brook, deep buried in the dingle's bed,
Lifts its long silent voice, and op'ning slow,
Life, Nature, Day prepare their buds to spread,
In that most pure, effulgent planet's glow,
Bright Lucifer, the son of Morn, the first sad heir of woe.

Hark, 'twas the note of some awaking bird!
Another joins: then spreads the twittering cry
In jargon low, still strength'ning, till are heard
Half-practis'd melodies, born but to die:
Faint trilling strains, that evermore supply,
By multitude and sweetness, what in power
Hath been denied them. From his kindred sky
The lark hath call'd the blackbird from his bower,
And the wild mountain breeze is waking tree and
  flower.

And higher still, and multiplied around,
From the Vale's bosom to the Mountain's brow,
Ascend and meet the airy tides of sound,
And mingling glide in one harmonious flow:
For now the Torch of Heaven is kindling slow
To its full golden glory, and extend
Earth's budding beauties to th' enamour'd glow
Of that bright Orb: and now his fires are kenn'd
Beac'ning thine awful crest, proud peak of Demawend. (4)

Nature hath risen from her trance, and joy
Still marks her rising, is her first employ.
Nature awakes in loveliness confest,
As late she sank in loveliness to rest.
The languor soft, enshrouding her repose,
Like elfin robes fell from her as she rose,
Radiant in life and smiles, and every vein
Rend'ring the heart its full throb back again;
As the pure tide recruited by her rest
Runs its glad round bright sparkling through her breast.
In all her smiles her freshness and the might
Of Heav'n-born beauty, as she meets the sight
Of Man, she calls him with her thrilling voice,
Diffus'd thro' earth, air, ocean, to rejoice.
For him her smile doth beam, her song doth rise:
For him Love's lustrous beacon, her pure eyes
Are lighted up to lure him with their ray
To peace that blooms where her sweet footsteps stray.
For him each full throb of that heart, each sigh
Whisp'ring of joys too bright to languish, pall, or die.
So broke the morn: so Nature woo'd to bless,
And vainly tempted Man to happiness.

Prometheus' Daughter with the dawn arose:
The bird whose note dispell'd her light repose
Had scarce his decent, russet plumage drest,
When her young foot the dewy greensward press'd.
And now with Dion on the mountain-brow
She stands, absorb'd, soul, mind, in cheerless woe.
Blind to that glowing prospect, deaf to all
The songs of bliss that round her rise and fall.
Would'st thou the cause divine? With me draw near,
List that deep voice which calls the heart-wrung tear.

" Indra, my mind is fixt. Could aught control
The firm and settled purpose of my soul,
It were that woe, sweet Maid, which but to see
Is torture, madness, misery to me.
But I am sprung of no ignoble Race.
Like thee (tho' more remote) my blood I trace
To kings and heroes of an ancient Line,
Who shed their life-blood in a cause divine.
Too long I've linger'd, trifling life away,
And burying powers not giv'n to feed Decay.

Henceforth I spurn th' unworthy sloth, and go
To take my grade in Earth's wide strife of woe.
Sorrow from ancient days hath been the lot
Of our scath'd Race, and yet forsakes us not.
To meet her step, unfalt'ringly I go,
Nor count th' ally of our great House my foe;
Nor ask a lot, aught differing from their fate,
To write Earth's noblest blood degenerate.

" Let Sorrow come, but with her there shall tread
A step not mindless of th' unburied Dead:
And mid the World's wide turmoil there shall be
One voice for Truth and Heaven-born Liberty:
One heart to dare, one hand that heart to aid,
One soul unshrinking, one untarnish'd blade.
Earth has her miseries, but compensates all
In that last gift, the narrow, peaceful hall."

" What dreams be these, my Dion? Whence art thou
So changed of late? What cloud o'erhangs thy
brow?

The hunter's hardy toil, the hunter's meed,
Supplied of late Ambition's highest need.
Whence hast thou learn'd for stormier joys to pine,
And count this impulse of thy soul, divine?
Oh! show me but a hope, the Truth we prize
Shall gain fresh lustre thro' the sacrifice,
And not to stay, but urge thy step, shall be
Her voice, who loses all in losing thee."

" Yes, Indra, I *am* chang'd. From that dread night,
When, scaling Demawend's sublimest height,
And downward gazing o'er the cloud-roll'd plain,
I heard that more than mortal minstrel strain,
And turning met the deep, unfathom'd eye,
And read therein a stormier destiny,—
Since then the change. Such portents greet them not
Whom Heav'n design'd to fill the peasant's lot.
They note some high design, they mark the mind,
Destined to sway the fortunes of his kind;
Their hopes, their fears, their interests to partake,
And self's strong fetters from the soul to break.

Would Indra bid her Dion basely drown
The general care in objects all his own,
Chasing from thought the deep debt handed down
Thro' a long line of kings?"

"No! Dion, no!
Prometheus' fate wants yet th' ignoble woe
Of counting one, in all his long descent,
With finite joys or selfish schemes content.
Go! since thy conscience points th' aspiring road,
Pursue the path our Race hath ever trod;
Confront like them privation, peril, woe,
And like them bind with Glory's wreath thy brow."

"There spake Prometheus. Light of my lone soul!
Did not dread Conscience urge her stern control,
No earthly lure could tempt from thee to stray.
But what hath great Prometheus' Blood to say
With those who dream life's languid hours away?
Where is the tranquil peace his son hath known?
The myrtle sceptre or the pillow'd throne?
Love were too blest a privilege to grace
The last scath'd relics of that Heaven-struck Race.

Or, be its voice allow'd, it ne'er may prove
The changeful strain, still blest, of mutual love;
But a deep dirge-like, woe-prophetic tone,
Whose burden tearless sighs, the lone heart's ceaseless
    moan."

"True, my heart's lord: a troublous lot 'tis still
Our fate, the fate of all our Line to fill.
Yet, not for fortune, power, or bliss, would we
Barter this high, tho' mournful Destiny,
While Heaven vouchsafes a spirit undeprest,
Serene in sunshine of a guileless breast.
But whither tends thy footstep? What the clew
Thine ardent Fancy prompts thee to pursue?"

"First to Elborus' summit, were't alone
To pierce the mystery of that Heav'n-pil'd Throne;
Consigning there to Nature's decent breast
His sacred relics, whose dread Shade will rest,
Perchance, when Earth receives the boon she gave,
And those bleach'd bones repose within the grave.

Thither I haste, undoubting there to see
The clew to deeds may stamp me worthy thee.
Light of my eyes, farewell! Thy Mother's tear
I dare not see: be't thine her woe to cheer.
Farewell—farewell!"
     She sank upon his breast.
So clings the woodbine to its long-lov'd rest:
Her fair arms twin'd in hopelessness of woe,
Her eyes uprais'd, that on his own do grow
Fixt in their tearless misery;—her hair
Back from her brow thrown wildly in despair,
With all its dense folds of the raven dye.—
Whoe'er had view'd her in the agony
Of that dark moment, had but little guess'd
Of the firm spirit shrin'd within her breast.
Whoe'er had known her when the pang was past,
Had little deem'd Affliction's wing could cast
So dark a shadow o'er that spirit, prone
Mid others' hopes and cares t' annihilate her own.

Attir'd as suits the mountain's hardy child
Dion set forth on venture lone and wild.

His couch the earth, his canopy the sky,
His curtain each wild breeze that rustles by,
And the bright stream in mountain freedom blest
The soothing symphony that lulls his rest.
In baldric broad, o'er his strong shoulder slung,
The quiver stor'd with deathful arrows hung;
The bow of power adorn'd his better hand,
And grac'd his side Prometheus' battle-brand,
That still from sire to son descending, ne'er
From Mercy's eye had wrung th' indignant tear,
Nor law infring'd, or human or divine,
To stain or dim the lustre of its shine.
Firm was his step, yet buoyant as the tread
Of untam'd courser in the Desert bred:
And o'er the mould symmetric of his height
The eye still wander'd with untir'd delight:
In every free unfetter'd motion guess'd
The dauntless spirit and the guileless breast.
And in the massive brow, the kindling eye,
The air severe of innate majesty,
Perus'd some legend dim of days bygone
When still Earth's charms could tempt celestials down.

Savage the scene Caucasian Wilds present :
Rocks that be mountains, clefts abysmal rent ;—
The torrent brawls in headlong fury on
'Twixt cliffs impervious to the noonday sun,
Whose firm foundations on Earth's nucleus rest,
Spann'd by the blue sky's vault, from crest to crest.
And on the Torrent's marge, where scatter'd spring
Tree, shrub, and wild-flower, scarce a living thing
Of animated Nature cheers the sense,
Aw'd by the sombre, drear magnificence
Of all around.   The Rock-deer spurns a glen
So prison-like in his free, roving ken,
Hangs on the dizziest verge, and, streaking there
With his light form the azure fields of air,
Seems like a Mountain Spirit, gazing down
From some supernal empire of his own.
The shaggy Bear, sole monarch of that wild,
Loves well the haunts where seldom man hath smil'd,
Prowls in his surly indolence along,
Or, stretch'd luxurious the wild ferns among,
Where chance the sunbeam hath an entrance found,
Lulls his rude nature to the ruder sound

Of the hoarse torrent, or the woodland spell
Of some chance songster of that joyless dell.

Days, nights were laps'd, and months had roll'd away,
When the dark Euxine stretch'd beneath him lay—
A wide expanse of waters rolling free,
With mountains scarp'd of rude antiquity,
Down whose abrupt descent the forest dense
Leads, mass by mass, its wilderness immense
Of gloomy foliage, like some torrent wide
Headlong hurrying in its joyless pride
Down to the subject sea. Beneath the frown
Of this dark mountain pile, the waves roll on
In pitchy blackness; but, where free to meet
The smiling Heaven, its azure soft they greet
With hue as pure, and mirror all its glow
In gleams that change for aye, as changeful breezes
 blow.

That glorious prospect of the deep-blue sea
Burst on his gaze, as Freedom greets the free

In heart and thought, whose limbs the chain hath
  bound :
And, as his eye glanc'd thrillingly around,
Perus'd its measureless extent, to where
Faint trac'd like spirits of the upper air,
The mountain peaks of the far shore do rise,
By distance blent and mingled with the skies,—
Feelings, and thoughts, and memories, long subdued,
Rose on his soul and sent the sparkling blood
Swift thro' his glowing frame, until th' excess
Of that high rapture marr'd its blissfulness,
And o'er its bounds emotion's tide did rise
And gush'd ungovern'd from his streaming eyes.

What saw he there? What saw Athena's son—
Her own unrivall'd, grace-arm'd Xenophon,
Her pride in eloquence, her boast in arms—
When mid barbaric hosts and dire alarms,
Thro' wilds beset with treachery, want, despond,
He led his exil'd band to Trebizond,
And climb'd its height, and shouted, " 'Tis the Sea!
Our own blest home, our world of liberty!"

Oh! not one Greek of all th' illustrious band
Kiss'd the white pebbles of that wave-lash'd strand,
Nor bless'd the glad blue waters as they lay
In full collected majesty of sway,
With more of fervour, with so wild a sense
Of feeling's wealth at once and indigence,—
As he who now first gaz'd upon the deep
Laving the land where his Forefathers sleep,
And view'd in fancy their dim shades arise,
An awful band, beneath their kindred skies,
Treading the shores they rul'd ere Time wax'd gray,
Or Man, degenerate, loath'd their godlike sway.

END OF CANTO III.

Canto IV.

THE VIGIL.

MIGHTY thy watch-towers, O thou castle-crown'd
Earth, our dread Mother! Thence thou look'st on high
Into his azure eyes, whose arms around
Embrace thee still—thy love, thy spouse, the Sky:
He whose firm faith hath seen Eternity
Gliding like River to its parent Main:
Thence thou behold'st each Star's unslumbering eye,
Watching thy loves, and hear'st thy cherish'd name
In every love-note breath'd by rolling Orbs of flame!

Himala's spires of sun-defying snow,
Gigantic Andes' tunnell'd crests of fire,
Mont Blanc and Rosa of the hoary brow,
And Schreckhorn's peak, so lonely, wild, and dire,
Old Atlas, doom'd by Jove's relentless ire
  To prop with stalwart strength Heaven's massive dome,
Parnassus, ringing to the Day-god's lyre,
And vast Olympus, Jove's redoubted throne,
Yield all in might to thee, Elborus, weird and lone!

For on thy savage rock Man's champion lay,
Chain'd in the Hell-born Furies' dire control:
Jove's vulture tore his quivering heart away,
And age-worn tempests did around him roll,
Heaping froze icebergs from the wintry Pole.
Yea, and Jove's thunder scath'd that awful brow,
Shook the firm mount, but not his firmer soul,
Which dread nor torture from its height could bow
While dismal ages slowly trail'd their mangled length of woe.

'Twas the first gray of morn, ere Night is driven
From her last stronghold in the realms of Heaven,
When at Elborus' base the pilgrim stood, (5)
And upward gaz'd, and mass by mass pursued
Its rude unsoften'd outline, as on high
It swelling fill'd the concave of the sky:
A structure wondrous, whose least building-stone
Had tower'd a mountain, had it stood alone;—
Whose firm cement the crudest atoms found
Of Chaos, when with fiery clasp the molten Earth he
    bound!

Hard is the toil that steepy Mount to climb,
Whose pathless bulwarks from undated time
Have hung in their immensity, unbeat
By pulse of human,—ay, of mortal feet.
Nature's wild flock that o'er the mountain stray,
And on each giddiest verge securely play,
View its vast highlands of the icy zone,
As a bleak world dissever'd from their own.
Between the clime where mountain flow'rets blow
And drear, void waste of everlasting snow,

Naked the rock, save where the lichen springs,
And o'er th' unshelter'd waste its mantle flings:
Truest of friends, whom age or wintry blast
To her first love but rivets doubly fast.

Three days with mightiest toil Prometheus' son
That mountain scal'd; nor yet the crest was won:
The slippery rock in vain his step defies,
The beetling cliff in vain a path denies;
The deadly avalanche with thund'rous sway
Down-plunging sweeps the toppling crags away:
And now from Kazibek's twin peak of dread (6)
The mustering storm its cloudy legions spread,
Like some long flock of eagles, scenting far
The steam of carnage in the step of war.
Caught by Elborus' peak that cloudy host
Close-clinging wheel in eddying volumes toss'd,
Until a dense murk atmosphere they form,
Big with the gloom of the suspended storm.

Then burst at once the blinding levin-flash,
And hoarse-voic'd thunder's volleying peal and crash,

From rock and cliff and cavern's darkling side
Deflected, mutter'd, deepen'd, amplified :
Till the last note is but the shuddering jar
Of subterranean thunder, buried deep and far.
Then rush'd the Whirlwind in its giant pride
And stripp'd the snows from half the mountain side.
Part, like some boundless virgin pall, outspread
Hung in mid-air for many a league, and shed
Its shadow huge far o'er the affrighted coast :—
The denser hoards, their feathery footing lost,
Rush from the summit to the vale below,
Rending a rocky deluge as they go,
And, as the fire-scythe mows brown Autumn's grain,
Sweeping the crackling forest from the plain.

It chanc'd his foot at that dread moment press'd
A rock which, jutting from the mountain's breast,
With sides too steep to bear the feathery weight
Of the hoar snow, stood there in naked state.
Clinging like shipwreck'd seaman to the mast
On which hope, fortune, life itself are cast,

He felt the Whirlwind as with Ocean might
Heave its swoll'n tides against the Heaven-built height;
He saw the Mountain-mantle caught on high
With snowy chaos blot earth, sun, and sky;
And felt the pinnacle his arms entwine
Reel wild as giant surfeited with wine:
Proof-arm'd by zeal 'gainst terror mid a shock
That marr'd Heaven's vault and rent Earth's adamantine rock.

Now, bold Adventurer, speed thee! Dost not mark
How from the bosom of yon tempest dark,
That seem'd so big with ruin, Hope hath sprung,
And Safety prov'd the birth of throes which wrung
The elemental World? Oh! speed thee on
The path which Whirlwinds have before thee gone
T' uproot th' impending avalanche and sweep
Each various death from that inviolate Steep.
Oh! speed thee! What be toil and peril now?
Thy foot is planted on the Mount whose brow
Is hallow'd to thy fancy? Once again
Spread to the steep thy chest and tensely strain

Each agile nerve. Enough, the height is won,
Thy hope fulfilled, thy mighty labour done,
And thy full heart and raptur'd mind may seek
Relief from thoughts that thrill and blanch thy storm-worn
    cheek !

Now at the crag he stands of loftiest height,
Around whose waist their zone the heavens unite.
Rent downward to the base by recent shock
Of the live thunder stood that splinter'd rock
In hoary solitude, and round its base
Distinct appear'd the Lightning's fiery trace,
Where the snow crust, abraded, gave to light
A cliff, long ages buried out of sight.

Cramp'd in the rock by thunders bar'd to sight
Four massive stanchions plant their fangs of might,—
Upholding each its chain of virgin gold,
Forg'd as for limbs of more than mortal mould.
The heavy volumes, thence descending, bind
With mockery vain th' impassive mountain wind :

For he, th' illustrious victim, he whose fate,
Whose matchless woes that mountain consecrate,
Free as his own unconquer'd spirit proved,
Hath found the freedom and the truth he lov'd,—
Long since enfranchis'd from each mortal pain,
Man's hate perfidious and ignoble chain.
And the poor wrecks of that once glorious form
Feel not the gyves, nor chill beneath the storm,—
Writhe not as stoops the Eagle to his prey,
Or, soaring, rends the quivering heart away.

What eye could gaze on those dread relics cast
E'en where th' illustrious victim breath'd his last,
On those ennobling chains, that granite stone,
Which saw his torture, echoed back the moan
Wrung from an agonized heart that still
Preserv'd inviolate the dauntless will,—
Nor one repentant, one reproachful thought
Deign'd to the pangs his coward foes had wrought;
What heart unmov'd such memories could sustain,
What eye glance cold o'er that recording chain?

Absorb'd in deepest musing, Night had grown
O'er the wide world and round that summit lone,
Ere Dion mark'd its progress. Cold and bright,
Unlike the aspect of an Earthly night,
So pure each planet, so undimm'd the sky,
So phosphor-clear the snowy hoards that lie
Immeasurably spread, reflecting fair
Each wandering ray that lights bewilder'd there,—
It rather seem'd some holiest twilight, made
Of each soft shaded light and lustrous shade.
Such ray impearls the Mermaid's deep abode
Beneath old Ocean's boundless crystal flood ;
Or binds the treachery of its chaste control
Round the waste circle of the icy Pole.

He felt his peril, as subsided slow,
Chill'd by the blast, his warm heart's vital glow,
And delving with his sword beneath the snow
A cavernous retreat, around him roll'd
His cloak of felt in many an ample fold.
Prepar'd beside th' untomb'd remains to keep
His hallow'd vigil on that haunted Steep.

It fell, that awful Night. O'er Dion's soul
Its tide mysterious did resistless roll,
Heaving its shapeless thoughts and phantoms dire
In billowy depths of mingled gloom and fire.
The past, the present, things familiar grown,
Objects of reason or of sense, were none,—
Or *but* existent dimly to express
The power, th' extent of that vast Nothingness.
Yet 'twas not darkness. He had hailed the Night
To quench in utter gloom his o'erstrain'd sight :
Shapes half develop'd fill his baffled eye,
Then crumbling join the murk profundity.

Nature seem'd all inverted. Mightiest war,
The toil, the terror, the terrific jar
Of all her struggling powers, Earth, Ocean, Sky,
Roll'd weltering round in maddest revelry.
And thro' the turmoil, thro' the giddy shock
And whirl and dissonance of Powers that rock
The Universal System to its base,
There crept upon his soul the sickening trace,

The trail abhorr'd of an all-blighting thought,
That this vast power and toil and strife were wrought
By and for nought. And then the thunders took
The loath'd idea: the murky welkin shook
To its deep-mutter'd murmur; and th' Abyss
Gave back the serpent thought in one long hiss
Of fiendish mockery. And on th' inverted eye
A shape of blindness, madness, mystery,
Rose o'er Heaven's mighty wreck: and while Despair
Blew like the icy North, freezing whate'er
Of life remain'd, the yelling dissonance
To attributes supreme link'd the blind name of Chance.

The tumult deaden'd; the o'ertravail'd mind
Sank into stupor, stunn'd, exhausted, blind
With th' ungovern'd strife: and like the weak
And sickly growth of Morn's distemper'd streak,
Along the lurid Heavens, thought backward trail'd
Its languid twilight length and strugglingly prevail'd.

Dark forms were round him, shadowy shapes and vast,
The awful spirits of th' unfathom'd Past,
In whose compare hoar Saturn's ancient sway (7)
Seems but the brief vain dream of yesterday.
The vasty Deep, the measureless Abyss,
Eternity's dark Realm, the Wilderness
Of Doubt and Error—each had hither sent
Its spirit envoy, whose dread form, unbent
By Immortality's dire burden, bears
With princely ease th' infinitude of years
Since Time from Order grew. Around they stood
A silent group, as pondering deep the flood
Of Past and Future. It relief had been
Their voice to hear, tho' terrible as when
Conflicting thunders shout, or direr far
Heaves from Earth's womb convuls'd th' intestine jar.
But they stand silent all. What make they here
With their stern eyes fixt motionless and drear
On that blood-hallow'd rock? Joy they to trace
His woes, who shook their Empire to its base,
Or homage to that mightier Spirit own?

Long had he gaz'd, ere conscious there was grown
From the dim mists which shroud that fateful spot
Another form and diverse. Those had not
One feature common to the human Race:
Each seem'd th' embodiment of thoughts that trace
Their being to the twilight of the soul.
But he who, now uprising, claim'd control
Of Dion's rapt attention, seem'd design'd
Th' ennobled type and sovereign of mankind.
Such the sublimity his port express'd,
That brow in calm, majestic suffering drest,
That eye's unfathom'd depth. Yet seem'd he worn
By woes the Mightiest only could have borne.
Oh! when is might so mighty as in woe?
Oh! where is majesty, save on the brow
That suffers all unbent; rend'ring again
The meek defiance of a high disdain,
Calm towering, like Heaven's star-ennobled height,
O'er Pain's worst torment, Fortune's black despite?
It was relief on that calm brow to gaze,
The sight to fill with those all-glorious traits,

Blending in harmonies that recompose
Th' unsettled fabric of the mind; like those
Which, heard on old Sigæum's haunted shore,
The wind bore mingled with the billows' roar,
While shapeless rocks to fair proportions grown
Round Ilium bind th' insuperable zone. (8)
Dim wan'd the forms. Exhausted Fancy's sight
Was clos'd or prison'd by succeeding Night;
Yet not until that glorious one had blest
With smile approving Dion's grateful breast.

'Tis morn. Earth wak'd to radiance bright and warm
Shakes off the mists that shroud her glowing form;
Which, part dissolv'd in Ether's flood decay,
Part roll majestic like dim ghosts away,
Surpris'd by Morning's waft. The World beneath
Bursts into life renew'd from transient Death;
Hearts that lay down in heaviness arise,
Blithe as the lark that warbling swims the skies—
Like him to that blue vault uplift the voice
Of a tun'd heart, and in their strength rejoice.

The hill, the vale, the blue unfathom'd Deep,
Sprent those with dew, *this* smiling out of sleep
As the young Breeze comes dancing o'er his breast;
Each, all in new, untarnish'd beauty drest,
To eye, to ear, to each rapt sense outpour
Their boundless bliss, glow, sparkle, and adore.

And Dion's vigil ceas'd. That hallow'd rock
Where the great Victim triumph'd o'er the shock
Of more than mortal woe, seem'd first to claim
As deathless monument of his high fame
Prometheus' relics. But the granite height
Uncloth'd of soil, unyielding to the might
Of Dion's sword, his pious wish defy:
The rock he searches with attentive eye,
Enters a cleft by recent thunder rent,
Abruptly plunging by a sheer descent
Into a cavern rude, the work entire
Of ancient Chaos' all-subduing fire.
There, decently compos'd, Earth's sacred breast
Receiv'd the bones of her great Son to rest;

And he, whose spirit was to earth allied
But in the bond which mightiest love supplied,
'Twixt Heav'n his birthplace and the Earth he strove
To rivet closer to that Heaven by love,—
Here, where blue ether and th' extremest trace
Of earth meet, mingling in a chaste embrace,
Has back to Earth restor'd what claim soe'er
She in his birthright with the Heavens might share.

His task complete, with peril all renew'd
The downward path Prometheus' son pursued
With lighten'd heart, but toil-enduring frame,
The torch of Heaven had twice relum'd its flame
And yet again was kindling, when his feet
Press'd the slope bounds where vale and mountain meet,—
The roots gigantic by that summit hurl'd
Deep mid the bowels of the groaning world.
His eye distent t' embrace the vision vast
Of mount o'er mountain rude confus'dly cast,
His thoughts, his spirit, from their converse late
With more than mortal company, elate,

He held his downward way, in pensive mood,
Unconscious of th' assembled multitude
His foot was nearing; nor that he was grown
The focus whither all-converging shone
Ten thousand glances: till the clangor loud
Of mountain cornet and the shouting crowd
Each wandering sense recall'd with sudden start
That forc'd life's current back upon the heart.

Close at his feet, outspread beneath his sight,
Where the Mount's undules and the plain unite,
A people's might lay gather'd, swelling wide,
Countless as foam-globes of old Ocean's tide.
It was a sight most startling, in the mood
Begot by Nature's sternest solitude,
By sights and sounds combining to declare
That mortal step was all-unwonted there,
At once in presence of mankind to stand,
The birth Cadmæan of the teeming Land.

But what that shout? What mean those bended knees,
Those clouds of incense wafted by the breeze,

What those triumphant strains? From side to side
His glance shot restless thro' the concourse wide.
All eyes concentrate their keen rays in one,
All voices, gestures thither tend alone;
Himself the mark of all. Incredulous still
He searches o'er and o'er the teeming hill,
But meets no rival there.
     " My fellow men—"
'Twas thus he spake, and Echo peal'd again
From crag and cliff the jubilant accord
Of welcome proffer'd to his op'ning word:
" Whence this vast concourse? What concernment deep
Leads forth a Nation to this haunted Steep,
O'erpeopling thus the desolate domain
Where mountain Spirits hold their silent reign?
And why on me those looks of wonder bent?
And what the purport of the shouts that rent
Th' empyreal concave? Is it strange to see
A mortal, burden'd with humanity?
Or come ye forth, as came your Sires of yore,
Prometheus' blood to honour and adore,

Then foully shed, and into exile chase
Each lingering scion of his kingly race?
If such your will, in happy hour ye come,
And Fate hath led my exil'd footstep home
In hour opportune: nor know I a plea
Why he should suffer and myself be free,
Who share (oh! were I worthier) in the tide
Of his rich blood, his sorrows and his pride,
And who, my task fulfill'd, his great remains
To Earth's embrace to render from the chains
By little hands impos'd, stand free to close
My sacred birthright in his mighty woes.'

Scarce had he paus'd ere, rising wild and high,
A Nation's shout of triumph rent the sky:
" Hail the pure blood of our anointed kings!
All hail the sacred Providence that brings
Our own great line of heroes back to sway
The realm whose grandeur pal'd in their decay.
Hail to our King! our great Deliv'rer see!
Hail Freedom's dawn, Day-star of liberty!

Thrice rose that shout: but when in Freedom's name
'Twas shap'd and syllabled, the struggling flame
Of liberty, so long o'erborne, represt,
Burst, a volcanic fire-flood from each breast,
With shout so terrible, that from on high
The bird of Jove, dim wheeling thro' the sky (9)
Fell stunn'd to Earth at Dion's feet and lay
Gasping in sobs the breath of life away.

That portent new inflames the wondering throng;
Their shouts redouble. Had Prometheus sprung
To life where stands his offspring, their delight
And triumph scarce had soar'd a loftier flight,
Nor had *his* awful Form with dread imprest
Or deeper reverence each devoted breast.
" A present miracle," they shout, they cry;
" Heaven seals and signs her ancient prophecy—
The victor vanquish'd, the oppressor slain,
The mighty victim call'd to life again
From his long trance, his awful, star-watch'd sleep
Of hoar, dim ages on the snow-clad steep.

The beak, his sacred suffering form that tore,
The eye suffus'd and redden'd in his gore,
The wing that flapp'd insulting that dread brow,
Lie at his feet, clos'd, powerless in their woe.
Bring forth the crown and sceptre never stain'd
By tyrant's touch, dread symbols unprofan'd,
Which Earth, aye mindful of her solemn trust,
Had sacred held with her Promethean dust:
Till ripe the hour, an Earthquake's might restor'd
The dread regalia for their rightful Lord."

Forth at the word, disparting from the throng,
The heralds file in marshall'd rank and long;
Compass with stately pace the sacred ground,
Earth's quadrate aspects linking in their round:
Then at his feet the crown and sceptre lay,
And would his form in purple robes array.
But Dion stay'd them.

     " Fathers, chiefs, forbear;
Not mine the brow this diadem to wear.
Tho' dread Prometheus' blood this bosom warm,
His rightful heir, a Maid of matchless form

And peerless mind, with every grace array'd.—
In exile nurtur'd dwells the sacred Maid.
Shout high her name, all ye who love the sway
Of great Prometheus: him in her obey:
' Indra, Prometheus' Daughter.' Yet once more
And once again, till Ocean's billowy shore
Catch the glad tidings as their murmurs reach
His breakers, battling with the surf-sown beach."

Thus shouted high the ever-wavering crowd,
Pleas'd to reverse a choice so late avow'd:
" Indra, our queen, our queen!" But, as the sound
Ceas'd, mid the echoing crags and gulphs profound,
And nodding forest, other murmurs ran
Thro' that vast concourse, toss'd from man to man—
" Prometheus' Daughter in a land afar,
Who shall our host lead forth to instant war?
Who guide in peace a people sworn to own
The sway of great Prometheus' race alone?
Thou must our sceptre bear: 'tis Heaven's decree,
By portent clear and ancient prophecy.

Our new-born rights thy fostering aid demand,
Our sword, our sceptre, court thy ready hand.
Raise thou our crown; our king, our captain be;
Firm fixt our choice, and we will none but thee."

" Friends, whom the pitying Heavens this hour restore
With my dread Fathers' tombs, old Ocean's solemn roar,
Gladly the truncheon proffer'd to my hand
In Indra's name I grasp: the chief command
Of your Battalia, and beneath her throne
The helm of State, until she claim her own.
In her renew'd Prometheus' self ye'll find,
Hers his high virtues, hers his God-like mind.
Each power, each gift of that anointed Race,
Prometheus' genius, Maia's * matchless grace;—
Until return'd the sacred Maiden claim
That throne, that diadem; in her great name
I guard, defend them, with your loyal might,
Your hearts and hands, and Heaven to back the right."

* Maia was daughter of Atlas, and niece of Prometheus; she was one of the Hesperides.

He ceas'd, and joyful, jubilant assent,
From Earth to Heaven the shouting myriads sent,
From Heaven to Earth reverbing. Forth to view
Disparting from the crowd each captain drew
His martial cohort—Men in training new,
Unskill'd as yet the changeful front to yield
For each dire mystery of th' embattled field;
But nurs'd in hardship, well inur'd to bear
Extremes alternate of the changeful year,
The Dogstar's fervor and the icing chill
Of midnight watches on the wintry hill;
Stern, iron Men, the mountain's hardy birth,
Whom in her fever-fit plethoric Earth
Sends forth, her veins of their fierce throb to free,
With specious watchwords arm'd, " Truth, Justice, Liberty."

In crescent form array'd their phalanx rude
Bristling with spears in breathless silence stood;
Then forth at once each flaming blade was drawn,
Dazzling the Day-star of the early dawn,

And sternly wav'd on high o'er each flush'd brow,
Then prest, in plight of his inviolate vow,
To each rude warrior's lips. No tumult then,
No shout of triumph rose from those stern men;
But a deep murmur, like the sudden jar,
Mysterious, given by Ocean from afar
On the still hush of Night, when far and wide
Calm lies each billow slumbering in its pride,
And Ocean's might reposing, mortals form
No thought unquiet of th' impending Storm.

No arms of proof array'd that hardy Band,
The brow no helm, the throat no gorget spann'd,
Each bore the various weapon zeal supplies
To ready hands and new-born energies:
The spear with which the savage bear is bay'd,
The tough horn bow, the legend-haunted blade;
Yet tho' no corslet flam'd upon the breast,
No nodding plume their martial zeal express'd,
A symbol worthier far the vows they swear;—
Look to the kindling eye, flush'd cheek, 'tis there.

Theirs the tried mail impervious to the dart,
Th' ethereal temper of a dauntless heart.

All this mark'd Dion, as with martial pride,
From rank to rank his kindling glances glide,
Girt with that throng of kindred hearts and hands,
On his own soil, beneath the shade he stands
Of that thrice-hallow'd Mount. His own dark Sea,
His Fathers' tombs, home, country, Liberty
At once restor'd. The thought his bosom fir'd,
Breath'd thro' his frame, his glowing tongue inspir'd
With more than human eloquence. They saw,
That throng, his step majestic; with deep awe
Hung, breathless, on his speech. The visible form
Of worshipp'd virtue, vigorous, youthful, warm,
Mov'd, breath'd before them. Earth an aspect new
Of fadeless verdure wore: the sky more blue,
Old Ocean fuller, mightier seem'd to be;
Earth's golden Age renew'd Truth, Justice, Purity.

END OF CANTO IV.

Canto V.

THE QUEST.

" Look forth upon the night, my child.　How shine
　The starry Heavens, that page of power Divine?
　Is Day's last beam extinct, Love, in the West?
　Sighs the night-breeze, or folds its wing in rest?
　And turn thee now, thy gaze to Eastward bend,
　Mark well the aspect of high Demawend:
　For if, unshrouded by the mist, his brow
　May in the stars' collective radiance glow,
　And my foreboding yet may be beguil'd:
　What be the portents of the Night, my child?"

" Clear is the sky, the evening Breeze at rest,
    All sounds be hush'd upon the mountain breast,
    The stars shine each in his appointed sphere,
    Bright as tho' Heaven had fram'd without a tear
    The destinies they guard. The Day-star's track
    Night hath effac'd beneath her pinion black :
    But far away to Eastward clearly rise,
    Trac'd o'er the darken'd canvas of the skies,
    The thousand years that blanch but may not bend
    The brow sublime of star-choir'd Demawend.
    And now uprising o'er his mass there glows
    A spot, a speck of brilliance ;—still it grows,
    Flinging its ray of ruddy light afar :
    How redly rises Eve's effulgent star !
    It rises not. It lingers on the crest
    Of that hoar mount, and while its glories rest,
    Like beacon-flames pil'd o'er the cresting snow,
    A blood-red tide floods all the World below."

" 'Tis the dread summons, Indra. Ne'er again
    Thy Mother rises from her couch of pain.

Yon beacon ne'er its lurid radiance gave
But one more victim fill'd Prometheus' grave.
I feel—*have* felt it—cold around my heart,
The coil of death. Life flutters to depart:
Yet, ere Eternity's dread voy'ge she try,
Feels the wing falter and the courage die.
O slavish Fear, most vile of all that swell
Our spirits' hostile ranks, thy funeral knell
Palsies each Virtue with its fatal tone,
Curdling the heart's warm life-tide into stone.

" Death, name of mystery, still from Reason's morn
Thy shadowy yoke my servile neck hath borne.
Now that thy form in closest view doth stand,
Now that I feel thy cold, remorseless hand
Send the ice-chill of torpor thro' my frame,
What buoys my spirit, as on wings of flame?
Oh! 'tis a hope I ne'er had deem'd to know,
Whose cloud-wrapp'd Heaven gloom'd black without a bow—
A hope that, like some glorious insect springing
To life and beauty from the cerements clinging

Round her pent form, leaves Earth's cold grave to rise
And bask, henceforth, in sunshine of the skies."

"Friend, mother, guide, my guardian from the morn
Of helpless, thankless infancy, when borne
In those lov'd arms, at that reverèd breast,
Thy voice my spirit calm'd, thy lips caress'd:
When thou wert all of Heaven on Earth to me,
And my vain self was all Earth's care for thee:
Sweet Mother, hush thee; thy deep woes have weigh'd
Thy spirit down beneath their baleful shade,
And thro' the gloom-haze of the past appears
The future, burden'd with remember'd tears.
Oh! well I trust far distant that sad hour—
Remote from thee Death's dark and envious power,
Whose victim, not the taken, but the heart
Left pining, crush'd, forbidden to depart."

"Draw nigh, my child; oh! think not 'tis in vain
I seek to warn thee of approaching pain.
My spirit ebbs apace; my labouring breast
Scarce heaves its sickening burden of unrest;

My sight is clouded. Nearer press thy face,
That I may see thee, feel thy sweet embrace;
That thy blest image be the last of sight:
For other forms are crowding; ancient Night
Hath set his captives free. Dost thou not view
Their dusky forms, a sad and silent crew?
How slow, how solemn! Ever thus they grace
The dying couch of our devoted race.
Dost thou not mark them, Indra?"

       "Nought I see,
Blest Friend, of none think, hope, but only thee."

" Heaven grant thou do not—Heaven preserve thy mind
From the dark gloom of horror, which I find
Slow creeping o'er mine own. Yet is there one:
Thou canst not but behold *him*. 'Tis thine own
Blest Sire. O thou, my soul's love, joy, and pride,
Lord of my youthful vows, I did abide
Long, long; for thee have mourn'd, and wept, and
 pray'd;
Dream'd thou wert nigh, till garish morn bewray'd

The bitter counterfeit, and caus'd me lay
My malison of misery on the day
And bless the pitying night. And thou art come
In thy majestic beauty: to thy home
Of sacred rest will bear me. We will dwell
For evermore in peace, with none to quell
The fulness of our joy. Ay! mark her well,
'Tis thine own babe: thy soften'd image see,
Glaucon, thyself—hope born in form of thee.
Why look'st thou sad? Shall we not thither bear
Our peaceful babe, where Heavens be alway fair,
And Man betrays not, not existing there?
See how she smiles on thee with love benign!
My Glaucon, take her to thy heart and sign
A father's blessing o'er her. Even now
Her rosy lips are struggling to avow
How well she loves thee. She will tell thee all
Her little dreams, and one by one recall
Her innocent, pure thoughts. Wilt thou not give
Thy heart of hearts to hear her, to receive
Her sweet disclosures? Ah! I dream'd of woe—
Of long, drear wretchedness;—that thou wert low,

My bosom Lord, in manhood's prime o'erta'en
By torture, death, too terrible to name.
And years of mortal suffering were past by,
Years of the heart's slow, wasting misery:
And our sweet babe, like some rich pearl, was grown
A mine of beauty on a shore unknown;
Smiling in purity of grace to bless
The bleak, wreck'd rocks, strown round in wretchedness,
To bless, to gladden—Thee? her sire?—Ah, no!
An orphan's doom was seal'd on her fair brow.

" And one was sent,—not thou, but of thy race,
Of princely form like thine, and awful grace;
Who with his wizard harp and minstrel sway
Wil'd our young Indra's destin'd lord away.
And then came Death, the last terrific foe,
Despair and gloom the burden of his brow;
He stretch'd his pall of horror o'er my sight,
And drown'd my spirit in excess of night:
And I had perish'd;—but an angel form
Came, smiling peace, where all foreboded storm.

Her fair hand rent that curtain of despair;
Her sweet voice harmoniz'd the jarring air:
Her smile won entry to the heart's dark core.
The blind depths own'd it and were dark no more.
Her finger pointed me to realms above.—
I look'd. This seraph wore thy traits of love.
It was our babe, our little one, whom thou
Fold'st in thine arms; the same her angel brow:
But she was grown in beauty, and her eyes
Were deep suffus'd with mysteries of the skies.
A wingèd seraph she. But thou art come—
My dream is ended—my dread slumber done.
Ah! what if life be but a feverish trance
Whose waking is eternity? Thy glance
Decays—is fading. Yet one moment stay,
While our blest babe I more securely lay
Within my bosom clasp. I follow thee,
I follow——follow——"

      Softly, languidly
She drew her circling arms around her child,
Gaz'd up to Heav'n, then back on her, and smil'd;

And by that clasp relaxing Indra knew,
And by the fixing eye and traits that grew
So sudden still'd in quietude of rest,
That life had parted from the fond, warm breast
That long was wont to throb for her alone.
Death! Death, thou stern destroyer! many an one
Thy ruthless hand hath stricken; but thou ne'er
Didst sever bond more precious or more fair;
Didst never leave so helpless in her woe
The sad survivor of thy murderous blow.
There still was eye of fellow-mortal near,
Some pitying heart, some voice to fill the ear
If but with jarring note; some tongue to say,
Thou art not yet an utter castaway.
Thou mayst go forth, unshunn'd, untaunted go,
No brand of outlawry on thy lone brow,
By reason of thy misery. Yea! still
Mayst thou partake the sunbeam, breeze, and rill
Untax'd of trespass, since not yet thou'rt thrown
On Man's chill pity, heart-wreck'd and alone.

Night was around her, and the Dead. There lay
A hush of dreadful stillness with the ray
Of the faint taper, that with sickly light
Spent its vain mockery on the void of Night.
Those arms, around her neck so fondly twin'd,
Seem'd, e'en in death, reluctant to unwind,
Resisted still the gentle force she tried,
For they were stiff'ning with life's icing tide.
She gaz'd on those still features: through and through
She read the scroll of memory spread to view
In their lov'd lineaments. Ah! who shall tell
What floods of hallow'd thought the bosom swell
At each sweet dream of her who from life's morn
Hath been the angel of our peace, hath borne
Heaven's law of love to man. Of her, in whom
We first believ'd of bliss beyond the tomb,—
When to her bosom clasp'd, all earthly woes
Were hush'd to rapture of the soul's repose,
And cares and griefs that threaten'd to endure
Through life ebb'd softly with the staunching tear.

Ah! who shall tell? For there is *once* on earth
An hour more woe-fraught than man's stormy
 birth:
'Tis when, dissevered from the womb once more,
Cast by the wave receding on life's shore,
Our early race of sanguine fancy run,
Our fairy voy'ge of hope and sunshine done,
Our buoyancy impair'd, and many a rent,
Torn by the brunt of hostile element,
To wreck our healthful confidence, we may,
Perchance, tempt once again life's stormy way;
But never, never, wheresoe'er we roam,
Return to sunshine, happiness, and home.

Thus lay Prometheus' daughter, till the star
That rose with eve had culminated far
In th' ethereal concave. Sorrow-drown'd,
Cold as the arms enclasping her around,
She lay. But now the portal's sullen jar
Call'd her lost thoughts and memory from afar,
As solemn, entering, vision-like, appear'd
A form from childhood's earliest dawn rever'd,

The sage who'd watch'd her virtues' germs to twine
And train each tendril to a branch divine;
The kind, the meek, the gentle, the sincere,
Born without guile; the man whose blameless tear
For others shed in worth transcended far
The spoils that tempt a greedy world to war.
His once tall form by weight of years deprest;
His eye, that beam'd the fervour of a breast
In sorrow school'd, yet fruitful to th' o'erflow
Of joy divine and love to all below:
That form approach'd, bent o'er her, and that eye
Pour'd forth the soul of tenderest sympathy.

" Father, whence, wherefore art thou come?"
                                        The mild
Old man replied : " Thou called'st me, my child."
" Alas! I call'd thee not, nor e'en in thought
Left this dread couch. Heaven's grace alone hath brought
Thy blessed step."
                  " My child, thine accents broke
My midnight slumber; but or e'er I woke,

Thy voice was silent and thy form was gone.
I rose and hasted hither, for thy tone
Jarr'd as in sorrow on my trembling heart.
And yet I guess'd not 'twas so sad a part
Thou called'st me to fill."

      He said. Anon
Hath loos'd the clasping arms around her thrown,—
That lifeless form compos'd to decent rest,
And rais'd a sacred anthem o'er the blest
Who die in peace; and solemnly consign'd
To Heaven's kind care that woe-distracted mind;—
Then Indra's ear and soul, deep-stricken, fed
With healing balm, the praises of the dead;
Prob'd the crush'd wound with kind, but searching art,
Till the numb'd tides well'd freely from the heart,
Till the deep healing gush of tears held sway
With might that hurried deadlier thrall away.

Three days to grief were giv'n. The early ray
Of the fourth morn scarce found its golden way
Through Indra's casement, when the orphan maid,
From slumber ris'n, her beauteous form array'd

In minstrel garb, look'd round, with watery eye,
On scenes rever'd from earliest infancy,
Sacred to household joys and memories dear,
Love's glance, Hope's promise, Sorrow's hallowing tear.

" O scenes of childhood, innocence, and glee,
My home that was, and never more must be!
She, who a daughter styl'd herself of late,
Leaves her heart's blessing at thy sacred gate.
Blest be thy threshold, hearth, and circling wall!
Blest while they stand, and hallow'd in their fall
Beneath the hand of Time, before the blast
Of mountain storm that, erst unheeded, pass'd
While pilgrims bless'd the ever-open gate.
Farewell! thou art not half *so* desolate
As the lone heart that mourns thee. Past the gleam
That sunn'd us both; our bliss a vanish'd dream.
But mine!—and yet I envy not thy lot
To stand deserted on this haunted spot,
When all that gave it grace and life are gone,
And thou a stranger at thine own hearthstone.

Farewell, sad refuge of my sires! this heart
Must burst—is breaking : thus and thus we part! "

She dar'd not trust her eye, her memory more :
She left the threshold, clos'd the sacred door.
What dread may daunt the soul o'er woe elate ?
The wreck'd in heart are paramount to fate;
The sands that meted out youth's bliss are run,
Indra's sad pilgrimage of Life begun.

And what her purpose? Whither would she go
Alone through this bleak world of strife and woe?
Of woman born art thou, and need'st to know.
The bee her thymy pasture knows; the flower
Her lover lord and his appointed hour :
The Breeze, Aurora's rose-encluster'd bower;
The exil'd Dove, her prison'd wing set free,
Knows but one end of her glad liberty :
Spring knows her own betroth'd and plighted star;
And e'en the Tempest, whose fierce love is war,
Knows when Orion riseth.   And shall she
Whose bosom Love hath sanctified, to be

His heaven-born fire's most pure and hallow'd fane,
List the low pleading of his voice in vain?

Yes! when the Dove her gentle home forswears;
Yes! when Aurora sheds forsaken tears;
Ay, when the Bee her thymy bank shall shun;
When the Rose-petals close against the Sun;
When, at the rising of her star, no more
Spring, laughing, wakes her flower-germs as before;
When fierce Orion, tyrant of the sky,
Calls his wild hurricanes and none reply;
When Nature's laws, upturn'd, inverted lie,
And, saddest, wreck'd sweet Woman's purity;
Then Love may plead,—plead in his low, deep tone,
Yet find his might decay'd, his reign of triumph done.

Beyond the garden-fence, his white locks strew'd
On the keen gale of Morn, Arcestes stood.
"Thy love, true friend, hath early chas'd thy rest.
Bless me, my Father, and I shall be blest."

"Would that the poor, weak blessing of a heart
That soon with earthly cares and woes shall part,
Could be a shield and shelter round thee spread,
Help to thy steps and shadow to thy head.
Together wend we, Indra. When o'erpast
Thy toils, attain'd thy heart's sweet rest, at last
These worn-out orbs in hope I'll tranquil close,
And thou shalt hymn my requiem of repose."

He would not be denied. They onward sped,
That ancient Man and beauteous orphan Maid:
But she now bore, in garb of minstrel drest,
The harp bequeath'd her by their mystic guest;
That harp, whose magic whirl'd the soul along
Resistless, chiming to her syren tongue.
They sought a path, less savage than the road
By Dion's venturous step of ardour trod;
Where shepherd tribes a scanty pasture find,
A race uncouth, but yet of human kind;
Lawless, or bending but to force alone,
But claiming two rude virtues for their own—

Good faith and hospitable lore. Nor they
Senseless to music's rapt, heroic lay.

Not half this mountain tract was travers'd o'er,
And distant yet the Euxine's classic shore,
When, worn with toil and bent beneath the weight
Of hoary age, Arcestes bow'd to fate.
So peaceful sets on Ocean's troublous breast
The Day-star sinking to his glorious rest;
Each glance benign upon the dim world cast,
Each sigh surcharg'd with blessing to the last;
And the bright track his pilgrim step hath strown
With glory, beac'ning to a realm unknown,
And op'ning through the sapphire-vaulted sky
The golden gate to blessedness on high.
Alone must now her pilgrim path be ta'en
Mid rugged wilds and yet more savage men:
Those to the mountain child familiar long,
These gazing, awstruck, on the Child of Song,
Whose stately air, retir'd, but lofty, mood,
And form of grace, in such mark'd contrast stood

With their rude lineaments. Whose song could sway
Their souls with might surpassing mortal lay.

Her theme was now th' illustrious exile's woes,
The sport of Fate; Earth, Ocean, Heaven his foes,
Yet victor rising o'er Earth, Ocean, Sky,
And Fate itself, by matchless constancy.
And ah! when dwelling on the one, deep thought,
That all his sorrows, suffering, triumph, wrought
That pure, unquenchable, exhaustless flame
That still burn'd on, through every change the same—
Which woe but heighten'd, luxury could not dim,
And peril but more sacred made to him—
His country's love. No heart those tones could hear
Of pleading pathos, but felt shadowing near
Ulysses' awful spirit, mightier far
In woe than conqueror in the ten years' war.

Or sang she him, Athena, whose dire fate
Seal'd his proud birthright of the good and great
Among thy children?—him who Plato taught
His lore divine; from whose pure spirit caught

His eloquence sublime, thy peerless son,
Chief of ten thousand heroes, Xenophon?
Sang she of Socrates, at once the boast
And condemnation of thy blood-stain'd coast;
The first whom Pallas' voice inspir'd to know
Herself, in Virtue's shape transform'd below?
Sang she the woe which robb'd a World forlorn
Of such bright Day-star of a purer Morn?
That deed, o'er which Medea's dreadful shade
Shriek'd her wild laugh and shook the reeking blade.

Oh! as absorb'd in gesture, eye, and thought,
Her audience rude th' unwonted numbers caught,
The inspiration of that matchless strain
Wrought in each heart and madden'd every brain;
And the stern hunter of the mountain, grown
Fir'd with ambition till that hour unknown,
Marvell'd that aught to his wild soul should seem
Dearer or worthier than his first, last dream
Of war and rapine, or that music's sway
Should steal the fierceness of his soul away.

Of Phocion, name scarce less rever'd, she sung,
Not less her glory from whose soil he sprung,
And, ah! not less her victim, whose red hand
Still pour'd the tide o'er that affrighted land
Of her best children's blood. O matchless queen
Of arts, and eloquence, and godlike men!
Whence thy perverse, unhallow'd fury, shown
On all whose names were worthy of thine own?
Which of thy noblest sons hast thou not sent
To death, to bondage, or to banishment?
So that in peace within thy walls to die
Might seem reproachful to the Memory
Else faultless deem'd. Or did thine artful mind
Ponder herein a subtlety refin'd:
On human virtue's frail and faltering zeal
To set the firm, irrevocable seal,
And make that virtue, when to Heaven 'twas grown,
By death's inalienable pledge thine own?

But most were mov'd their ardent minds when he,
Laconia's patriot, and Thermopylæ

Inspir'd her lay: and mountain bosoms glow'd
With fire heroic as the numbers flow'd;
And the small Band, self-offer'd at thy shrine,
Fair Liberty, once more in serried line
March to irrevocable death.   Their tread
How firm, how solemn are the glances shed
Around them, as a last farewell they take
Of home, friends, country, for that country's sake.
Their silent march no murmur'd voice betrays;
The clash of steel alone, the martial blaze
Of their own sun from arms and armour thrown
Mark their stern path to Hades and renown.
But, in each bosom, settled as the Deep
Ere yet the tempest o'er its surface sweep,
Home's early joys, remember'd hope and trust,
Their friends, their altars, and their fathers' dust,
In awful power repose.   On either hand
To mourn, to envy their high privilege, stand
Laconia's martial youth: and aged men,
Rever'd as their own altars, feel again
The bounding glow of youth, and long to lay
On that high fane life's fast-departing ray.

And Sparta's maids, a beauteous band, are there.
What heart, the freedom of those smiles to share,
Would not stir Glory in Death's rugged lair?
White robes their forms, their brows white garlands
    bind—
Robes, blossoms, spotless as each vestal mind:
Each arm outstretch'd; each chisell'd brow the shrine
Of holiest ardour in a cause divine;
Each tender cheek how pale! save where appear
As through the cleft pomegranate's crystal clear,
Soft hectic streaks, and in each eye a tear:
Such tear as many a Spartan eye bedew,—
Such as Leonidas himself might view
Unblaming. Tear well fitted to thy rite,
Relentless Nemesis, dread daughter of the Night.

Thus sang Prometheus' Daughter. On her song,
Entranc'd and mute, her audience feasted long:
But when the tramp of warriors meets their ear,
And flaming arms and nodding crests appear,
And eyes flash out, as from the deep Sea's wave,
The fires that beacon and adorn the grave,—

And as the mountain pass they dauntless scale,
And pour their free song on the mountain gale,
And banquet cheerful as the guests decreed
Of gloomy Dis and th' illustrious Dead:
No more her audience curb'd their martial pride,
But, rising, pac'd the Cot with loftier stride;
And clash'd their arms and mingled in the fray,
So Fancy taught them, of that glorious day.

Thus chang'd her theme. But whatsoe'er its vein,
No mood of lightness mingled in the strain;
Nor did the spell-bound Shepherd, as her eye
Brought o'er his soul the deeds of years gone by,
Presume of that lone minstrel to require
One thrill of gladness from his wondrous lyre.
But as she onward sped, the mountain breast
'Gan offer startling tokens of unrest;
Each hamlet muster'd at the Elder's door
Its chosen youth; their thoughts, looks, language, war.
Struck with the portent, she her speech address'd
To one whose locks of age his rank express'd
Mid those rude Shepherds.

"Father, what alarms
Are mustering thus your chosen youth in arms?
No gauds be yours, no spoils to tempt the hand
Of lawless conqueror or the robber band.
Your riches health, your heritage stern toil,
Freedom your birthright, poverty your wall;
The sweeping avalanche and earthquake's shock
The sole invaders of your eyrie rock.
Whence, then, this martial concourse, this array
Of warriors arm'd and mustering for th' affray?
Is not the world at rest?"

"Alas! my son,
When *was* the world at rest?—Since time begun
Of quacks and madmen still th' alternate prize,
While strength foils virtue, knaves outwit the wise.
But thou a stranger art, or shouldst have known
The tidings strange that o'er our hills have flown;.
The portents dread that have to Earth restor'd
Prometheus' Race and edg'd Prometheus' sword
To Death's red harvest. If thou, then, wouldst hear
A tale of marvel, fitting minstrel ear,

Enter and rest thee in my lowly cot,
And be it ours from thy sad heart to blot
The homeless Wanderer's woe."
                              With grateful look
That thrice repaid the boon, the Maiden took
Her welcome seat beside that lowly board;
And while the matron spread her rustic hoard,
Fresh milk, and barley cakes, and flesh of deer,
And press'd with kindest zeal the simple cheer
Upon her anxious guest, that aged man,
Loquacious, thus his promis'd tale began:

" A stranger, thou, my son; yet wheresoe'er
Thy lips first drew the breath of vital air,
Whether in lands where Ganges' strength is roll'd
O'er India's sparkling gems and sands of gold;
Or where the snorting steed of Scythia first
Quells in Tanaïs' rills his fiery thirst,
And neighs his welcome to the new-born son
Of Ocean, strength'ning as his might rolls on;
Where'er thy birth, no Nation but the fame
Of great Prometheus has enroll'd his name

First of Earth's heroes. Since his Race afar
Were chas'd to exile by our evil star,
The land, distraught by turns with civil strife,
Or foreign war, the fetter and the knife,
Hath wept in sackcloth and repentant mourn'd
The heaven-sprung Race whose faultless rule she scorn'd.
But still a hope surviv'd. From days of old
Sages and seers had in their lays foretold
That once again, as from the womb of Time,
Prometheus' fire should burst, Prometheus' line
Once more a hero yield. The day, the year,
By mystic symbols shadow'd, had drawn near,
When portents strange throughout our land retrace
The hope which ages might not all efface.

" A mound there is with pine-trees shadow'd round,
Amid whose dust by curious eyes are found
Gems of small price and ancient coins that bear
Prometheus' name. Tradition fixes there
The ancient palace;—but a desert now
Marks the lone spot, and there tall thistles grow.

That spot the shepherd and the labouring swain
Shun when eve's shadow lengthens o'er the plain;
For many speak of sights and sounds unblest,
Whose memory strikes pale terror through the breast.
Few months be past since that lone, haunted mound
We wondering saw with fiery column crown'd.
A splendid pyramid, which not the blast
Of the wild tempest from its base could cast,
Which not the whirlwind ruffle. High and clear—
The cause to each of marvel and of fear—
By day, by night it stood, nor stood alone:
For, gazing anxious, tower'd the snow-gemm'd crown
Of dread Elborus; pillar'd there was seen
An answering beacon, piercing the serene
Of heaven's blue vault. Full forty nights they stood
Shedding o'er all the land their lurid flood;
Each on his neighbour gazing, deem'd to view
The hand of death in that pale, livid hue;
Each caught from other the infectious chill,
And gaz'd by turns upon the Giant's Hill*

---

* Elborus is so called from the gigantic spectre traditionally said to haunt it.—See note 3 at the end.

And back to that lone mound. Then came the shock
Of the blind elements: the Earthquake's rock
O'erthrew the populous city. Thrice it came,
Earth pouring from her breast the liquid flame,
And uttering her dread thunders. When 'twas o'er,
All eyes those beacons sought, but found no more.
Then one, less fearful, climb'd the Mount's ascent;—
Its mass the Earthquake to its base had rent,
And in the chasm's gorge had open laid
A flight of marble steps of ample grade,
Erewhile the palace' access; now o'erstrown
With shatter'd cornices and shafts o'erthrown.
Descending here, for Fate his footstep led,
Wide halls and courts were open to his tread;
As fresh, as fair in beauty all appear'd,
As if the court that moment had been clear'd,
And from his vacant, gem-encluster'd throne
That hour the monarch to repose had gone.
And o'er the throne a glorious halo shed
The jewell'd crown of th' illustrious Dead.
Twain its chief gems, "The Mount, the Sea of Light:"(10)
Alike ascrib'd to that dread arm of might,

Which of their golden fruit despoil'd the trees
And gem-dropt fountains of th' Hesperides.* (11)

"The dread Regalia thence with care convey'd,
Each sought his father's spear or battle blade
To guard those sacred relics from the hand
Of him who reign'd the tyrant of the land.
Near and afar the joyful tidings sped :
The vale, the mountain heard, and every head
Once more in hope was rais'd. That news awoke
The peasant crouch'd beneath his servile yoke ;
The shepherd dreaming on the mountain side
His dream debasing of the tyrant's pride
And his once happy land. Th' untoiling steer
Untended now may wander void of fear
Through the green pasture. The deserted flock
Choose their own browse upon the thymy rock ;
But none shall now their wandering steps recall
As down the vale Eve's deep'ning shadows fall ;

---

* Hercules.

Nor pen their helpless young within the fold
From howling wolves or blast of midnight cold.
Peasant and swain alike, the serf and lord,
Their peaceful homes have left to grasp the sword.

" No clarion blew, no gorgeous banner shone,
No circling edict summon'd all as one.
Yet by a common impulse undefin'd,
All turn'd their steps to that dread height, where shrin'd
Prometheus' ashes lie. One anxious night
Crowded with portents pass'd beneath that height.
When morning dawn'd, the rising Sun cast down
The awful shadow of that mountain lone
O'er half the Euxine: They beheld *him* come
For whom they'd watch'd, and wept, and pray'd—for whom
The womb of Time had travail'd sore and long,
Foretold of sage's speech and prophet's song:
Prometheus' great descendant, cast like him
In more than mortal symmetry of limb,
In more than human beauty. From that hour
Hath dawn'd an era new. The tyrant's power

Pal'd, as on high rose great Prometheus' star;
Pal'd, as his name was voic'd of mountain war.
Yet, not the regal diadem will don,
Nor fill the vacant throne, Prometheus' son.
In Indra's name the regal edicts flow,
The vacant diadem for her fair brow
Is sacred held. To Persian lands afar
Speeds the high embassy, but threaten'd war
Musters our mountain youth. Such, Minstrel, be
The causes wondrous of the stir you see.
Nay! all untouch'd thou'st left our rugged fare:
Would we could tempt thee with a cate more rare!
Rest thee, young Wanderer; think not hence to go
Till morn breaks cheerly o'er yon mountain brow."

So spake the ancient Man, nor deem'd his guest
In that strange tale so deep a stake possess'd,
Nor that, beside his hearth in lowly state,
His queen, Prometheus' matchless daughter, sate.
While she with throbbing heart and flushing brow
Ponder'd each word that thrill'd her bosom through.

Joy, pride, surprise,—for Dion pride and joy,
By turns, at once her wilder'd thoughts employ;
And love, such love, so chasten'd, rais'd, refin'd
In loftiest musings of a spotless mind,
Elate o'er time, chance, passion's heady sway,
The world, its mortal taint and fading ray;
And yet so mingled, tangled, sweetly sown
With childhood's joys and promises unblown,
That like some partial shower bow, hung between
Earth's flowery mead and Heaven's high vault serene,
Its beauteous clasp, for envious clouds more bright,
Links Earth's best glory with the realms of light.

END OF CANTO V.

Canto VI.

THE DEFIANCE.

High rode the Sun thro' Heaven, and, bath'd in light,
Slept the deep Euxine wide outspread to sight:
Sparkling, as flash by flash his billows play,
And his huge volume basks in noontide ray.
Afar in distance, mid the Heavens you trace
(The Heavens down-bending to that soft embrace)
Where ends th' Immense, where opens the Sublime,
Where dim Eternity joins hands with Time.
And nearer, where the watery gulf below
Meets the full floods of light from Heaven that flow,

Another flood, the buoyant waft of air,
The while sweeps lightly in broad mazes there.
And nearer still, where, dancing o'er the sand,
Wave courses wave from Ocean up the strand,
White wreaths, flung graceful by those Naiads, lie
Mid the dark rocks and sea-drift heap'd on high.
But who shall give the Ocean's voice to song?
The myriad harmonies sublim'd in one,
The dim, mysterious, whisper'd secrets given
'Twixt the hoar Deep and th' eternal Heaven?—
Murmurs so faint, we doubt if 'tis the ear
Of sense attests them and in sooth we hear,
Or if some latent sympathy alone
Appeal the heart in likeness of a tone.
So bask'd the Waters.   High above them frown'd
Rude mountain heights with tangled forest crown'd,
And highest, rending Heaven's blue vault, thy brow,
Elborus, guards a world of wintry snow.

Wild is the scene and vast: yet not alone
Primæval Nature here upholds her throne:

For hither thronging multitudes resort,
To swell the pomp of great Prometheus' Court;
Their offerings, homage, tribute, proud to bring.
Or but to gaze, enraptur'd, on a king
So late restor'd as from the womb of Time,
And feast their eyes upon that form sublime,
Till round them rise in seeming years bygone
The shadowy Past and all its dim renown.
And hither Indra came—her tried disguise
Secur'd her well from mark of prying eyes,
Secur'd from Dion's ken. How swell'd her breast
As, mingling with the crowd that onward press'd,
In vassal guise her Dion's feet she sought,
The veriest unit of his princely Court!

No hall of State the work of mortal art,
No guarded precincts from the World apart,
No marble tesselate its aid affords,
No grim array of serried pikes and swords,
But on a massive granite rock, o'ergrown
With stains of Time and lichens many an one,

A lion's tawny spoils beneath him spread,
The pine's rude arms wide waving overhead,
The mountain peak above, the sea below,
His regal pomp enthron'd on his dread brow,
Th' illustrious Regent sate. Beneath his throne
Reclin'd the Elders of the State, men grown
Hoar with the frost of counsel. On their right
The chief in arms, stern Rulers of the fight,—
Young, ardent spirits, given, like Pallas' birth,
All arm'd and radiant and resolv'd, to Earth.

Simple, yet graceful, in his garb of State,
The least of those who Dion's bidding wait
Were costlier clad. And while around him glow
Rich ermin'd robes and gems,—a dazzling show—
His state, superior to such trappings vain,
Casts into shade that rich and glittering train;
As hilt of gold with flashing gems inlaid
But foils the blue gleam of the Damask blade.

High on the terrac'd rock she mark'd that throne,
Of genii builded in an age unknown.
Dion fills but the footstool of the shrine;
Its sacred seat, Prometheus' daughter, thine.

Pale in the crowd she stood, their hope, their queen,
O'erlook'd, unnoted: she whose voice had been
The clarion of all hearts, whose lightest will
Thousands had rush'd delighted to fulfil.
Unmark'd she stood: the while her flashing eye
Undazzled pass'd that glittering pageantry,
To seek, to fix, to feast on him who bore
The traits, the features reverenc'd evermore—
Her childhood's friend, companion, brother, guide.
How blent with woman's love her woman's pride
Thus to behold him, by his virtues thron'd,
So well adorn the right all bosoms own'd.

And this their fathers' land, their fathers' dust
From ancient days had here consign'd its trust,
Mingled perchance with every mountain pine
And wild-flower basking in the sunny shine,

The turf beneath their feet, the rocks around,
The torrent gushing past with tameless bound.
Her fathers' spirits (could she doubt it?) there
Walk'd the deep Ocean, throng'd the viewless air,
Came on the shadowy whisper secret borne
By vassal elements at wake of morn;
Or when, at eve, a holier calm hath blest
The winds and waters with the trance of rest;
Or when, conflicting both, wild thunders roll,
And awful voices shake Man's failing soul.

She gaz'd where stood that sacred, mystic throne
His generous hand reserv'd for her alone.'
One word of hers had potence to restore
Her land, crown, bosom's lord, to part no more.
But was it from *her* lips the word should flow,
At which her Dion's sov'reign power must bow?
At which, descending from his virtual throne,
His star must homage yield before her own?
Was it not bliss sufficing her, to be
Th' unseen Palladium of the Brave and Free?

To move in mystery like a spirit there,
Felt as the presence of their vital air:
Their queen, their guardian angel, though unknown,
Dispensing peace and blessedness alone?
To feast on all his glowing virtues still;
To watch, perchance to shield from threaten'd ill:
In secret counsel of the snares that lie
Beyond th' horizon cramp'd of kingly eye:
And thus, beneficent, unseen, unknown,
Exult in consciousness of joys foregone?

But hark! but hark the trumpet's clarion bold,*
Toss'd from the Euxine's rocks and caverns old,
From crag to crag reverb'd; now swelling high,
Now lost mid breaker's moan and zephyr's sigh
Along the surf-sown margin. "Warder, say,
What from thy watchtower, beetling o'er the spray,
Meets thy lone eye?"

---

* The Arabs have no trumpet. These, therefore, must have belonged to the guard of honour appointed to meet the envoy.

"My Lord, from early morn
My sight, o'erwhelm'd, the boundless waste hath borne
Of flood and mountain crag. Oh! weary they
Who lonely watch where restless billows play.
But now they come, a small, a stately Band;
I see them winding o'er the Ocean sand.
Slow is their march; the billow bounds to meet,
Then falls in foam-wreaths at their coursers' feet:
Not whiter seen than that which serves to fleck
The glossy velvet of each haughty neck,
Each ample chest, as curb'd, though not subdued,
They champ the polish'd bit in restless mood,
And, pawing high, but ill their fire restrain,
Or brook the bondage of the jewell'd rein.
Wild on the breeze the sable banner's fold
Swells, a black storm-cloud 'neath the crescent gold."

"The Khalif's well-known standard. Warder, say,
Thou that keep'st reck'ning of the wild waves' play,
Comes nought beside along the watery way?"

" Far, far to East, to West, the icy Pole
   Spreads the deep Ocean waste, the weary billows roll.
   The livelong night that waste my soul hath fill'd
   Of moonlit furrows by the strong wind till'd:
   The long drear night, the sultry blaze of day;—
   Oh! weary lot to watch the sleepless billows' play.
   Nought mid that waste of waters deep I see
   Save the lone skiff that wanders far and free:
   The anchor'd galley with its sail unfurl'd,
   And Rome's grim eagle mid the hazy world.
   While eastward far a sable speck still grows
   With each white wave that up the sea-beach flows."

" Enough! three missions come: due honours speed,
   And each in turn to instant audience lead.
   Soldiers we be,—brief form and brief debate
   Suit best the genius of our infant State."

Near and more near the martial murmurs swell
Up from the sands where restless billows dwell;
In partial bursts receiv'd, as some chance rent
Through the steep cliff affords them free ascent.

Then, as the cliff is scal'd, in lengthen'd time
Prolong'd the measure of the martial chime,
Tok'ning the labour of the steepy road.
And now the summit of the cliff is trod,
And full and free as bursts the seaward view,
Burst those wild notes in mountain freedom too,
Dance o'er the billows, light and unconfin'd,
Mount the blue Heaven, float o'er the viewless wind,
And from Elborus' awful summit hurl'd,
Return like voices from a distant World.
Then sudden cease; and in their place succeeds,
Mid the sea's moan, the measur'd tramp of steeds
And ring of harness, as in fair array
The Envoy threads that life-encumber'd way.

An aged warrior he: his turban fold
Not whiter than the beard of snow which roll'd
Wide waving o'er his breast. A tunic green,
Beneath the white folds of his Aba seen,
Betrays his sacred birth: and round his waist
In shawl of green his jewell'd arms are brac'd.

Ample his garb, beside, of spotless snow.
Time had worn furrows o'er his lofty brow,
Matur'd and settled, but not quench'd the high
Enthusiast courage of that deep-set eye;
Nor from the features' high, sharp outline driven
One trait of haughty pride that towers to Heaven.
Brief was his reverence and his greeting rude,
As thus confronting Dion's throne he stood.

" Thus saith the prophet's Vicar (on whose brow
  Be blessings multiplied in boundless flow):
' Our ears amid the prayers that hourly rise
From faithful lips to twice a hundred skies,
Have heard of Treason: yet restrained our might,
Nor bar'd the sword, reluctant still to smite.
If, then, unask'd our will, ye have o'erthrown
The ancient rule for sceptre of your own;
If in idolatry most blind have made
An idol altar to some unknown shade,
And that a woman's, ye have foully done:
Yet hear the terms of grace our will makes known.

Destroy th' accursèd altar. Whom ye will
Depute the seat of royalty to fill,
So he be Man. Throughout your land proclaim
Islām, the one true God, and Prophet's name.
Be the sword sharpen'd, bent the sounding bow
On him th' accurst, who, hearing, fails to bow
And take the pledge of peace. This do and live:
Our faith, our pity, pleads, and we forgive.'"

He said, and ceas'd: throughout his audience rose
Hoarse murmur'd sounds indignant: aged brows
In stern displeasure lour'd, and youthful eyes
Flash'd the keen lightnings of incens'd surprise;
And youthful hands by warrior instinct stray'd
Tow'rd hilt of dagger keen or battle blade;
And swell'd from man to man the answer deep,
As when wild, fitful gusts old Ocean sweep,
Waking the myriad voices of his might.
Dion gaz'd proudly on the throng; his sight
Kindled intense, as if the lightnings thrown
From eye to eye converging fill'd his own:

Awhile he gaz'd, then in a voice whose thrill
Did those wild waves of Discord sudden still,
The haughty Envoy answer'd:

" We have heard
Of him, whose voice thou art, each boastful word.
Bear back our final answer. Ere was known
On Earth thy Prophet's law, thy Khalif's throne,
Heaven to our Sires did sacred rights bequeath,
The soil they tread, the freeborn gales they breathe.
Ere yet went forth the Desert's tameless child,
Your great progenitor—ere yet the wild
Of Araby the voice of dweller heard,
Save her steed's neigh or clang of Desert bird—
Our Sires chose one to guide their infant State,
In war their chief, in peace their magistrate.
Their heroes rul'd; truth, virtue, love had sway,
Till bigots chas'd that chosen race away.
Years wax'd and wan'd: the Arab Prophet came,
Proclaiming discord, kindling murder's flame;
Our hapless land, betray'd, divided, rent,
Not scatheless stood, th' unrighteous armament:

Their upstart king, loath'd, hated of his own,
Crouch'd to the crescent for his tottering throne.
But when Time's womb Prometheus' heir restor'd,
The land her fetters burst and bar'd her sword:
That heir, a maiden, great Prometheus' own,
With all the hero in Prometheus known.

" Hence learn, no shrine, but throne confronts thee here,
And to the haughty terms of truce ye bear
Take back our brief reply.   Allegiance none
To foreign State our freeborn spirits own.
With them, with thine as equals will we treat,
Or prove your equals when our war-blades meet.
Nor will we, blest in freedom, o'er the mind
Of one, freeborn, the yoke tyrannic bind;
Nor on ourselves assume the burden given
To one weak conscience, by the will of Heaven.
Thou hast our answer,—we desire not war,
Yet wield the swords our dauntless fathers bore.
We covet peace: yet spurn it, if allied
To one base thought that shocks our freeborn pride."

Full, clear, and deep the princely accents fell,
As when wild rolling o'er some cavernous dell
Of ancient Caucasus, the thunder low
Fills the rude glen till all its bounds o'erflow:
And vibrates to its core in stern assent,
Each rock, each cliff, each time-worn battlement,
Till, wak'd the lowest chord, in one long sweep
Nature's dread organ peals its volumes stern and deep.
So swell'd that voice, so wak'd from breast to breast
Reflections keen of those high thoughts exprest,
Till ran from man to man the stormy sound,
And with the whirlwind's potence swept around;
And each unwittingly his couch forsook,
And on the Envoy hurl'd his dazzling look;
And to and fro that wood of plumes was sway'd,
As the strong gale of passion fitful play'd,
Like pine-boughs tossing in th' autumnal glade.

Unmov'd the Envoy saw around him glow
Emotions powerful as the gulf-tide's flow.
In calm, stern voice he spake, as o'er the land
He stretch'd in sign of wroth his naked battle brand.

"Thus saith the Prophet's Vicar (be his reign
With blessing crown'd!): 'Since ye our peace disdain,
Receive our wroth, our curse, to blight and slay;
Terror by night, the scythe of Death by day.
Enough, the sword of vengeance is gone forth,
Death's tramp I hear, dread Azrael's shout of wroth."

He ceas'd, small reverence made, and turn'd to go,
His former path retracing calm and slow,
Regain'd his steed, all social rites declin'd,
And shook his sable banner on the wind.
He came as comes some vulture from afar,
Herald of carnage, harbinger of war;
Is past, as from some death-devoted land
The scout, forerunner of the locust band.

Ere yet the martial clangour died afar,
Mid breezy tides and tumbling breakers' roar,
Up the steep, toilsome path, at headlong speed,
The Scythian spurr'd his wild, deep-chested steed, (12)
In strength and freedom glorying. Far behind
He, snorting, leaves the laggart mountain wind.

Loose o'er the disc of his broad buckler slung
The deathful bow and rattling quiver rung,
Mingling their music with the tinkling sound
Of silvery plates the war-steed's neck that bound;
While toss'd on high each shaggy mane is borne,
Like thund'rous cloud by adverse currents torn,
And quails the slender spear, as bound on bound
Speeds the wild desert steed;—cliff, rock, and glebe resound.

Free and intrepid was the horseman's mien,
As might his race and nurture wild beseem:
A son of Nature, in the rude tent bred,
From realm to realm by wandering shepherd led.
Where'er the circling Heaven its curtain draws
Around the green Earth's breast; where'er the laws
Of Night and Day the heavenly guardians keep,
And Titan seasons scale th' ethereal Steep;
From those high realms where, wheeling round the sky,
Arcturus urges still the huntsman's cry,
Nor sinks to close the ever-burning eye;
To where Antares from the Scorpion's heart
Sheds death, and glows the Scorpion's fiery dart,

There his wide dwelling. Boreas scatters there
His dripping wing, shakes far his snowy hair;
And here, Hyperion, glorious as of old,
Floods Earth and Heaven with tides of molten gold.
The circling seasons, vassals of his need,
Call forth the tender herb his flocks to feed;
Nor mountain wall, nor rivers, ocean's band
Curbs his free step, nor bounds his native land.
His greeting paid, in rude, uncultur'd tone,
Thus spake far Scythia's child, the Desert's tameless son:

" The Lord of many Lords, whose realms comprise
All spread beneath the Sun's far-darting eyes;
From the bleak frozen zone to where his might
O'er Nature sheds intolerable light;
He wills thee greeting. Rumours of thy war
And petty change of State have reach'd his ear;
But charg'd of thee with humble tribute, none
Hath kiss'd as yet the threshold of his throne,
Whether 'tis fear the duteous act denies,
Or conscious indigence in those dread eyes.

Wherefore to pity mov'd, he bids thee know
His fulness, like the shoreless ocean's flow,
Lacks not the wealth of each untitled rill
His bliss to perfect or his depths to fill;
Yet not the less doth fealty's pledge require,
Those symbols of his sway, earth, water, fire.
So 'neath his skirt securely shall ye dwell
When War lets loose on Earth the fiends of Hell."

He ceas'd, and while the glances of the Brave,
Flashing around, indignant protest gave,
Calmly, in conscious dignity serene,
Thus Dion answer'd:—

"Thou whose manly mien
Beseems a son of Liberty, whose speech
The creed which slaves receive and tyrants preach,
Know that the dust by our free step imprest
Once built the shrine of many a noble breast;
Know that no wavelet, sparkling, bounds along,
But bears a burden in the general song
Of liberty; no flame but vaunts *his* might
Who brought to Man Truth's consecrated light.

"Think ye to strangers lightly we'll entrust
Our fathers' sacred, venerated dust?
Think ye we'll banish one glad wave, whose song
Doth to the Past and Memory's lore belong?
Or that to foreign hands we'll e'er consign
The hallow'd emblem of a fire divine?
Come ye as guests? Full freely shall ye share
Our cup, our hearth, the fruits our furrows bear.
Come ye as foes? Our waves our dust shall hide,
Our fire consume the robber and his pride.
Choose ye of these, and may sound wisdom bar
The famish'd wolves and slaughter fiends of war."

Awhile amaz'd the Scythian envoy heard
That bold defiance of the terms preferr'd;
Then from his belt a bearded arrow drew,
And at the Regent's feet the emblem threw:
"Take then our wroth, the arrowy death that flies
By day, by night; the vengeance that but dies
When root and branch consum'd in Death's red fire,
Nought breathes t' incense or feed th' avenger's ire.

The Scythian bow is bent. Your mountain height
The neighs of thousand thousand war-steeds fright,
Ten thousand thousand thronging hoofs rebound,
And Hell's dark caverns quake as rocks the shuddering
    ground."

He said, and like his own swift shaft was gone
Ere Echo ceas'd to mouth that fiery tone.
Sprang to his courser's back with vigorous bound,
Nor curb'd his fire as fast consum'd the ground.
Silence succeeds as his last hoof-sound dies,
And each asks anxious at his neighbour's eyes.

That silence Dion broke. "My fellow-men,
Born and baptiz'd in liberty again!
Why gaze ye thus, as each would fain inquire
His neighbour's thoughts, or scan his spirit's fire?
Have ye not each to other prov'd full well
How true the temper of resolves that swell
Each dauntless breast? Or did ye think to find
Allies mid foes and robbers of their kind?

Or would ye taint your glory, stain your sword,
By truce degrading with a robber horde?
Or buy with servile homage at their hand
The right to breathe on this your native strand?
Come, foreign war! If such be Heaven's high will,
Come all the world in arms our coast to fill:
Be but our hearts like those our fathers bore,
True to themselves, untainted to the core;
Be but their virtue ours as are their brands,
Their sacred birthright and their strong right hands.
Those foes external shall but fence us round,
As monsters guard the Hesperian garden's bound:
As hurtling waves the Pearl of Ocean keep
From caitiff kites and snatchers of the Deep.
Oh! never while Prometheus' fire within
Burns bright and clear. Oh! never, while to win
Our own hearts' tribute be our dearest aim;
Never, while breathing Indra's sacred name,
Guarding your heaven-born rights, her ancient throne,
Inspir'd of thoughts she would not scorn to own,
Grac'd by her guardian angel's presence blest,
Th' aspirations of th' undaunted breast,—

Never shall slaves or robbers' hands efface
One sacred birthright of our free-born Race."

She heard—ah! heard she not those noble words
Which swept all-powerful o'er her bosom's chords,
Stirring a tumult of blest thoughts within,
Till to her eyes the welling transports spring?
Thrice, thrice repays her every toil and woe
Each wingèd word that thrills her spirit through,
Each proof of excellence in one so dear,
Each precious earnest of his truth for her.

Scarce Dion ceas'd, ere, swelling soft and clear,
Music's light strain stole o'er the ravish'd ear:
So gently breathed, the Siren of the Deep
Ne'er lull'd old Ocean to his charmèd sleep
With more assausive art. That languid strain
Died on the breeze, and rose to die again:
Like the lisp'd dreams of infant Orpheus' rest,
When at Calliope's young matron breast
Rich floods of harmony his soul oppress'd.

The flute, the hautboy, rich and mellow horn,
Their plaining notes together blent, and borne
On Ocean's waft, with many a liquid thrill
Of Delphic harp th' unwarlike concert fill.
While Nature's organ, matchless in its tone,
Man's voice, the power of many powers in one,
Perfects the swelling peal. And who be they
That lead their choir from out old Ocean's spray?
Comes she the Paphian queen of becks and smiles,
Of love and beauty, from her chosen isles?
Where night and day soft clouds of incense rise,
And the heart's flames are fann'd with frequent sighs.

Nearer the chorus swells. Distinctly now
On Dion's ear the Delian numbers flow.
That melting strain so languishingly stole,
Lull'd the charm'd sense, dissolv'd the failing soul.
They sang the triumph of the Queen of Smiles,
Love's witchery soft and gay insidious wiles.
They sang of hands and hearts together blent,
Of lives dissolv'd in love's soft blandishment,

In Cnidus' grots where languid brooklets flow,
Red roses bud and flowery myrtles blow,
And breezes, cloy'd with perfume, fluttering by,
Waste all their vigour in the frequent sigh.

And now so near the pageant, all might scan
Th' unwarlike group whence those smooth numbers ran.
First march'd the minstrel Band; a motley crew
As the mixt regions whence their blood they drew:
Each in his robe of spotless white array'd,
With massive gold on neck and arms display'd.
Follow the Troop whose hands the banner bear,
The warrior helm and panoply of war
(A silver spoil with ductile gold inlaid):
The nodding plume and jewel-hilted blade.
Succeeds his courser in superb array,
Majestic, pacing to the measur'd lay.
And then the ivory chariot, richly wrought,
Inlaid with gems in Orient regions sought,
And drawn by steeds of Andulusian strain,
Silver their bits, of silk each snowy rein:

All grace their movements: curb'd, but not subdued,
The generous ardour of their stainless blood;
Docile as two young fawns, twinborn they move,
Their proud crests arching, join'd in playful love.

On the high chariot's easeful throne of state,
In languid grace reclined, Argyllus sate.
Loose flow'd his costly robe; his better hand
Scarce held, on cushion propp'd, the silver band
His steeds that rein'd. Few winters o'er his brow
Had past, and all unruffled in its flow
Had been life's course; yet wearily had prest
The weight of luxury o'er a sated breast:
The Incubus of pleasure mock'd in vain
By any title that implies not pain.
That cheek unting'd of health, unbronz'd by toil,
Those languid limbs, whose vigour of recoil
Is sapp'd and wasted. That dull, hollow eye,
Whence Hope's bright sparkle ne'er again shall fly,
Nor courage beam—
     O Mistress of the world!
Whose strong right hand the bolt of ruin hurl'd

At every crest of pride : whose iron wing
Crush'd the throng'd nations in its mighty swing,
And ground their gold, their brass, their iron sway
As 'neath some chariot-wheel the fictile clay
Of potter's hand: and art thou fall'n so far?
Is this thy pride in peace, thy bolt of war?
Comes this vain silken insect to present
The fall'n, lost glories of thy firmament?
Thy haughty Consuls', thy stern Tribunes' pride?
The adamantine spirit that defied
Alike all mortal power; and mightiest still
When most opprest beneath the heaviest ill,
Uprear'd above the wreck of tower and dome,
Crush'd but unbent, the haughty front of Rome?
O thou Camillus, saviour of thy land,
Man of the dauntless heart, the iron hand!
O thou Marcellus, thunder of the war,
Rome's all-subduing, keen-edg'd scimitar!
O Caius Marcius Coriolanus! known
Where'er brave deeds or generous acts were done,
Rome's proud, unmatch'd, uncompromising son.

O Marius, Mucius, Brutus, Cato, where
Hide ye your ashes mid your land's despair?
Hath ev'ry spark that noble dust which fir'd,
With your majestic, glorious course expir'd?

A smile, contemptuous of the scene survey'd,
About the Envoy's languid features play'd;
The rude and simple pomp which decks that throne
As far unlike the luxury of his own,
As iron Rome, stern mother of the free,
To Rome th' enslav'd of vice and luxury.
Smooth flows the envoy's speech in phrase that trips
Select and artful o'er his honied lips:—

" Rome still hath noted with approving eye
An ancient Nation's strife for liberty :
Rome, free herself, who freedom would bequeath
To all who share the gift of vital breath.
Keep ye but firmly that ye've nobly won,
Uphold the course your glowing wheels have run,
Succeeding ages shall your name revere,
And history's page glow bright in your career.

But know ye this? E'en now around your land
The Arab hordes in threatening myriads stand?
So vast their numbers, with the breath alone
Of their proud steeds they cloud the risen sun;
With their thick-prancing hoofs of fire efface
Of this fair land each mutilated trace.
Fierce is the onset of their matchless horse,
Unseen, till trampling down the hostile force.
Forth, as strong eagles stooping from the sky,
They rend their prey ere yet they meet the eye—
A rushing cloud, an earthquake, and no more:
The very steel gleams *but* suffus'd in gore;
The neigh of furious steeds, the crash, the roar,
As of a thousand tempests hurl'd ashore:
Glance round,—an army trampled and o'erthrown,
Earth drunk with blood, the dreadful tempest gone.

" Or be your phalanx staunch, and each firm row
Of triple spears impervious to the foe;
Around you wheeling as the falcon flies,
Safe from your wrath each vantage point he tries,

Yields as ye press, and if your dense array
Show but a ripple in its onward way,
Thro' that weak point, ere man to man may close,
Pours in a torrent dense of fiery foes.
Pursue? Ye might with equal ease o'ertake
The glance of lightning quivering o'er the lake;
As safely chase the pestilence, to wreak
Your nerveless vengeance on the foe ye seek.
That steed, twin brother of the Desert wind,
As fleet, as fiery, and as hard to bind,
Is vanish'd ere an onward rood ye've prest:
The Parthian* sting stands quivering in your breast.

"Such is your foe, and for each patriot brand
A thousand hostile swords wave o'er your land.
The States around you mark your certain fate,
Your certain fall, like hovering vultures wait;
Rome only, touch'd with pity, grace ordains
T' exchange for her free name the proffer'd chains."

---

* Parthia was, at this time, a province of the Arabs.

"And what Rome's purpose if this grace we crave?"

"Then will she stretch her sceptred hand to save,
　Muster her iron legions from afar,
　And grant you captains skill'd to rule the war;
　Nay, should the pastime please dread Cæsar's might
　Himself may deign to sway the field of fight."

"And what if we despise the matchless grace
　To be Rome's toys; to give her armies place
　In our free land; th' arena where a king
　In idle sport the bolt of war may fling;
　Pond'ring at ease the orphan's, widow's moan,
　As fathers, husbands, friends are round him strown?
　What if such boon hath nought to tempt our eyes?"

"Thou triflest, Prince. It were nor safe nor wise
　To spurn Rome's proffer'd grace. One only hand
　Can pluck from ruin's verge your hapless land.
　That Power, despis'd, may seize the land ye throw
　Thus at the mercy of her deadliest foe."

"This then our high alternative, to yield
  To Rome our rights, without one stricken field,
  Or fall as heroes fall? Our lot is ta'en,
  To wear Death's freedom rather than Rome's chain."

And thou, gay insect, wing'd from thy sad home,
The bloated carcase of once mightiest Rome,
Didst thou not tremble as thy lily hand
Presum'd to grasp the consecrated wand,
Which once Lucullus, Brutus, Scipio sway'd?
Did those soft limbs not shudder when array'd
In that dread garb the iron frame which bound
Of Marius, Pompey, him with laurel crown'd,
Rome's all surpassing, matricidal son?
And com'st thou in the robe in which were won
The Punic spoils, Numidia's blazing crown?
From which the Gaul's gigantic host o'erthrown,
Fled, howling, to their wilds: Which entry won
Through thine inviolate phalanx, Macedon;—
And from the Thracian to th' Iberian shore,
From Libya's wilds to where the surges roar

Round Thule's utmost isle, resistless sway'd,
Hail'd with deep awe and tremblingly obey'd.

To his pavilion on the surf-sown coast
The young Argyllus and his train are past:
There, while soft luxury steeps each sense opprest,
With guile and treachery swells his artful breast.
Then murmurs rose. The Arab, Scythian foes,
Threat'ning their land, what madness caus'd them close
Their gate 'gainst succours of imperial Rome?
What hope their mountain hold could dare alone
The world in arms? Was not the Khalif's might
Alone out-trampling Liberty and Right?
Such the strong feeling which pervades that throng,
And shap'd in words finds birth at Chiron's tongue :
Free in his thought, as dauntless in his soul,
No dread of misconstruction could control
His speech sincere. A lover of his land,
None ever doubted of the heart or hand
He gave to Freedom's cause.
     Him Dion heard,
And answer'd swift: "Chief of the stainless sword,

What words be these?   When was the eagle's wing
Found ineffectual from her brood to fling
The downward-glancing bolt?   When call'd she one
Of all the alien tribes around her throne?
Or suffer'd to her eyrie's wind-rock'd home
The vulture bald or dastard kite to come?
Are *we* less noble, less resolv'd than she?
Have we no home, no friends, no liberty?
Or is it to prolong life's slavish round
Of sense, breath, motion, that our limbs are bound
In warrior steel?   Then have we bled in vain,
To rend a tyrant's, forge a bigot's chain.
Oh, think not Victory doth in numbers trust:—
Mycale's strand, Plataea's trampled dust;
The wave that murmurs in its glory o'er
The Persian spoils on Salamis' proud shore;
The voices of the Mighty, slumbering on,
Hymn'd by the surge of deathless Marathon;—
All, all, as one, the glorious truth attest,
That Victory shrines her in the Patriot's breast.
That the base fires of rapine shar'd among
The hearts of myriads who to conquest throng,

Must pale, decay, before th' ethereal fire,
Intense, concentrate, our dread rights inspire;
Whose every arm the levin-burden bears,
Of a land's vengeance and a nation's tears."

A tumult strange those thrilling words excite,
Opinions diverse, clashing in their might.
Part, by the terrors mov'd which round them press,
To truceful deeds their anxious thoughts address.
But in each nobler breast the slumbering flame
Of freedom kindled at each glorious name
Of Grecia's hero strand. "Oh, let us rise,
Friends, brethren, warriors! if the crowded skies
Be black with tempest, 'tis that they may show
In hues more bright the lustre of that bow
Which our great deeds shall frame. To Death we owe
One debt, to children and to country one,
And one to Virtue. If we can atone
In this great sacrifice the claims of all,
Blest is our lot, and triumph crowns our fall;

And after ages, pointing to our strand,
Our names shall number with th' illustrious band
Who living aye, from age to age inspire
Great deeds, and tend the hero's spirit fire."

" Shades of our mighty Race—dread Powers that reign
O'er souls which slavery never shall profane,
True to the sacred heritage bequeath'd,
We guard the land ye trod, the gales ye breath'd,
The rights ye guarded. When we can no more,
Or robbers slay, or grasp the blades ye bore;
When, spite of virtue, wisdom, valour, all
Freedom's blest fabric totters to its fall;
On that dread ruin, at thine altar's base,
Our wives, our friends, our little ones we'll place,
Light high the funeral fire, ascend the pile,
And leave Earth's slaves our ashes and our smile."

Such glowing words bear down each faltering doubt,
Till the old Euxine's cliffs reverb the shout
" Of Indra and our country !" Indra heard
Her name in plaudits blended with the word

To Freemen dearest. In her heart that fire,
Intense and stainless, brighter rose and higher;
Till Difficulty crouch'd and Danger smil'd,
And nought seem'd arduous to fair Virtue's child.

And one there was, whose zeal outstripp'd the rest,
Whose plaudits spoke a more than patriot breast;
Who joining loudly in the thrilling shout,
Chill'd the heart's glow with many a whisper'd doubt.
One whose dark, devious path seem'd spangled fair
With gems that Innocence and Virtue bear.
No voice like his indignant to assail
Each vice unpopular that taints the gale:
No glance so keen, detected guilt to spy,
And drag unmask'd before the public eye.
Thus deck'd in seeming Virtue, Virtue lent
To him her power, but not her pure intent,
Self his sole worship. Such was Proceus. Few
His motives scann'd, but Dion read them through.
Hence Proceus' hatred, bas'd on selfish dread:
But Dion's thoughts to realm remote were fled;

He noted not how Proceus' felon eye
Jarr'd with the plaudit patriots peal'd on high;
A moment false to country, self, and them.
Shades of the Mighty, pause ere ye condemn!
A moment's wandering of the thoughts t' atone,
His soul till death is freedom's and your own.

END OF CANTO VI.

Canto VII.

THE DETHRONED.

Dread Nurse of Mystery! Queen of the Ebon Throne!
Night, eldest-born of Chaos! Thou, whose hand
Sways the dread realm Man vainly deems his own,
And rules, despotic, each dire phantom Band
That throngs the dim coast of the silent Land:
Oh! thou that questing still the bright-hair'd Sun,
Shalt at the end outstrip his car and stand
Infolding with thy wing th' arena won,
The Heavenly zone where late his wheels of glory run:

Ere those vast circles thro' the Concave hurl'd
The mystic mazes of Existence spun;
Ere o'er the gloom-depths of th' inanimate world
The brooding Spirit in dread silence hung,
A conflict troubling, whence fair order sprung,
A war whose fruit was harmony: didst thou
Reign o'er the murky mass, together wrung,
The crush'd, blind Chaos, wrapt inert below,
Th' abyss in whose blind depths Life's germs lay coil'd in
    woe.

And when thine ægis rent, the golden shower
Wing'd from the Day-god's bow, incessant rain'd
O'er half the rip'ning world, thy hold of power
Latest arm'd, these mountain wilds remain'd,
Where mighty Caucasus the war sustain'd
'Gainst Order and the Light. And still thy throne,
Majestic most in ruin, hath disdain'd
To compromise the rude, scath'd grandeur grown
Up thro' the skies, and down to black-wav'd Phlegethon.

It is the shadow of thy wing that fills
Silent the Chasm's gorge. It is to thee
The distant torrent from his hundred hills
Lifts the long silent voice. It is to be
Nestled beneath thy wing, that ev'ry free
Grim child of thine forsakes his cavern'd hold:
Roars the gaunt lion in his joy to see
Thine eye of gloom: and each gigantic fold
The fire-ey'd dragon hurls, volume o'er volume roll'd;—

And monarch eremite the deep-voic'd owl
Exulting shouts his vespers. And from far,
In council group'd, the jackal senate howl
Their various watchword of the sylvan war,
Then, sudden ceasing, to their beat repair.
And surly loitering on his rock-grav'd track
Joys in thy shadow deep the burly bear,
And prowls the margin of the lakelet black
To view, mid stars of Heaven, his grim form render'd
    back.

So greets old Caucasus the reign of Night,
But other sounds the cavern'd wilds affright.
Hark their unwonted clang: the steely shock
Of arm'd hoofs battling with the pavement rock.
He comes. Who comes? That haughty front, that eye
Which swarthy glows: that ruin'd majesty
And port no more august. Those features, cast
In mould, once glorious; but, the hour is past.
That raven steed, so wild of eye and mane,
Whose hoofs of fire Earth's contact base disdain.

He comes. His dark form shadowing e'en the gloom;
The night-breeze ruffles not his hearse-like plume;
Cold gleams the steel upon his warrior breast,
Rigid his mien, but not in pledge of rest;
For, flash by flash, those burning eyeballs roll
And mark the tempest of an awful soul.
Mark, at their flash the lion stills his roar,
Droops his proud mane, nor lashes as before

His sinewy flank. But meek as unwean'd child
Resigns the kingship of the savage wild,
And stealthy stalking, mingles with the night.
What presence this the fearless can affright,
The lawless bridle with unsanction'd chill?
Spirits there be in many a tunnell'd hill
Of Kawf's dread chain, but prison'd all and bound
In cavern'd adamant of gloom profound,
Secur'd with spell Iblee's proud will must own,
The inviolate seal of sceptred Solomon.
And Genii haunt each vasty chasm there, (13)
Or cleave with pinion strong th' imprison'd air,
Vast shapes of gloom: or brood in secret mine,
Where vainly sought Jumsheed's rich treasures shine.

Not such the stranger horseman. Each wild thing
Knows the dark port, the vast o'ershadowing wing
Of such, nor trembles at his presence drear:
A spirit prouder, mightier far, is near.
Not at his tread the yawning rocks unfold
Their wealth of gems unsunn'd and virgin gold;

Not at his word th' ephemeral dome may spring
Worthy the palace of the Genii King,
But hearts of adamant his mandate own,
And human spirits build for him a loftier throne.

Yon antre vast receives him : and the shock
Of jarring hoofs is sepulchred in rock.
But through those cavern'd aisles their murmurs swell,
Where sullen pools in frozen silence dwell.
Stern are his features, as, dismounting slow,
He lights with steel and flint the taper's glow ;
Tends the hot steed, his sole surviving trust,
Chafes his stiff limbs, allays the fire, the dust
His throat that parch with water's fresh'ning tide,
Spreads his scant store of date fruit bruis'd and
    dried,
Then restless roams the cave.

                            " Ye shadows deep,
Worthy of Erebus.   Black waves that creep
From Earth's last nucleus.   Dismal shapes that flit
Where light scarce enters.   Mysteries dire unlit

From your first being by the prying eye
Of mortal man. If, in Earth's breast there lie
An access to the Deepest, and the Lord
Who deepest reigns, ye must that path afford."

He said: and from his jewell'd scabbard drew
The blade, as rock-stream glimmering cold and blue
In the faint ray: and from his arm gave flow
Life's ruddy current to the pool below:
That pool so black, whose sullen waters keep
The trancelike torpor of unhallow'd sleep.
Slow fell the purple drops, dispersing wide
Throughout the blind depths of that sullen tide;
While with keen blade outstretch'd and frenzied eye,
And form dilating in its majesty,
Erectheus stood.
    " Spirit, whose ruin'd state
Mine own resembles! whom, in power elate,
I ever honour'd:* and to whom I come,
Fall'n like thyself, as to some friendly throne

---

* There is a sect in Persia, the Yezidis, who honour Satan, and almost worship him.

For counsel and for aid. Not fall'n so low,
But that, like thee, I bear a regal brow,
And claim some worship from th' internal host,
Whose fealty forfeit, all indeed were lost.
Come from thy fiery throne. Some honour due
From thee to him, who ne'er till now did sue
Or God or creature. If, as mortals tell,
Thou lov'st the pledge of ruddy slaughter well,
'Tis thine. Or if thou can'st so near thy throne
Endure a spirit haughty as thine own,
Who can do aught but bend; thou hast in me
A pent Volcano, charg'd with misery,
Blood, terror, woe, to Man's detested brood.
Come from thy depths; the all-unfathom'd flood,
Th' abysm of blind terror. If in me
Thou find a quailing heart, a trembling knee,
Be all the boon denied. Great Spirit, come
From the black depths which shroud thy fiery
    throne."

'Twas silence all. But in the lakelet's brim
A secret power 'gan stir. A vapour dim

First rose in filmy column pale and high,
Then a pure flame, too bright for mortal eye.
Then, whirl'd by force unseen, unfelt, the fire
In spiral volumes brighter gush'd and higher;
And when once more unclos'd Erechtheus' eye,
There stood a form of matchless majesty
Where the bright flame had been. Youth, beauty, grace
Held their high triumph in that glorious face,
That free, ethereal form. Such traits become
No spirit exil'd to eternal gloom;
Least the dread king of Orcus and of Night.
Well might they designate a Child of Light,
But for one discord marring the design,
Yet ruffling scarce *one* undulating line
Of woman's perfect mould. On that pure brow
Was thron'd command, and the deep eye did glow
A lambent sea of mystery. As they stood
Confronted, separate by the murky flood,
Better that mortal match'd in ruin'd state
The desolate pomp of Hell's dire Potentate,
Than she, that wondrous, fairest, summon'd Thing,
Whose beauty, startling Night's reluctant wing,

Hung like some isle of Light, mid the profound.
She might have been *their* queen triumphant crown'd,
Who, fairest of their sex, lent willing ear
To the love-pleading of a Heavenly sphere.

All musical, yet deep, the accents fell,
" Mortal, thy wish?" But thro' each inmost cell
Of heart and memory tumult strange awoke,
Thrilling each sense as thus Erechtheus spoke :—
" The master-spirit of th' Abyss I sought,
Fair Thing, not thee. Think'st thou one stormy thought
Pent in this breast could company with thine?"

He paus'd, abrupt, confounded ; for each line
Of feminine gentleness was past away,
And that broad brow, above the vivid play
Of the keen lightning glance, impended now
Like some down-gliding avalanche of snow,
That late repos'd, swath'd in prismatic light,
A fairy treasure on the mountain height,
And now, mid thundering rocks and lightnings hurl'd,
Prepares destruction for th' affrighted World.

More dire the change, that thro' the discord wild,
Traits of that startling, dazzling beauty smil'd,
As thro' murk shadows brooding in a lake
Thrill'd by the thunder's jar, bright ripples break
In lines of silver. Every ghastly care
Pent in his breast had found reflection there.
Yet woman's still those traits, as woman's prove
When her heart maddens unrequited love.
Again the Vision spake, tho' chang'd her tone:—
" Mortal, thy wish?" Erechtheus' doubts were gone.
He answer'd deep, and Hell the sound reverb'd.
" Vengeance."
    " On whom?"
        " On all. The ruthless sword
Of indiscriminate ruin."
      " Is there none
Thou would'st except? Friend, sister, lover, son?"

" Friend, sister, lover! Ha! the names full well
Suit the bleak echoes of the caves of Hell.
The time hath been I too could mouth each name,
Nor deem'd that mockery in the accents came,

For I was powerful, noble, wise, renown'd,
And at my beck were wealth and honour found.
But Discord rose, rebellion shook my throne:—
Then was it virtue to pull tyrants down.
'Twas wise at least t' anticipate their fate,
And build fresh fortunes on their ruin'd state.
A Tyrant! Yes! The power was mine, and still
I rul'd the Nation with a lordly will;
Else had I been more abject than the herd
Who curs'd the yoke their slavish necks endur'd.
Yet I was kind, was bountiful, and threw
My gifts ungrudging to the villain crew;
Crush'd but the noxious reptiles in my path,
Nor grudg'd life's boon to things beneath my wroth.
But past the lethargy: and they who view'd
The slumbering lion in his couchant mood,
Shall—— But enough. Our present will made known,
Spirit, what answer from the fiery throne?"

" Thy will! poor child of dust. Allegiance swear,
Bend thy proud knee, prefer thine humble prayer,
Then meekly bide our will."

"Hah! is thy might
So vast? So curb'd thy knowledge and thy sight?
Claim'st *thou* of me allegiance, still denied
To him who made thee and thy boundless pride?
What, bend to one not second e'en in sway,
And change for thine the fetters rent away?
Is knowledge power? If so, what trust in thee,
Whose sight grasps not the World this eye can see?
Spirit, my purpose, in thy coming, done,
Return and worship at thy Master's throne,
No lord of mine. Henceforth I rest my trust
For power malign on instruments of dust;
Thy peers in knowledge, yet content to be
My slaves, nor fealty dreaming of, from me.
Deeply I err'd to deem Hell could impart
A power more dark, more potent than Man's heart.
Back to thy lord:—and henceforth would ye sway
Stern, mortal hearts, trust solely in the ray
Of thine excelling beauty. Time hath known
Worlds, for a stake less glorious, lost and won."

He said. And o'er that wondrous count'nance glass'd
Tides of emotion deep successive pass'd.
Seem'd it as there the Stygian billows hurl'd
Their spectre myriads o'er some Eden world.
Erectheus' self appall'd might scarce endure
A glance, that search'd the hidden realm obscure
Of the dread soul; his eye beneath it fell,
His heart an instant paus'd; then in the swell
Of pride rebounding rose. His glance borne down
He rais'd indignant: but the Form was gone:
A spire of flame its jet effulgent bore
Up from the spot, where stood that form no more;
Then, leaping to the roof expir'd, and left
Thick gloom without—within, a spirit reft—
Of what? Of all. The presence that anon
Had part and parcel of his being grown,
His world of sympathies:—unlov'd 'tis true,
Yet precious deem'd and mourn'd when borne from
  view.
He call'd her—but his voice, reverb'd and thrown
From rock to rock, until each anxious tone

Had caught the cavern's demon gloom, came back
Unanswer'd. O'er that pool of waters black
He stretch'd again his glaive, again gave flow
The ruddy lifestream to the tide below,
And utter'd words of power. But, no reply,
Save the lone echo's hellish mockery,
Into the void of silence, darkling fell.
He shook his blade, and every fiend of Hell
In turn defied. Low yells of distant mirth
Rippled the pool and thrill'd the steadfast Earth.

He seiz'd the taper, and with hasty stride
Press'd toward the spot where rose by turns and died
That mockery wild. Scarce might the trembling ray
Warn him of pools and fissures deep that lay
Before his random step. But onward still
The sounds allure him. Seeming now to fill
The space around: now dying dim and far,
Scarce thrill night's silence with their sullen jar.
Now turns he, startled by a frantic cry:
The warm breath smites him, but no form is nigh.

His whirling blade wounds but the airy tides,
And mockery wild his fell intent derides.

Thus onward urging still his steps, he came
To a black chasm's verge. The taper's flame
In the dense night a blood-red speck appear'd,
Whose rays were stifled as the verge he near'd.
Th' abysm black nor sight nor sound affords
To thrill sensation thro' her hidden chords.
A void, wherein the shuddering sense was thrown,
Its pole-star, compass, helm and pilot gone:
While self, dilating that dire void to fill,
O'erflow'd, an ocean fathomless of ill.

Downward that pit might pierce the hidden keep
Where Death's dire secrets with Oblivion sleep;
So dead the hush, 'twas torture to sustain
A nerve's least thrill, the tremor of a vein,
A restless thought, that plunging like some stone
Into the bosom of the Dead Sea thrown
Despair's cold thrill stirr'd sluggishly and lone.

At length the trancement broke. Far, far below,
Thousands of dreary leagues; perchance where flow
The sluggish waves of Phlegethon, a beam
Of faintest light upon his eye 'gan stream :
So dim, no nerve in darkness less intense
Had been its herald to the frame of sense ;
And yet so welcome. Round its fickle hue
The rallying spirit to a focus drew
Its powers suspent, while aye in bulk it grew.
It grew, as twilight grows in Arctic skies,
Languid and sickly on the watcher's eyes.
A space, perchance an hour, and it is now
A spark distinct amid the void below—
An equal space, and plainly was discern'd
A globe of dazzling flame that fiercely burn'd
In ever-changeful hue. Now nearer grown,
It shows a sphere of flames tumultuous thrown
Like breakers raging round some islet coast :
And now, so swift its progress, sense is lost
In the delirious whirl, the lightning flash,
The rush, the roar, the madd'ning, deafening crash

Of fire-tides battling with the waves of night,
And hurtling madly with an ocean's might.
Around, the gloom-tides clos'd. Their pitchy shroud
Strangled each ray that from the fire-orb flow'd,
Which, in its own fierce flame consuming, gave
No gleam to tinge the black chaotic wave.

Erectheus gaz'd. Undazzled was his eye:
His ear receiv'd a groan of agony:
Came it from thence? or from his own firm heart?
From each, from both. He felt the burning dart
Of horror infinite. He saw—he knew
Himself, his being, in the flames that drew
His spell-bound gaze; his essence molten there
In quenchless fires of horror and despair.

Awhile, that burning Orb, self-pois'd, delay'd
Within the chasm's gorge, as slow decay'd
The upward impetus:—then, plunging, sped
Beneath, collecting potence as it fled.
It sank; and with it sank Erectheus' eye,
His heart, his mind; the very constancy

That had so much endur'd. He needed not
A voice to warn him. There he read his lot,
His fate—for ever.
    And an answer came,
A whisper from that whirling globe of flame,
" For ever."
    And whilst, drown'd in pitchy shade
Of the dread Gulf, those sinking fires decay'd,
He sigh'd, " For ever." And an echo lone,
Sole echo of that pit, gave back the tone,
" For ever."
    Guardians of the human race,
Depute of Heaven with your high thoughts to grace
Man's petty need, and your dread ægis spread
Around his sinking spirit,—were ye fled
One, all in that dark hour?
      Scorn'd, defied,
There linger'd yet one seraph azure-ey'd
About his ruin'd heart. Her accents broke
His spirit's sullen trance and gently woke
The sole sweet chord that in his bosom strung,
Felt Hope's vibration, whilst the World was young,

From that fair hour renew'd the hallow'd strain,
And brought the Past on Memory's waft again.
O buried joys! O fancies ever new!
Springing to grace the spot where being grew;
Soon were your petals scatter'd by the blast,
Yet lives their odour, precious to the last.
And oft the foot of Guilt in mid-career
Hath met of those sweet germs one leaflet sere
Strewn in his path, and turn'd aside to spare
The hallow'd symbol of an hour so fair.
And thus, Destruction's baseless chasm spread
Before his step; his stern and desperate tread
Crumbling its verge, Dreams of the olden year
Chain'd his mad step, delay'd his fierce career,
Unmann'd his spirit; gave him once again
The power of choice—to be, as he had been,
Or burst the bonds of Darkness.

       Deep he sigh'd:
" Oh! had this mood stol'n o'er me ere the pride
Of pomp and power had left me, lonely cast,
Like stranded bark that never to the blast

Again its sail shall spread, again give flow
Its silken streamer, as the light gales blow.
But now, to crouch because the wing is rent;
To prostrate the proud spirit, while unspent
Its vital energies; to yield to Power
The claims denied in Fortune's palmy hour—
Hell's blackest shade like sunny gleam would show
Compar'd with such deep infamy of woe."

He ceas'd; for rising from the gulf there stood
A meteor flame. The comet's hue of blood,
The comet's glaive-like form it seem'd to bear,
Such as, when streaming on the midnight air,
'Tis by pale Nations view'd. Now closer grown,
A wavy scimitar, self-pois'd, it shone
O'er the black chasm's void. Upon the blade
Which flam'd intolerable light, there play'd
Blue, necromantic characters—" The sword
Of indiscriminate ruin." Fate had heard
His dire appeal. That sword before him hung,
Wooing his grasp.
    Fierce o'er the verge he sprung

Into the blind abyss, the hilt to clasp,
Death infinite beneath him. Had his grasp
Fail'd of its fateful aim, he ne'er had risen
From the black, hellish womb of the abysm ;
But thro' Earth's centre plunging to those seas
And isles where roam th' unblest Antipodes, (14)
And thence returning, only to renew
The downward plunge Earth's murky nucleus through ;
Librating thus while Ages roll away,
Helpless, uncheer'd of sun or planet's ray ;
But settling, aye by gradients sure, tho' slow,
Down to Earth's centre dire of gloom and woe,
Shudd'ring to close e'en that all-torturous flight
In blank inanity's more awful night.

Such had befall'n, but that his warrior hand
Grasp'd firm the hilt of the enchanted brand,
And, buoyant o'er the frightful gulf upborne,
He trod its gloom-tides, as some velvet lawn
At midnight hour is trod. Throughout his blood
The touch of that dread sword diffus'd a flood

Of stern and fiery zeal. Exulting high,
He wav'd it o'er his brow. The torturous cry
Of human myriads, mingling with the yell
Of mocking fiends, fill'd the black gorge of hell.
No spark of mercy kindled at the cry;
No softness, drawn in helpless infancy
From the sweet bosom, stor'd with life for him,
Answer'd that challenge dire. The twilight dim
Of human sympathy, so long o'ercast
By passion's storm-wrack, was for ever past;
And such fierce joy as deadliest foemen feel
O'er victims strown in thought beneath their steel
Scorch'd his consuming heart. With loftier stride
And eye red gleaming in its murderous pride,
He left the Chasm; lighted on his way
By the dire weapon's baleful, blood-red ray.

END OF CANTO VII.

Canto VIII.

THE AVENGER.

TO PONTUS.*

Thou dark, portentous flood, whose plombless caves
Earth's adamantine skeleton explore,
Engulfing far beneath thy rolling waves
Records of Ages past for evermore.
There, where thou treasurest up the hallow'd store,
Their scaly folds thy living monsters trail:
O'er brazen beak of many an antique prore,
Which plough'd the Deep ere Argo loos'd her sail,
The Mermaid smooths her sea-green hair and lifts her
    plaintive wail.

---

* The Euxine was anciently so called.

O'er many a brazen shield of warrior old,
Whom vengeful Juno scatter'd o'er the Deep;
When ten years' toil had sapp'd the Trojan hold,
And dire Achilles slept the leaden sleep:
Thro' gorgets' silver clasp green serpents creep,
The sea-dog whelps in fierce Oïleus' targe,
Rots the keen blade which caus'd the widow weep,
And they who rally here, and they who charge,
Are Proteus' scaly troop; plum'd wave and iron marge.

From wintry dungeons, hated of the sun,
Their icy fetters rending to be free,
With bound on bound five river giants run
To meet and blend, and be absorb'd in thee.
Here huge Tanaïs* hurls his billowy sea,
Clanking the ice-links which around him cling;
There hoarse Borysthenes † roars out his glee,
And Tyras ‡ and his mate rude greeting fling,
And deep, majestic Ister § rolls the tribute of a king.

---

* Tanaïs, the Don.   † Borysthenes, the Dnieper.
‡ Tyras, the Neister; his mate is the Bog, the ancient name of which is doubtful.   § Ister, the Danube.

Rugged thy vassals of the watery flood,
And strange and wild the peoples of thy shore,
The grim Sarmatian, quaffer of Man's blood,
With paint deform'd and terrible in war.
Here, on his wild steed wanders evermore
The quiver'd Scythian, restless as the wind ;
The frantic Thracian wastes thy western shore ;
And here, his home in Earth's dark bowels min'd,
The dim Cimmerian darkly dwells with Chaos old and
  blind.

The snowy Desert sent its tempest forth,
To meet the whirlwind from thy mountain caves ;
They wreck'd each frail bark in their frantic wrath
Disclos'd thy mysteries, heavenward hurl'd thy waves ;
And where thy flood, abhorring, shakes and laves
Old Colchis' haunted, venom-blighted shore,
Medea's sorcery sun, moon, stars enslaves ;
And, high above the elemental war,
The wail of prison'd ghosts wild rises evermore.

And downward gazing from his throne of clouds,
   The mountain King, Elborus, fills the sky:
   His regal feet the thunder-pall enshrouds,
   His shafts, red fire-bolts, glittering as they fly;
   His voice the thunder's deep-ton'd majesty,
   Hurling the deadly avalanche afar:
   But his dread brow, o'er storm-clouds lifted high,
   Dwells where no dissonance his peace may mar;
And culminates, his crown to gem, Heaven's bright,
   ascendant Star.

   The old Man bask'd before his hermit cave,
   The mossy rock a welcome shelter gave:
   For thro' his veins no dancing life-streams play,
   And his dim eye scarce drinks the cheerful ray.
   Past like th' autumnal waft each bosom true
   To early plight; his joys be dim and few;
   Yet many thoughts crowd o'er his spirit lone,
   His cares be many. They commerge in one,
   One beauteous dream, that at the midnight hour
   Revives the past with all its buried power;

One blessed sungleam, finding yet its way
Thro' portals barr'd against the blaze of day.
The grey dog fondly at his feet reclined,
Slumber'd the while or snuff'd the mountain wind;
Or, wistful gazing, sought the eye so dim,
Yet priz'd beyond day's cheery light by him.
Men say the shadows of the future, glass'd
O'er the seer's eye, at times be dimly cast
On his, that ancient friend, so grey, so wan—
Sole, sad remembrancer of joys bygone.

Sudden from rest his head the grey dog rais'd,
And down the sunlit glade intensely gaz'd,
Then deeply bay'd; yet Echo scarce replied
Ere the glad note in utter silence died:
In that deep bay a friend the prophet knew,
But marvell'd whence the awestruck silence grew.
At length his ear a footstep faint discerns,
And his dim eye with sudden radiance burns
Of warrior steel, and his heart-pulses own
The thrilling music of a voice unknown.

Save for his land, hope, fear long laid at rest,
What means the tumult of the old man's breast?

"Peace," said the Voice, " its sacred halo shed
O'er the white locks which grace the patriot's head.
Or doth the spirit world absorb thy care?
Or for thy country hast thou yet a prayer?"

"A prayer, my child? Oh! yes, while this old tongue
Is with one prayer, one faltering blessing strung,—
That prayer, that blessing, one their end and aim,
Shall fondly vibrate but my country's name.
Peace to the messenger of peace: dost bear
Tidings may glad the patriot's anxious ear?"

"The Arab from his desert, from his wild
Threatens our realm the frozen Scythia's child.
Rome calls the towers of Constantine beneath
Her strong sea-eagles to the feast of Death.
O'ercast our native heaven; afar and near
Rolls black the thunder. Patriot, dost thou fear?"

"Great is the Khalif's might. The Scythian host
Countless as waves that lash our iron coast.
Rome is an eagle, whose vast eyrie, furl'd
Mid clouds, bears fragments of a mangled world.
But, greater than the triple host is she,
Heaven's child, fair Virtue's nursling, Liberty.
When sapp'd our Virtue, Heaven no longer dear,
My prince, then ask the old Man of his fear."

"Thy prince! Thou wanderest, Father."

"Did I say
My prince? Not oft these wither'd lips betray
A thought which links the great Prometheus' son,
And our blest, suffering country's cause in one."

"Thou know'st our King, this Dion? Is he, then,
Worthy the sceptre of the first of Men?"

"Call him not king; dishonour not a name
Shall soon rise highest on the scroll of Fame.
Ay, o'er th' imperishable names of song,
Th' immobile rocks that breast Time's current strong,
Pass thou thy glance, the noblest theme recall,
But know thy Dion shall o'ertower them all."

" *My* Dion ? "

     " Said I thine ? By this I know
My country's friend, each lawless spoiler's foe.
For to love Dion is sworn friend to be
To country's cause, Truth, Justice, Liberty.
And tho' ofttimes a spirit sway my tongue,
And dark words mingle with the Old Man's song,
Yet Heaven from error guards the voice erst known
To Man, promulging oracles her own."

" Compose thy thoughts. Thine aged steps I'll guide
Where yon bleak height no lurking spy may hide.
Fear not to lean upon an arm so frail,
'Twill not beneath a patriot's burden fail.
Alas! how many an arm scarce match'd in might
With treason bands 'gainst liberty and right ! "

" My son," the old man said, withdrawing slow
His arm and gazing on the stranger's brow,
" Who art thou, that my spirit feels thy might,
And stands rebuk'd and awestruck in thy sight ?

Dim are mine eyes, and turn'd on thee discern
But plumes that wave and flashing rays that burn
As 'twere from warrior steel.   But when mine ear
Drinks in thy voice, far other forms be near:
Visions of glory and of old renown,—
Land of my love, ah! can they be thine own?—
Foreshow thy future as thy wake they throng,
Turning Time's jarring dissonance to song?"

" They can—they shall," replied that thrilling tongue;
" 'Twere impious but to doubt.   I, too, pertain
To country, freedom, truth's august domain.
But now our ancient virtue was thy boast.
Alas! foul treason mid our warrior host
And in our senate lurks.   Anon they bear
O'er the deep Euxine to the Roman ear
Terms which resign our fleet without a blow,
And pave a golden highway to the foe.
Their bark I found.   Their youthful pilot I
Hold captive—at the helm his place supply.
The deep, dark Euxine, guardian of our coast,
Shall reap one triumph o'er the traitorous host."

"And thou?"

"And I their hideous crime atone,
Of freedom's fane the humblest building stone.
But list thee, Father. Obstinate in ill,
Nor threat nor hope can move the captive's will;
Nor star nor landmark can I learn to shape
Our fateful passage toward Sinope's cape;
The very watchword lack I. Grant it be
(My last, fond hope) reveal'd, old Seer, to thee,
Recall from Earth thy thoughts."

The old man rais'd
His eyes to Heaven, and fixedly he gaz'd,
Like one whose spirit soars awhile to prove
Congenial commerce with the World above.
Stay'd on his staff those bloodless hands are spread,
The thin, grey locks stream backward from his head;
Ic'd their mobility, his features grow
Rigid as granite of the mountain brow,
Chisell'd by tempests. Sudden from his eye
So glaz'd and rayless, flashing lightnings fly,
Convulsive spasms shake his aged frame,
Then nerve its powers with more than earthly flame:

The drooping form uprises in its might,
And towers colossal on the awestruck sight;
The deep lines channell'd o'er his cheek and brow
Are flooded first, then drown'd beneath th' o'erflow
Of supernatural light. His arms, no more
Drooping and nerveless, but replete with power,
Are stretch'd on high, and round th' horizon move,
Where sleeps the land, fond object of his love.

"Oh, yes!" he cried, " upon her brow it lies,
Heaven's dew of blessing with its rainbow dyes.
I see, I see her in her budding bloom,
A maid awaken'd from the silent gloom,
The trancelike torpor of long ages: free
Her step in grace and virgin dignity.
On her fair brow the warrior's crested helm
Conceals Prometheus' ancient diadem.
Dread lightnings quiver in her sceptred hand,
Her eye is throne to Virtue's high command:
Beauty and grace her matchless form invest
With terrors, own'd of every throbbing breast.

Truth waves the banner o'er her head, and shine
Her virgin footsteps with a grace divine."

He ceas'd. The eye that dazzled with its light
Like meteor's blaze flash'd, set in sudden night.
Fail'd from his limbs the momentary fire,
His features' glow and youthful grace expire,
Totter his knees. Or e'er the youth could stay
His sinking form, extended cold it lay
Gasping for life. Vain seem'd each tender art
To re-allume the embers of the heart.
And when his hermit-cave, half borne, half led,
He gain'd, and sank on his rude leafy bed,
'Twas long ere Calthas ventur'd to inquire:
" Time presses. Duty onward becks, my sire.
Say, was the word reveal'd?"
"Not to the Seer,
My child. Yet speed thee on, with heart of cheer,
Assur'd that signs shall pilot thee along
And words of credence shall imbue thy tongue.
Alas, that fate so sad should threaten thee.
Is thine arm skill'd to cleave the billowy sea?"

"It matters not. But I the pilot's lore
Have learn'd in wandering late the Euxine shore.
Farewell. Remember Calthas."

"Dark our day
And full of woe, when price like this must pay
Our country's freedom. Heaven requite the boon
With after bliss. Farewell! my son, my son."

Day wan'd ere yet the youthful warrior stood
Above the Euxine's blue, far-rolling flood;
Intensely gaz'd where wide those waters flow,
Then diving sought the shelter'd creek below,
Where from each cliff the nodding forests brood,
And form at noon a twilight solitude.
Here slumber'd on the tide a fairy skiff
Mid shrubs and wild-flowers of th' inverted cliff;—
So still, no ripple trembled from its side
With silvery cleft the mirror to divide:
Folden her sail; her oars the rude deck strow,
The seagull perch'd upon her idle prow;
The silence of the forest gain'd a tone
More deep from presence of a thing so lone,

Late redolent of life—now dead as be
The rocks which wall that armlet of the sea.

A searching glance young Calthas round him threw,
Then stepp'd aboard, his cloak around him drew,
And on the gunnel silently reclin'd,
Liv'd o'er the scene with memory-haunted mind.
Before him spreads his own, his fathers' sea.
Around, his forests and his hills are free.
Ah, why hath Heaven to Man the boon denied
Of spirit, fetterless as mount and tide?
Why, rather, Man, hast thou the boon forsworn
To which with ocean-flood and mountain born?
Why must each dawn of freedom lour opprest
With deepest boding to the patriot's breast?

So Calthas mus'd. But soon his thoughtful mood
Was chas'd by footsteps from the tangled wood.
Onward, in number five, th' intruders came.
The first, of martial air and giant frame,
Whose firm yet careless step accorded well
With the bold glance which dazzled where it fell,

And brow as iron-bound as rocks that brave
The blue Ægean's far resounding wave.
His step was on the plank when sudden stay'd
By one whose mien the courtier's craft betray'd,
Who, cautious glancing as he forward press'd,
In honied tone the watchful youth address'd.
" Art owner of this bark, fair youth ? "

"Not I;
Your pilot simply."

"Thou shouldst know where lie
Rock, reef, and whirlpool ? "

"In the night hath sprung
A hidden reef: the whirling tides be strong.
But we, like Ocean-waves, the rock will leap,
And with the whirlpool spoil the wealthy Deep.
Art answer'd ? "

" Youth, I am. Fair comrades, cheer ;
Staunch is our guide, ye now have nought to fear."

" And when *had* we to fear ? " a deep voice said,
Of foreign accent.

"When we doubted aid
Of Tywold."
"Truce to honied words. You slow,
Scarce-crawling chief, what chains the laggard now?
Thrust off from shore; for boys we tarry not,
Nor female ballast need to trim our boat.
Seize thou yon oar, Demetrius. This for me;
Now float we freely o'er the dark blue sea.
Youth, mind the helm."
Soon shot the gallant skiff
From rocks and shadows of the sheltering cliff,
And currents false that swathe the mountain round;
And like a sea-bird, scap'd from prison-bound,
Flutters with joy awhile the snowy sail,
Then fills its bosom with the rising gale,
And o'er the dancing waves, mid showery spray
Bears the light craft upon her fateful way.
And now might Calthas more at leisure mark
His fellow voy'gers in the destin'd bark.

Familiar to his eye was one whose traits
Once stamp'd on memory, Time might scarce erase.

He sate reclining in the weather bow,
His right hand propp'd and shaded his pale brow,
His lofty front with furrows scarr'd, and fine
Of his sharp profile every chisell'd line.
Th' habitual sneer his plastic lips that dress'd,
At fitting season could be all supprest,
For he the statesman's, patriot's rôle had play'd,
And Proceus' counsel still the senate sway'd.
His restless glance, a serpent of the soul,
With stealthy glide from space to object stole,
The thoughts of men now plundering; and anon
Wand'ring the circle of the heavenly zone,
Weighing the airy currents and the host
Of black clouds mustering on the mountain coast,
Or searching some unguarded pass, to dart
A pleasing, mortal venom to man's heart.

In strongest contrast rose upon the sight
The rugged form and superhuman might
Of Tywold. Nurtur'd in a foreign land,
A daring spirit and a matchless hand
Preferr'd him early to a chief command.

But Nature with the fires that fus'd his soul
Had blent the pride that will not brook control.
And, stormy as the prison'd blast that raves
To rend its freedom from dread Ætna's caves,
The jar of anarchy, the battle's din,
The camp's rude licence—these were life for him.
He might have scorn'd his inmost thought to mask,
Had any dar'd his confidence to task.
His shrewd, keen spirit grappled at a bound
The fact, which Proceus quested like the hound;
Swift deeds his speech: and his th' instinctive might
By which the Forest King maintains his right.

"Confusion to the laggart breeze," he cried,
  As he the bellying sail impatient eyed.
  "Has the old Euxine in his thousand caves
  No storm to drive our vessel thro' the waves,
  The life-blood thro' our veins?"
                    "Now, heaven deny
That prayer," cried Brastus, glaring on the sky.
"Seest not, e'en now, o'erstrained the creaking mast,
The billows curling in the freshen'd blast?

And yon black clouds the mountain peaks that deck
And gird the waist of giant Kazibek:
Methinks our fortune we may hug, if there
Destruction lurk not in the tempest lair."

" To *speak* of tempest on the curling wave
In open boat is Fate's worst plague to brave."

Full on the speaker Calthas' glance was turn'd,
And read in sullen eye, that smouldering burn'd
Like charnel meteor, and in lips comprest,
A grov'ling mind, a grossly selfish breast,
A spirit hingeing, doggedly and slow,
On sordid greed or slavish dread of woe.

" I," said a voice of giddy folly, heard
Thro' the dense tangles of a snowy beard,
" I ask'd the Seer our fortune. His reply
Hath right good zest of mirth and pleasantry.

" Madman," cried Proceus, off his caution thrown,
" Consult the Seer! whose inmost heart is known
To Dion the Impostor?"

"Fear not thou,"
Mimas replied, with disconcerted brow.
"I veil'd in tropes our voy'ge; inquir'd the fate
That might the Fawn (so nam'd our bark) await,
Who to the Eagle's fostering wing would fly.
'Twill stir your mirth to hear his sage reply;
How think ye fram'd?"
"How, how?" cried Brastus, fear
In voice and gesture quivering.
"Thou shalt hear:
'For fawn of treacherous heart the lair is strown
Mid coral pastures of a shore unknown.'"

The old man's chuckle died upon the ear,
And left an awestruck pause of silence drear,
And startled looks, that each from other seek
Relief, yet add but pallor to the cheek;
Proceus himself an instant sate aghast:
Tywold alone no portent could o'ercast.
Proceus the silence broke.
"No prophet's eye
Need we to read the aspect of the sky.

Yonder the tempest rages, hurrying down
With giant stride from his dread mountain throne.
Tempest and midnight gloom be portents plain;
Who reads them not hath gift of sight in vain.
Seek we yon port, there anchor'd ride till morn,
Then speed, with mast unshatter'd, sail untorn:
So, wisdom, heedless of an old man's prate,
Shall, full forewarn'd, elude th' impending fate."

The old man laugh'd, and Tywold's frown grew dark,
But eager join'd their comrades of the bark
In vote with Proceus. "Youth," he said. "give way;
Put round the helm and seek yon shelter'd bay."

" At peril of your life," exclaim'd the stern
Deep voice of Tywold; "wave nor wind shall turn
My course while holds unshatter'd sail or oar.
Let him who dreads the tempest swim ashore."

His haughty, stern, commanding spirit sway'd
Their meaner souls: their very fears outweigh'd.

In silence they pursued their voy'ge, or heard
Alone, like clang of some ill-omen'd bird,
The old man's laugh. Abruptly Tywold broke
The silence; each half started as he spoke.
" How saith the Consul? How should bear at dawn
His fleet?"

" Beneath Sinope's cape 'tis drawn,"
Proceus replied. " Our own lies moor'd, beyond
Hieron's cape at wave-lash'd Trebizond.
Dwindled Rome's mighty soul since Cæsar's day;
Nor dare her huge Triremes provoke th' affray
Unlicens'd by our will, with that frail fleet
Equipp'd in haste their hostile brunt to meet."

" Now, by the fiends, a coward scheme! I'll none
Part or emprise with any dastard son
Of Rome. My wrongs shall ne'er confounded be
With spite of slaves whose wrath is treachery.
No night-bird hiding from the blaze of noon,
But a grim eagle that confronts the sun,
My vengeance; banding not with miscreant things,
But shaking its lone thunders from its wings,

Nor earthward stooping from its cloud-built throne,
Save in his strength to strike the mighty down."

"A hero spirit!" tauntingly replied
The Tempter. "Flight sublime of virtuous pride!
Were't but consistent, youths unborn should smart
Till grav'd the noble lesson on each heart."

"Consistent! Ay, no more will Tywold band
With coward heart, false faith, and woman hand."

"But traitor to his chosen federates prove?"

"Peace, wretch! thy venom cannot Tywold move:
Wouldst thou his course divine, shape first thine own,
Then say thus, never crawl'd Hermanric's son."

"The Regent's fleet is destin'd."
      "This right hand
Shall destiny outweigh."
       "Oh, thou shalt stand

The hero of the fight. The Regent's grace
Shall condescend on Tywold's brow to place,
Perchance, the second crown of oak, or yield
(For all love change) the first-fruits of the field.
His princely tongue shall praise thee. When is known
His pleasure, who shall venture to postpone
Tywold to Chiron's or young Theseus' name?"

"Serpent, thou sting'st adroitly. Whence the claim
Of this young upstart fame and fate to dole
To valiant spirits? Can his arm control
Like Tywold's the wild battle? Hath it been
Like his in fifty stricken fields, still seen
Where fiercest tumult rag'd?"

"Not so, yet one
Bright field of his thy fifty hath outshone:
So prate the wise. I heard a lover plead
At maiden's feet his cause: the myrtle shade
Conceal'd me well. 'If,' said she, 'I accord
This amaranth sprig, full keen must be thy sword,
Full bright his fame who wields it.' 'Maid,' replied
The youth, 'this pledge shall flourish in its pride

High o'er my crest, more terrible by far
Than Tywold's plume, red comet of the war.' "

" Well! and the maiden was content?"

" The maid
Shook, like some wind-wav'd flower, her graceful head.
' Is such thy highest and thy proudest aim,
To emulate the scarce remember'd fame
Of a barbarian, who at best was known
For savage valour and rude might alone?
Canst thou no more?' "

" All this the maiden said?
How answer'd he?"

" With Chiron's name. The maid
Still bent her brow. Young Theseus' deeds. She smil'd,
But still withheld the boon."—

Burst forth the wild,
Long stifled wrath of Tywold. " Theseus' might
Preferr'd o'er his, who train'd his arm to fight?
Taught his young hand the warrior blade to wield,
His eye to search the teeming battle-field?

A noble, brave, and graceful youth. But he
Preferr'd to Tywold?"

      " Stay, thou yet shalt see
Tywold avenged. The maid withheld the prize.
The youth, despairing, vow'd the task'd emprise
Past human prowess. To the faint belong
No virgin wreaths, no meed of poet's song.
Hast never heard how fled from mortal might
Erectheus' self, the terrible in fight?"

" Erectheus never fled," stern Tywold cried,
With shout had drown'd the thunder in its pride.
" He never fled. On that accursèd strand
Long strove we, crest to crest and hand to hand,
Till sudden sunder'd by the rush of fight.
But thro' the press I chas'd his plume of night,
Death clos'd upon his wake like waves that sweep,
Tracking some monster of the vasty deep.
Just then arose the cheery battle cry
Of ' Indra.' Dion swept like tempest by.
He play'd the captain's part, I'll n'er deny.

His eye each pass explor'd, his charge laid low
The staunchest squadrons of the stubborn foe:
But ne'er attain'd Erectheus. Him the throng
Of flight dragg'd (slaughtering friend and foe) along:
Till, as he strove to rally up the war,
A chain of elephants that fled the roar
Of the Greek-fire the struggling hero bore
Mid the deep river, cumber'd with the slain,
And spoils and trophies of the battle plain.
Erectheus never fled. A hero true,
Worthy his fame. Thy silly tale pursue."

" 'Tis clos'd. The youth who fear'd not Tywold's fame.
Nor pal'd at Chiron's or young Theseus' name,
Dismay'd, the novel pledge refus'd. 'Fair maid,
Keep thou thy proffer'd meed of fame,' he said,
'Reserv'd for him whose tongue hath learn'd to shine
In boastful triumph truth denies to mine.'
So spake the lover. Youth, the helm put round;
For Trebizond our changeful bark is bound,—
So wills the valiant Tywold."

Answer'd stern
That warrior: "Stripling, venture not to turn
Our course, an' thou'rt not weary of thine own!
Tywold is then the scorn of maidens grown,
The mark our beardless youth o'ershoot with ease?
Curse on the lifeless sea, the laggart breeze!
Can yon black thunder-cloud yield nought but gloom?
Or lives the once proud Tywold to become
Of his own elements, the free, the strong,
Scorn'd, as the byword of each feeble tongue?"

A blast came roaring from the cavernous wild,
Where mount o'er mountain to mid-heaven is pil'd:
It came, upcurling every billow hoar,
Then, rapt on high, the crumbled Ocean bore;
It smote and hurl'd the fragile bark afar,
Full on her quivering beam, as 'twere in war
With dread Leviathan. Pal'd Proceus' cheek;
Curses and prayers, mixt blasphemy, did reek
From the foul lips of Brastus: and, upborne,
Like shriek of some wild demon of the storm,

The old man's laugh above the turmoil dark
Was heard, while each clung desperate to the bark,—
All, save stern Tywold. From despondence sprung
That chief, exultant—joyful greeting flung
To the wild herald of the tempest grim,
Sent, as in answer of his doubts, to him.
His tall form stay'd against the creaking mast,
His red plume tossing in the furious blast,
His brow dilating, kindling his dark eye,
His arm outstretch'd to that black, thund'rous sky,
He seem'd the Genius, terrible and lone,
Of Tempest, gazing on his cloud-pack'd throne.

" Oh, ever thus, thou fetterless and wild,
Swift Spirit of the Waste, hast thou beguil'd
And scatter'd all my coward doubts afar:
Thou fearless element, whose conquering car
Grinds into dust the Ocean, and hurls down
The rocks Eternity had grav'd his own,
Thou, thou art Tywold's friend, and in the roar
Of thy wild storm he freely breathes once more."

"Youth," he exclaim'd, to Calthas turning, "yield
  To mine the helm thy frail arm scarce may wield:
  'Tis Tywold's hour, but thou shalt near him be,
  To point our pathway o'er the trackless sea.
  Shake not thy head. My will is law. Whene'er
  Slacks the strong gale the helm shall be thy care."

The wind still rose; the rainy torrent pour'd;
In deep, hoarse peals the stunning thunder roar'd;
Thick gloom enhanc'd the firebolt's dazzling might,
And fast that gloom was black'ning into night.
Toss'd the frail bark amid that turmoil rude,
As lives some name of note on memory's flood.
Furl'd all her sail, save one slight strip of snow,
That, like a sea-gull, flutters o'er her prow.
Great was their peril, as with headlong bound
Their fairy skiff the trough of ocean found;
Or, toilsome, climb'd th' impending watery steep,
To stream from thence her beacon o'er the deep.
Each heart bestow'd in secret many a curse
On Tywold's haughty soul and will perverse:

Each, save the youthful patriot's. Fondly he
Look'd on the wrathful sky and troublous sea,
In hope that Heaven might their deliv'rance store,
Permitted to his own right hand no more.

And now Night's sceptre, stretch'd o'er sea and sky,
Lent to the tumult stern her majesty.
" Youth," Tywold said, " our bark thou seem'st to guide
By doubt undazzled o'er the murky tide;
Yet long hath land defied mine aching sight,
Nor hangs one star her beacon on the Night.
What then the index of thy course?"
        " Yon jet
Of flame on high Elborus' summit set,
And that lone star o'er far Sinope's cape;
'Twixt these the bark her venturous path must shape."

All gaz'd in mutter'd wonder: then, in deep
And deathlike silence. Thro' each heart 'gan creep
The vital tide; chill fear the brain oppress'd,—
The very laughter of the old man ceas'd.

Their eyes first sought the Star's, the Beacon's light,
Then, on the pilot's features grew their sight.
No jet of flame, no star o'erhangs the coast,
The snowy sail itself in gloom is lost.
Yet each, distinct, the pilot's form discerns,
His features' mould, the very flush that burns
His else pale cheek, illum'd with light that glows
As thro' his veins the lifetide ebbs and flows.
Paus'd each scar'd heart. That beacon first flam'd high
When, rising from the dim obscurity
Of unrecorded Time, Prometheus' star
Climb'd the blue vault and chas'd Night's gloom afar.

And hence, Prometheus' banner pennon nam'd;
And ancient prophecy its might proclaim'd
O'er every foe. E'en Tywold's dauntless breast
That portent mov'd. The youth he thus addrest:
" Too young art thou for base deception's art,
And thy clear eye betrays no guileful heart.
Hold by this beacon, since thine eye can read
Its ray, and Fate no better helps our need.

The rather trust it, since thou says^t it glows
High o'er the Mount, whence my wild tempest
   blows."

Dread is the sov'reign majesty of Night,
When with the elements she links her might,
And her black sceptre scares the seraph sleep
From the lone wanderer of the vasty deep.
But dreadful more to traitor hearts, who there
Meet Terror banded with the fiend Despair.
The monsters of the deep, disturb'd from rest,
Heav'd their dire forms above the billow's crest.
Here measureless Leviathan—around
Their bark his arms a wildering forest wound.
Here Hydras hiss'd with fork'd and fiery tongue,
And ghastly Mermen from their elf-locks wrung
The briny wave, and madd'ning descants sung
That, mingling with the storm, to frenzy stung
Each fear; and like that fiend which haunts the crest
Of precipice, the fatal plunge suggest. (15)
And here, like coral reef to Heaven upgrown,
The monstrous Kraken lifts his star-gemm'd crown:

His spectral eyes two moony circles form,
Red as her light when wading thro' the storm.
His jaws a furnace, barr'd with fangs that grow
Tall as the mast o'er some high galley's prow—
His bulk a mass, immeasur'd of Night's gloom,
Formless as Terror, rayless as the Tomb.
Here things half fish, half ape, around them mow,
And mopping beck them to their caves below.
And sea-dogs howl, and, if the raving blast
An instant pause, they hear, with hearts aghast,
A deep conch sound, the dirge of spirits driven
From Earth by Ocean, and by crime from Heaven.

But, at the morning watch, the tempest's might
Seem'd soft'ning fast in that all-gentle light.
The gusts less mad o'er furrow'd Ocean sweep,
Each white crest ruffling of the billowy deep.
Each turn'd his own or neighbour's fears to jest,
As rose Sinope o'er the watery West,
A stain of liquid purple, whose soft hue
Match'd nor the azure sky nor ocean's blue,

Seen as the labouring bark from trough profound
Of Ocean crests the billow at a bound.
Each deem'd already won that wish'd-for soil,
Already reap'd his treachery's promis'd spoil.

" Fair youth," said Tywold, " wondrous is the course
Thy skill hath shap'd: but past the tempest force,
And thy young eye must weary of the deep:
Recline thy limbs, and snatch the needful sleep."

" Full soon for me the pillow shall be prest,
And long my sleep, and deep shall be my rest.
But, never satiate of the view, mine eye
Devours yon purple mounts, that chequer'd sky,
Those free glad billows as they heave and fall—
How beautiful! alas, how fleeting all!"

" How beautiful! Nay, stripling, thou art one
Of wayward fancy. Oft I've gaz'd upon
Those toys of sea and sky as kindred things,
Unfetter'd as my own rude spirit's wings.

But beauty ! Now my stormy soul requires
In that idea repose to its stern fires.
Strange that a form so soft should shrine a mind
Which beauty owns, where Tywold greets his kind.
But rest thee, child. My own dim, aching sight
Assures me thine must weary of the night."

" This is no fitting hour. My lids must close
But in the long, deep trancement of repose.
Yield to my hand the helm, and take thy rest,
If thou canst slumber with unlighten'd breast."

" Ne'er doubt it, child. But with a soul like thine
Methinks or crime or rest had ne'er been mine.
Take heed, poor youth. On treachery's deadly sea
Nor beauty beams nor peace is stor'd for thee.
I know not why; thy voice my heart appeals
As 'twere with memory's tone. Thine eye reveals
Scenes of past years, long buried out of sight,
Since Death untimely shed his hopeless blight.
But thou hast earlier enter'd paths of crime,
And deeper woe and ruin must be thine."

"Deliberate is the choice, repeated not.
But thine—I mourn o'er thy perverted lot:
Form'd for high aims, to dare, to do, to be,—
Had I one tear, it were devote to thee."

"To me! Nay, heed me not. My destin'd part
I fill, Heaven's legend on the lion's heart.
Thou wilt not rest? Then be the helm thy care.
Kind youth, those swift and sudden gusts beware
From yon high mountain. Loth were I that ill
Fell the sole heart can throb for Tywold still."

Wrapt in his cloak, the warrior cast him down
At Calthas' feet, and with a speed unknown
To pamper'd eyes, is lock'd in slumb'rous rest,
Known by the long, deep heavings of the breast:
The pilot's eye in painful reverie
Dwelt on his form. "Alas! and must it be,
That generous soul, in this its dark, warp'd plight,
The first dread offering to my country's right.
But 'tis a fate I share. Nor must regret
Teach me stern virtue's dictates to forget."

From time to time, as o'er the swelling sea
The fair Fawn bounded tamelessly and free,
The rushing gusts from mountain tunnels still
Tax'd the young pilot's prompt and watchful skill.
The crew half slumbering o'er the planks repos'd,
Save one: that old man's eyelids never clos'd;
And ever and anon those eyes of stone
Young Calthas met, fixt, fasten'd on his own.
At length his loud, discordant laughter broke
The silence. Starting, all save Tywold woke.
" There, there it blazes, high, and higher still,
The blood-red beacon on the Giant's Hill."*

All gaz'd in awe, where tower'd the giant height
Of dread Elborus in his cloud-rob'd might:
Despite the risen sun, the distance vast,
Distinct that fiery jet to Heaven was cast;
Morn in its ray grew lurid, as when dies
The star of Day mid thunder-burden'd skies.

* Mount Elborus is so called.

The pilot turn'd.   He saw with foam o'ercast
The Deep uprooted by the trampling blast.
Of his lov'd mountains, one last hurried look,
Of the blue Deep, the cheerful Daystar took,
Stirr'd Tywold with his foot; then sudden cast
The veering shallop broadside to the blast.
Then came at once the shock, the frantic cry
Despair reserves for Man's last agony ;
Outvoic'd by peals of frantic laughter thrown
From wave to Heaven, from Heaven abhorring down
And ere the mingled yells have ceas'd to scare
Each pitying spirit of the Flood and Air,
The boiling surge amid its yeast upheaves,
As Autumn blast the swirling forest leaves,
Wrecks of the shatter'd mast and plank uptorn,
And direr freight, the drowning swimmer's form.

And Calthas sank beneath the briny wave,
Alike the traitor foul and patriot's grave,
His soul commending to the hand that gave.
He rose, the wreck a moment buoy'd him o'er
The troubled Deep and stunning billows' roar.

The cry of Proceus pierc'd his dizzy brain,
As sank that traitor ne'er to rise again :
The yell of Brastus, mingling with his prayer
Of blasphemy, o'ertortur'd by despair,
And direr yet the laughter shriek that raves
From Mimas, strangling in those deathful waves.

Cumber'd with crested helm and corselet's weight,
The mighty Tywold struggled hard 'gainst Fate;
Despairing not when Hope forgot to show
Her torch, man's beacon o'er this waste of woe.
The pilot's touch a moment's respite gave,
(When ask'd he more?) ere plunging to the wave.
That moment freed him from his warrior cloak,
And now his touch the morion's clasp hath broke ;
And his red crest, the terror of the fight,
Old Ocean hides for ever from Man's sight.
An effort more, the corselet, frequent tried
In fields of fight, sinks gleaming in the tide.
But far the shore, the drifting wreck remote,
Death calls. The whirlpool opes his famished throat,

Then wherefore near the drowner's clasp delay?
Why counts his eye the foam-globes of the spray?
He deems to view, mid Ocean's plumage hoar,
The silvery helm their youthful pilot wore.
Back from his arm the scattering billows fly;
'Twas but the Dolphin's scale that mock'd his eye;
Oh! tarry not, strong swimmer. Mighty thou,
But mightier Ocean's boundless ebb and flow,
The tyrant winds be mightier. "Youth," he said,
" Thine eye for Tywold one kind drop did shed;
By the stern tempests of my wilds, I swear
Thy life to rescue, or thy death to share."

Scarce ceas'd he, ere the wave regurging brought
Almost within his arms the form he sought.
Swift as the serpent coils the stockdove, round
The sinking youth his sinewy arm is wound;
Droops o'er his shoulder strong the languid head,
His own exulting o'er the wave is spread.
Ne'er in his highest triumph so elate
With conscious might to wrest decrees from fate,

As now Eternity beneath him spread,
And Hope attenuate to a single thread,
Seem'd the wild wind its fury to control,
Aw'd by the fervour of that dauntless soul.
Lull'd is the blast, the wreck swift drifting by
Now rests and grows upon the swimmer's eye,
As buoyant merging o'er each billow there,
He shakes the spray showers from his tangled hair,
And soon above the shatter'd plank he stood,
And drew his burden, helpless, from the flood.
Dweller by turns on land or sea, his care
Soon reallum'd the life-spark smouldering there;
The helm remov'd, *had* loos'd the corselet's band,
But the youth's grasp was fasten'd on his hand,
And so imploringly appeal'd the glance,
Then first awaking from its death-like trance,
That he forbore his purpose kind, and gave
His care to aid their passage through the wave.
He saw with joy that still the current bore
Their wreck slow drifting tow'rd the distant shore;
He saw that, hush'd the gale, the sun beam'd warm
O'er his young comrade's drench'd and death-cold form;

His haughty spirit, which in woe had known
But the stern power transmuting wave to stone,
Which peril ne'er had shaken from its rest—
That spirit proud relenting fires confess'd:
The past return'd, the blighting present gleam'd;
Was this the Future youthful promise dream'd?
" Alas!" he sigh'd, " those aspirations high,
Gush'd they to waste their fickle mockery
O'er th' unfruitful desert?" Gloom profound
Obscur'd his spirit, as he gaz'd around.
Could he not stir to rage his slumbering might,
And rend the Daystar's passage through the night?
His own rude passions like the steed control,
And reassert the empire of the soul?

A sigh the stillness broke. He turn'd—his eye
Fell on the beauteous youth reposing nigh.
Basking he lay in that warm sunny light,
To Tywold gloomier than the void of night.
The shatter'd wreck asylum per'lous gave,
Nor screen'd his person from the drenching wave,

That o'er him shower'd too oft in restless spray.
Extended o'er the folden sail he lay;
The eye, too glorious for Earth's lustre, shone
In fixt and anxious sadness on his own.
It seem'd to read his heart. " Alas, fair child,
And canst thou sigh above the ruin wild
Of this rude spirit? Hast thou yet for me
A kind thought, tottering as thy footsteps be
On verge of ruin more profound than mine?
If Heaven, indeed, hath marr'd a pure design
To form so perfect join'd a treacherous heart,
Who shall the angels credit? But thou art
Victim to some foul plot. Thou shalt not fall
In thy young blood, disowned, abhorr'd of all.
Thy form I've rescued, thy young mind I'll save
From worst than tomb on Earth, or watery grave.
" Alas!" he cried aloud, and smote his brow
With his clench'd hand; " and is it even so?
Shall the foul vulture's heart soft pity move?
Quits he the carnage to reclaim the dove?"

END OF CANTO VIII.

Canto IX.

THE SNARE.

Night swathes the mountain, night the valley wide
Fills to o'erflowing with her boundless tide,
That, like the waters of some shoreless sea
Engulfs its billows in Infinity,
Bears sense aloft where worlds innumerous roll,
And to the realm of spirits wafts the soul.
But o'er the mountain brow Night's hush is risen,
With sounds of life that jar the vault of Heaven:
The rush, the sullen tide, deep, dense and strong,
Of battle steeds, and the mail'd martial throng
Of turban'd riders.

                    From yon craggy height
The drowsy goatherd, starting, eyes the night
With wond'ring glance. " The stars of Heaven look down
Serene and calm, each from his sapphire throne;
The moss-wreaths drooping from the pine-branch
    high, (16)
Wave but as beauty's tresses to the sigh
Of dawning love. The Ocean lies afar,
Whence through earth, air rolls on this deep, con-
    tinuous jar,
'Tis Ocean's might. Oft have our sires declar'd
How Heaven's dread standard o'er our mountains bar'd,
Ocean his strength upheaving rent asunder
His rocky bonds, and hurl'd his billowy thunder
High o'er Elborus' brow. My slumbering bride,
My helpless babe, uprouse ye. Death's black tide
Rolls on. Up, up, the mountain brow we'll scale,
And when o'er Earth the watery floods prevail,
Die in one long embrace."

                        Forth, trembling, sprung
His beauteous Bride. The web at random flung

Round the young babe she to her bosom press'd,
Scarce offers shelter to her tender breast
From the ic'd mountain blast.   Her raven hair
Streams o'er her shoulder.   Each white foot is bare,
And in the starlight gleams."

       " My love, my lord,
With thee to live, to die.   But must the sword
Of Death our young, our tender bud cut down?
Lead, lead, I follow.   Hark! how hurry on
Those fatal tides, mixt with the frequent neigh
Of steeds, and one wild shout.   Away, away."

" Alas! no death is here, which he may flee,
Who to his country true, and worthy thee,
Would live or perish.   'Tis not Ocean's tide
Whose voice to Heaven is lift; but hosts that ride
Tumultuous as his billows.   Thou hast heard
Our Prince's mandate to each mountain horde:
Thou know'st our country's need.   Sweet Life, farewell,
And thou blest land where yet the noble dwell,
Where dwelt my Sires, receive th' oblation free
To their dread shades, thyself and liberty."

He rush'd from her embrace. Down, down the steep
She hears from rock to rock his frantic leap.
The causeway gain'd, beneath a wayside oak
He seats him, shrouded in his shepherd cloak,
To wait the coming host. A foot-fall light
Sounds near. " What, ho! thou wanderer of the
    night;
Thy name, thy purpose? Till thou answer, stand."
A clasp of softness binds his rugged hand,
Around his neck a fairy arm is thrown,
The cheek, best lov'd, burns, blushes on his own.
" Alas! what madness brings thee?"

                            " Madness caught,
Jarthon, from thee, from all. One selfish thought,
One timorous doubt at this, our country's need,
Would brand me traitress to the patriot creed
By our great Prince promulg'd."

                            " And what would'st thou
Mid warrior ranks? Thy sex, thy youth, the glow
Of thy soft beauty? Hast thou heart to see
Thine infant mangled mid the barbarous glee
Of the rude soldier? Canst thou brook to be

The victim of his lust? Fly, Miriam, fly;
This is no task thy lofty zeal to try."

"Not so. Each terror weigh'd, I trust Heaven's arm
To shield our blest, our infant hope from harm;
Or if my soul must wither in his woe,
In freedom's cause, will needful strength bestow.
Alone, thy word will doubtful credence gain;
But when, wife, babe, thy sponsors they retain:
Then lead thou on; and though thy fateful tread
Tend to the sunless mansions of the dead
Secure they follow. 'Gainst thine honour's wrong
Keen is this blade, this woman's heart is strong."

She ceas'd; for now those thronging sounds of fear,
The tramp of steeds and clash of arms drew near.
First the Moowuzzin rode. His voice supplied
The need of trumpet-note, the course to guide,
To urge, to sway that boundless battle-tide.
Full on the night, from time to time arose
That sonorous cry, more dreadful to thy foes,

Islām,* than wildest burst of martial strain :
" Great is the one true God !"   And ere again
In silence fail'd the voice, 'twas peal'd on high
In one deep-ton'd, prolong'd, and thrilling cry
Of the dense host from league to league outspread,
Till every echo of the mountain fled
In that dread shout to heaven, and every star
Trembled that hallow'd name from lips to hear
Foul with the pledge of murder.

                           Leading on
His martial band, array'd in arms that shone
In every ray the stars of heaven bestow'd
On the night gloom, the aged Chieftain rode ;
Ukhbur his name, late envoy to the throne
Of great Prometheus' Daughter.   Never shone
Arabia's blazing sun with fiery dart
On sterner brow or bolder zealot's heart ;
And time, that chang'd his raven beard to snow,
Quench'd not the dire volcano stor'd below,

---

      * The faith preached by Muhummud.

But to youth's searching zeal the wisdom lent,
The stern resolve, th' unchangeable intent,
Th' inveterate spirit, growth of after years,
When Hope her smile forgets, and Woe her tears.
Swift at his signal, to his bridle rein
Dash'd Khoosroo, Prince of Lar's rock-strewn domain:
" Ho! stir yon slumberers; bind and hither bear."

" I hear, obey. But one seems frail and fair;
An infant fills her arms."
      " If Moslem, spare;
If Infidel,* meet cradle rocks below,
Where yon fierce torrent hurls its crest of snow."

Aghast the mother heard. Her suppliant eye
Sought the young Chief's to whom that stern reply
Was render'd. He a human heart possess'd,
He saw her clasp to her devoted breast
Her slumbering babe. He thought of twain afar,
Babe, mother, sunder'd by the fate of war.
" Swear on thy babe's salvation thou'lt not flee."

---

* Kawfur, infidel.

"So help him Heaven."

      "Enough, his life is free;
 Great Ulla grant to thee, to him, to know
 That truth divine, sole hope of man below."

 In question brief stern Ukhbur's voice is heard:
"Thy name? thy calling? See each lightest word
Bear truth's severest test, or they shall throw
Thy carcase o'er yon cliff to feed the crow.
Thy name?"
    "Is Jarthon. Where have liv'd, have died
My sires, dwell I upon the mountain side;
My flocks, my care."
      "How haps it thou art found
By the wayside, no fleecy charge around?"

"Chieftain, nor lordly head, nor lowly brow,
 But must to circumstance and suffering bow.
 A mother's hallow'd life of us demands
 Our hearts' warm sympathy and ready hands;
 For this our cot we left. Thine arm'd array
 Hath ta'en us, resting, by the foot-worn way."

"Now answer me sincere. From hence not far
The hostile forces camp in guise of war.
Lead me but thither; and henceforth no more
Forsake thy home to list the torrent's roar,
Or brave the icy blast on moor or hill,
With ruddy gold thy shepherd scrip I'll fill;
Or, for Islam, if thou thy creed resign,
Broad furrow'd fields and pastures shall be thine."

"O Night of a blest star! Yet, Chieftain, know,
'Tis no unwarlike crowd, no woman foe,
Whose lances like a leafless forest grow
In the deep valley soil."

"Content thee, hind:
Our Prophet's banner floats upon the wind;
God and the Prophet's name speed every blow,
And true believers *but* demand to know
Where Kawfur* armies hide. Lead boldly on;
But mark me—guile's least symptom to atone,
I hold thy wife's, thine infant's life, thine own.
Nor vainly hold."

---

* Idolator, infidel.

"E'en so! The foeman's might
Ye seek. Be't mine to guide your steps aright.
Had I a life for ev'ry foe ye'll see,
In this great cause I'd stake it. Follow me."

"Enough, lead on. Time presses. As we go,
Describe the force, guise, posture of the foe."

"A mountain shepherd I. As shepherds skill
To speak of war I speak. With kindlier will
I'd tell of flocks and herds, or lead ye where
Sleeps the cool pasture screen'd from midday glare,
Deep bosom'd in the dell, or caves disclose,
Where from the living rock pure crystal flows.
Or teach you how, upon the mountain side,
With stakes and thorns inlac'd a circle wide
Around our fold we pen. Or lead your foot
Where the clear lake imbathes the mountain root,
And mount and sky a world inverted stand,
And heaviest dews refresh the flower-sprent strand:
But warriors view our arts with scornful eyes.
Not far from hence a deep, wide basin lies;

Steep mountains heavenward wall its circuit round.
Once o'er a vasty lake those mountains frown'd,
Of depth unfathom'd and unmatch'd in gloom:
But in some age remote their prison doom
The waters burst thro' channel sapp'd below,
Where yet the torrent raves in ceaseless flow.
But yester morn a straggler of my flock
Led me to scale the valley's heaven-pil'd rock.
What time, emerging from his rest, the sun
That mountain's eastern ridge with toil had won,
And flung from thence far downward, o'er the tide
Of rolling mists his level glance of pride.
Those rolling mists the genial glance obey,
Majestic rise and greet the star of day;
And thro' their rents upon my wondering gaze
Flash'd back from lance and brand innumerous rays,
Lighting the vale throughout its wide extent;
And from the mighty host beneath was sent,
Borne on the swelling air-tides, a deep hum
Of life, like that which, sporting in the sun,

The insect myriads raise. At times combin'd,
And hovering slow upon the morning wind,
The eddying vapour blotted all from sight:
At times, when still'd that breeze, the hush of night
Slept o'er the basin vast. Then fitful rose
Sounds as of parted years that haunt us in repose."

" Sought ye the camp?"
                       " Chieftain, I sought it not:
Heaven smiles benignly o'er my peaceful cot,
War and its camps I dread."
                       " There be, who say
This Dion marshals there his doom'd array.
Know'st thou of this?"
                       " At least his banner flies;
Gay shows the mountain in its rainbow dyes."

" Then, are the passes guarded?"
                       " Even so:
Yet o'er those heights myself a path can show
By which, if brave your warriors, ye may win
The very life-key to the foe within."

" Doubt not our daring. Thou the pass should'st mean.
  Through which the torrent mines a path unseen? "

" The same—the very rocks that bridge it o'er,
  And stand aye list'ning to its deaf'ning roar.
  Oft, as a child, I've sat the livelong day,
  Lull'd by those sounds, to watch the flaky spray
  Now madly whirl, now shoot with arrowy flight
  'Twixt the black rocks: while still my dazzled sight
  Return'd to where commenc'd each bright career
  To find fresh foam-bells hurrying in the rear,
  And with fresh gaze pursue. But those old years
  Come o'er my spirit with the might of tears."

Answer'd a deep, stern voice: " Right fitting mood
For him who trafficks in his country's blood."

The startled peasant turn'd. That voice of might,
Replete with mockery, shed a sudden blight
O'er his scar'd spirit. As some keen ice-dart,
Rent from yon wintry peak, had cleft his heart.

Beside the Arab chief, a horseman rode;
Sable his arms, his cloak, the steed he strode.
High o'er his morion, black as midnight gloom,
Swept the stars' trembling lamps his sable plume,
As 'twere to blot from Heaven their sacred light,
Drinking but blackness from the gulf of night.
Proud arch'd the charger's crest: his fiery eye
Blaz'd as the Dogstar's torch in sultry sky,
When Famine rides the gale and flock from far
The vulture legions to the scent of war.
Thro' his wide nostril on the bleak night-blast
A torrent mixt of fire and vapour pass'd;
And his wild neigh o'eraw'd with music's might
The thousand thousands thronging to the fight,
As rose its regal clarion on the night.
And now they thread a valley deep and wide,
Where the strong billows of the mountain tide,
That long had sent their murmur from below,
Side with their steeds in broader channel flow.
Not farther distant than the eye might ken
Rose the bleak bulwarks of that fateful den,

Which, as they near'd, in straiter bounds comprest,
High flung the stream its billows of unrest.
Then Ukhbur spoke :

"Great Prince! A twofold aim
Be ours. Yon mountain's ridgy crest to gain,
And thro' the pass our thronging squadrons guide.
Choose thine own part."

Erectheus brief replied:
"Mine be Death's ampler banquet."

"Haste thee, then,
Young Khoosroo, lead thine own brave mountain men
Up the steep path. Thence sound our battle-cry—
God and the Prophet's sword, vengeance and victory."

At once full thrice a thousand warriors sprang
From their fleet steeds, their arms and armour rang:
Jarthon, their guide. Against the rocky height
Their agile limbs they bend, soon lost to sight
Mid bush and crag, or seen in dwindled wise
As specks t' enhance the mountain's giant size.

Meanwhile the Arab host in phalanx deep
Paus'd in the shadow of that mountain keep.
Slow wan'd the Night; the Scorpion's fiery train
From mount to mountain bulwark stretch'd immane,
Hung silent, filling all the narrow'd sky
With baleful glory. Dire Antares' eye
Sheds beauteous death;—and side with him the Star,*
Once monarch of high Powers, but since the war
Of heavenly Potentates, despoil'd and given
But the malign decretals of high Heaven.
Slow wan'd the night. Before, above them lower'd
The massive mountain whose high ridges tower'd
Sublime; but midway through that bulwark's side
Down to the base was rent a fissure wide,
Through which the raving torrent thunder'd forth,
The huge rocks grinding in its stormy wroth.
Those massive rocks, the corner-stones, whereon
Nature builds high to Heav'n her mountain throne,
Span with groin'd vault the ever-boiling spray,
And prison Night amid the blaze of Day.

---

* Saturn, the most baleful of the planets.

Into this frightful den, where torrents roar,
And dismal sounds from pitchy blackness pour,
Erectheus spurr'd his steed. O'er slippery rock,
Through flood and foam, amid the giddy shock
Of wave and barrier, his undaunted horse
Held through the hellish pass his onward course,
And his stern rider through the tumult bore,
Unscath'd and reckless; but alone no more.
What horseman follows in his gloomy track,
Array'd like him, in panoply of black,
Arms, cloak, and plume? The stunning din around,
And plunging steed, and pitchy night profound,
Absorb'd Erectheus; till his snorting horse
Paus'd at a rocky barrier in mid-course.
And a faint breathing made the presence known
Of one that dar'd, unsanction'd and alone,
His gloomy footsteps dog.
                            He turn'd and drew
His deathful scimitar. Its blood-red hue
Intensely glow'd, illuming that dark cave
As with a comet's blaze: "What wretch would brave
Erectheus' wrath? Speak, or in silence die."

High flam'd the sword, but fell not, for reply
Most eloquent was render'd. From his brow
That seeming horseman pluck'd the morion low,
And sate defenceless 'neath th' impending sword.
Down o'er the corselet in rich showers were pour'd
The golden ringlets: from the deep, full eye,
Where azure strove with Night's intensest dye,
Flash'd back for every ray that war-blade shed
A flood of living light that changeful play'd
With all the rainbow's hues. Unhelmèd sate
The beauteous stranger 'neath th' impending fate:
Unhelm'd—yet did not Mulcifer of yore
In Ætna's fire and Stygian billow frore
Forge the bright helm, the triple crest endow,
Which nodded dreadful o'er Achilles' brow,
Of temper so ethereal as the gold
Whose molten waves from that bright brow were roll'd.

" Whence, beauteous Vision ? "
       " From the fields of air;
From the full orbèd Sun; from caverns where

Burns his mysterious essence, which his eye
Shall ne'er explore; from meteor orbs that fly
Paling the mortal world; from stars that roll
Burning their circles round the icy pole;
From Ætna's cavern'd tunnel; from the hills
Of Bankoo, rife of thousand fiery rills;
From cavern'd Caucasus' dread halls—I come."

" And what thy purpose? Doth the certain doom
Of thousand thousands not suffice thy lord?
Or bear'st thou spell to edge the flaming sword
To its red harvest?"

" Mortal, that dire blade
Is not of *him* I serve. Fain would I aid,
Warn, counsel of thy fate, impending near;
But waste no accent on reluctant ear.
In scornful mood once bad'st thou me begone.
Touch'd by thine after penitence, I come
Once more. Form but that prior wish, and ere
Thy lips can mould it in the plastic air,
Ten thousand leagues dispart us."

"Be thy will
Aught else; but linger thou around me still,—
Sole object which the fast-consuming pest
Of vengeance leaves uncanker'd in my breast."

"Brief the allotted moments. In thy hand,
Mortal, thou bear'st a fatal gift, the brand
Of vengeance double-edg'd, which none may bear
Unscath'd, save those who spirit-nature share."

"Welcome the scath, so but the ruin fall
Deep, wide, uncheck'd, and pitiless on all.
What recks the panther, struggling in the Deep
With dread Leviathan, of tides that sweep
In giddy whirl around? Doth he not know
His death, destruction to his scaly foe?
Deep in the monster's fiery eyeballs sink
His dreadful talons: fetter'd by a link
Firmer than death, he drags him down below,
And counts death sweet, in torture of his foe."

"Sweet to Man's stormy nature is the draught
Of vengeance—sweet the ruddy mixture quaff'd
By Beings higher of degree ; but light
Is finite vengeance to th' eternal blight
Which swift succeeds :—an instant's giddy glow
Of joy inebriate, bought with endless woe.
Leave to brute instinct such. A loftier view
Be thine. Thy vengeance barter for a new
And glorious destiny. Come, share my throne,
The rule of spirits, fiery as thine own :
Exempt from death, disease, and gifted high
With powers to which man's might is vanity.
Ten thousand such—the least more mighty far
Than the vext elements, whose thund'rous war
Shakes the deep-rooted earth. These watch and
   wait
My beck and form, the legion of my state.
My nod commands them to the farthest star
Of the dim Galaxy, or where his car
The Northern War-king rolls. Dismist of me,
They search the secrets of the plombless sea,

Which mortals Heaven design, or plunge below
Earth's adamantine crust, where rooted grow
Elborus' snow-capped towers."

"Yet, beauteous thing,
With powers so vast above, below to wing
So strong a flight, to search, command, explore,
How lack'st thou passport to this bosom's core,
As thy late claim to homage doth imply?
And say how hides thy potence from man's eye,
Which grasps whate'er event is casual hurl'd
From Time's dim ocean to the natural world?
If o'er man's spirit thou possess no sway,
If the blind elements no law obey
Of thine; if Satan's self be not thy lord,
In what consists thine empire? What the chord
Of sympathy 'twixt human hearts and thee?"

"Mortal," replied the voice, "the world ye see
Is but a moment's pageant. Your vain sight
Ye turn bedazzled from the Sun's dim light—

That sun, a spark mid myriad sparks to me.
The waves immeasur'd of Eternity
Cast a few spray showers on your insect coast,
To form Time's pool, that ocean of *your* boast—
A pool, the first regurging wave may sweep
Back to the plombless basin of the deep.
The eternal billows, on th' eternal shore
Aye hurling, lend faint thrillings of their roar,
Dimpling your motely shallow in their might,
Where spreads each ring a cycle in thy sight.
But the blue firmament hath charge on high
To shield the Finite from Infinity;
From gales that o'er Heaven's gulf eternal sweep,
And each dire scale-arm'd monster of the deep.
Peopling that shallow with his atom brood,
The petty tyrant of a spray-shower's flood,
Reigns man, minutest embryo of a race
Amongst the mightiest in the realms of space.
Lord of a mystic empire, barr'd with care
From subtlest spirits of the sky and air,

Who for admission vainly ply. But one
Can solve that mystery, that dominion lone,
Man's heart, peruse, explore."

"The gloomy king
Of Tartarus?"

"Thou err'st; that sullen wing,
Erst with Archangels mating in compare,
Oft soars in view, but may not enter there.
Dost then inquire how hides our might from thee?
That insect eye an atom's frame *may* see,
But with an atom is o'erwhelm'd and blind
To each vast outline of the master mind."

"If such thy power, thou doubtless dost fulfil
  Some fitting part. Is that thou term'st thy will
  Free and unfetter'd? or hast thou a lord?"

"All creatures have."

"Save Satan."

"Him the sword
Compels, reluctant; most a slave, when he
Strives 'gainst his yoke and struggles to be free."

"Then are *all* slaves."
"All serve. The mightiest those
Whose motive love; the meanest, who oppose
Almighty will."
"Ibleess* high honour bore
Among the highest."
"*But* he bears no more.
Foremost in zeal, until ambition crept
A serpent to his heart, and seraphs wept
O'er the terrific ruin. Thenceforth hate,
Implacable, immortal, blasts his fate,
Rebellion hopeless, pride still kindling war,
And Terror thundering in her iron car
O'er the yet haughty spirit."
"Be mine still
That haughty heart, that majesty of will;
Th' indomitable spirit, sceptre lone,
Realm, terror to all else, and dire dissocial throne.
All, all but fear—Heaven's mightiest ne'er should dart
One bolt of terror to Erectheus' heart."

---

* Satan.

Pale grew the form before him. The arch'd brow
Lost all its majesty; and drooping low,
As stricken to the death her heart had been,
Sank the full flashing eye beneath its screen
Of night-fring'd snow. Much marvell'd he that one
Of such high presence and commanding tone
Should thus succumb. More marvell'd what might move
A nature thron'd man's sympathies above.
Drooping she sate, her war-steed drooping stood:
Beneath tumultuous rav'd the murky flood;
And Night encas'd her, as some priceless gem,
In triple jet of Death's black diadem.
Thus motionless she sate with drooping brow;
The heavy lid gleam'd ghastly as the snow
Which wintry Death sheds o'er Earth's tenderest flower.
Wonder to fear gave way; Love's mighty power
For one soft moment sapp'd the granite stone
His heart that cas'd, and in the melting tone
Of love he call'd her. Strange to his own ear
His accents sounded; yet seem'd they to cheer
The stricken heart before him. Leaning low
On her small hand the pale, transparent brow,

Whilst with her charger's raven mane were roll'd
The bright rich tresses of immortal gold,
She with one effort shook her spirit free,
Uprais'd the eye and spake; but chang'd the key,
And syllabled with effort each low word,
As infant voices by the dreamer heard
At the dead hour of night.

      " If yet remain,
Mortal, one bond thou dost not all disdain;
If yet my presence thou wouldst not affray;
If to have left my own high realm, to stray
Around thy path, forsaken most and lone,
Give claim to recompence; forswear this tone,
So terror-fraught to mind of higher soar,
Which of Heaven's might may some dim gleams explore."

    •

" And was it terror? Can a thing like thee,
Great mid eternal Essences and free
From mortal taint, thus shudder but to hear
Heaven's might defied?"

      " Else would such greatness bear

Strong challenge. Mightiest lights intensest burn,
And most profound their awe who most discern."

" What then thy grade ?"
      " Exalt beyond compare
O'er embryo Man. Less than the least who dare
Enter the Courts of Heaven."
       " Thine Author ?"
         " One
Is author of *all* being."
     " And thy throne ?"

" In space, among the countless worlds that roll
Spangling the firmament from pole to pole."

" Be there material Worlds beside ?"
       " There be,
Countless as foam-globes of thine insect sea."

" Peopled ? Of whom ?"
      " Some peopled, others still
In embryo chaos. Mortal beings fill

The first, of various order, power, degree,
None all-conforming with humanity."

" And what thy work ? "

" A mystery."

" What thy name ? "

" A mystery."

" And thine origin ? "

" The same."

" Canst thou to mortal eye the power convey
To view thy state, and those who thee obey ? "

" At least, I may the utmost compass fill
Of thy mind's grasp. Mortal, if such thy will,
Give token."

Scarce th' assent was given,
When the black arching rocks shot up, till Heaven
Seem'd spann'd and circumscrib'd within their bound,
And the pale stars a middle region found,
Where the blue ether hung, a crystal sea,
Far, far beneath th' o'er-arching canopy

Of the black cavern'd vault. Waist-girdled stood
By the high Heaven's ethereal azure flood,*
Forms semblant of humanity, but wrought
On scale so far transcending human thought,
That fancy, whelm'd and daunted by th' excess
Of her own vanity and nothingness,
Shrunk back abash'd. The least of that dire band
So vast, it seem'd the hollow of his hand
Might serve for basin to the rolling main;
Seem'd it, the sole of his dire foot might drain
The Ocean's blue abyss. Around their Queen,
All bow'd. On her transcendent brow were seen,
Not jewell'd gauds, but gems that costlier shine,—
The regal signet grav'd of hand divine.
On her, bewilder'd, turn'd Erectheus' eye.
Before him dwelt, in all its majesty,
That form of beauty; but it seem'd no more
As that which relative dimensions bore,
As aught of substance to be grasp'd, defin'd,
Compar'd or weigh'd; an image of the mind,

---

* The atmosphere, which we call heaven, is about forty-five miles in depth, or rather height above us.

Vast or minute as that the mental ray
Illum'd the while.
    Thence chanc'd his eye to stray
Tow'rd a pellucid cloud that, soaring long,
Scarce reach'd the feet of that majestic throng.
From Ætna's crest, or Kawf's drear solitude,
Oft had Erectheus in such mirror view'd
His image swell'd to Titan bulk—and now
But a dim speck discerns. Above his brow
His hand he spread, to shade from his strain'd eye
Th' excess of grandeur; and may thus descry
In that small speck his own most minish'd form
Portray'd exact, but by strong contrast shorn
To atom insignificance.
    He sate,
That haughty soul, awhile annihilate;
The wroth, the terrors of the insect thing
Before him glass'd! O Ridicule! thy sting
To haughty minds more dreadful than the dart
Dipp'd in Lernæan gall to plant the heart
With the dire serpent harvest. Dead he sate,
Sunk his high front, his courage desolate:

That last lone virtue, prostrate and debas'd,
Shatter'd the idol, the sad shrine defac'd.
But that one left not, whom all else had fled,
But that Love's flame above that Altar dead
Still flutter'd fondly and would not depart,
Man's last, dire foe had triumph'd o'er his heart.
But Love, Heaven's finish'd boon—Love, in array
Of female loveliness, was nigh to stay
The utter wreck. In accent soft and low
His name was murmur'd; and a sudden glow
Relum'd th' expiring torch, and, blazing high,
Thrill'd through his heart and lighten'd from his eye.
In the vain insect form before him stood
His mortal coil, his debt to flesh and blood.
In the bright being who invok'd him shone
His spirit's majesty—*her* throne, *his* throne;
Her vassals his; their wondrous power his own.
High o'er the pomp of grandeur round him sprung
His soaring spirit, and imperious flung
Its haughty glances down: and boundless grown
His thirst of power, already deem'd that throne,

So easeful won, too poor a prize to fill
The boundless measure of his lordly will.

Again the Vision spake. "As mortal sight
Hath grasp, I've shown thee of th' excelling might
Of these my vassals;—not, indeed, confin'd
By limits: free, impassive as the mind.
But that with bulk thou still confoundest might;
And mightier far than thou canst judge from sight
Those vassals be. Mortal, no words need tell
What deeds have utter'd, that I love thee well;
Not with the fading, transitory glow
Of mortal heart, but the full, fervid flow
Of my own glorious element. My state
Is less than Heaven design'd thee, ere thy fate
Thy will perverted, and destruction spread
A hell before, around thee. Then I sped
Arm'd with a boon, erst granted me, to bear
A choice, till now ne'er breath'd on mortal ear.
But Time decays. Relentless Fate on high
Whirls the red thong, and round her chariot fly

The yelling Furies. Each her prey demands,
Drops her black gall, and wrings her wither'd hands.
Now, once for ever, be thy choice made known,
Or finite vengeance or a fadeless throne."

"Spirit, thou know'st me not. Erectheus' will
Hope never swerv'd, nor shook the dread of ill.
Once form'd, Caucasian rocks not firmer stand
Against the trembling touch of infant hand.
Read in this blade th' irrevocable pledge
To him who fram'd its all-destroying edge—
Read in its Stygian temper that which arms
My purpose 'gainst e'en might of Heavenly charms.
Erectheus' pledge for good, for ill, once given,
Stands firm, despite the highest bribe of Heaven,
The blackest curse of Hell. Nor think, fair thing,
Thy sphere, how high soe'er, could bound the wing
Of my aspiring, while a higher stood;
My course on high a fiery lava-flood,
Involving all in ruin; chiefly thee,
The sole, blest link existence holds for me."

" Love spurns conditions. Cast but from thy hand
Th' insidious pledge, and at thy side I'll stand
In all thy daring; though thou hurl the brand
Of thy defiance at a mightier far,
And the blue Empyrean feel the jar
Of the dire strife, so but with finite foe."

Grim smil'd Erectheus. " Little dost thou know
Ambition's lore. My foot upon the neck
Of conquer'd monarch, think'st thou aught could
    check
My upward spring? Think'st thou th' angelic host,
Th' embattled Seraphim, should o'er me boast
Their ranks inviolate——"
                              He more had said,
But the bright pageant clos'd in sudden shade;
Vanish'd the splendence, majesty, and might,
And left him, shrunk, as by enchantment's blight,
Into himself. Seem'd as with thund'rous shock
Night's fetters clasp'd him, and the iron rock
Clos'd, crashing round. And o'er the din a cry,
As of some bursting heart's last agony,

Transfix'd his soul. Too well he knew that tone;
In the wide universe, perchance, but one
Had thus half bow'd him to relent.
                              Not long
Entranc'd he sate; for now the warrior throng
Through the black gorge are plunging; and the neigh
Smites him of frantic steeds. Away—away!
Abhorr'd each murmur that reminds his ear
Of Man's existence, or betrays him near,
And to his soul the humbling memory bears
Of *his* sad birthright to Man's grov'ling cares.

He spurr'd his steed, but mid the shadows black
Of that rude cave soon lost the onward track,
Involv'd mid alleys, numberless and blind,
That through the bowels of the mountain wind.
Perplext he turn'd, his steps retracing slow
Mid broken rocks: but paus'd, as burst the glow
Of torch and steel abrupt upon his sight,
Through sudden arch. There rode, in pride of might,
Earth's chosen warriors. In successive throng,
Crowded and countless, swept the files along.

Struggling with densest Night, the flickering glare
Of torch infrequent on the prison'd air
Scatter'd a sickly hue; through which did glide
On leathern wing ill-omen'd birds that hide
Their shrieking forms in Night. But from each
    fold
Of turban white or shawl besprent with gold
Th' uncertain ray an instant's splendour flung,
Flash'd from each blade, and like a halo hung
Round the dim outline of the snorting horse;
And the white foam uprising in their course
Sparkled and gleam'd as glows the troublous line
Where Ocean's restless, Earth's still might combine.

But his strain'd eye, distent o'er Nature's bound,
For those wild forms no mightier semblance found,
Than of the busy motes that countless stream
Thro' cavern'd shade, on some chance sunny gleam.
Was it for such his vengeance had been stor'd?
On such vain atoms must his wroth be pour'd?
And had he scar'd for ever from his sight
That lone lov'd form, to wreak his little spite

On these poor worms? E'en to the inmost soul
Dwindled he felt and blighted. Darkly roll
His troublous thoughts. His downcast glances fell
On the dire blade. The gloomy lord of Hell
Then had he curs'd, defied. A whisper small
Bade him the terms of that dire pledge recall,
By whom invok'd. To sudden madness stung,
He spurr'd his horse and 'mid the concourse sprung
Of the arm'd host. Back fled, in wild affright,
Steed, rider from his path: no fiend of night
Such panic dread had struck. The foremost ranks
Together crowd, until their coursers' flanks
In a dense mass are wedg'd, and breathless shrink
From his dark form as from the chasm's brink;
Nor life resume, till his last plunge is o'er,
And the hoarse torrent lifts its voice once more.

END OF CANTO IX.

Canto X.

THE EVE OF BATTLE.

No gleam to streak the mountain's ragged crest;
The Sun lies buried in the distant west:
The Stars in awe usurp his mighty throne;
Their many sceptres feebly mimic one:
With trembling grasp each wields the golden wand,
And longs to yield it to a sterner hand;
For eyes so pure and hearts so gentle scan
With pitying dread the demon wrath of man.

That basin deep, whose waves have ebb'd away,
And given a lake's dark secrets to the day,
At Dion's feet expands its chasm wide,
And still seems pregnant with the crystal tide;
For fires innumerous yield their vapour white,
And through the vale diffusive stream their light;
Paving with pearly rays the cavern'd gloom,
Thus virtue sheds effulgence from the tomb.
Dark towers the mount above that murk abyss
In splinter'd crag and naked precipice.

Here sate the Prince. His couch the turf supplied,
Refresh'd by well-springs from the mountain side;
His warrior cloak, about him careless cast,
Excludes the mountain's ic'd and searching blast;
His glittering helm with all its plumes of snow,
And rich cuirass the turf around him strow,
And at his side Prometheus' battle-brand,
Ne'er yet profan'd by false or feeble hand.
Around him strown, upon the mountain breast,
His warriors lay in attitude of rest;

Or, group'd in circles, commun'd of the fight,
Which Morn should herald with its earliest light.
Farther than glance mid that deep gloom might go,
Is peopled dense the mountain's rugged brow;
But not a watchfire gives the foe beneath
A warning beacon of impending death.

Dion apart from e'en his chiefs reclin'd;
His country's fate weigh'd heavy on his mind;
His anxious thoughts each varied feature scan,
Each frail point strengthen of his complex plan.
The morrow's dawn shall see triumphant wave
His country's banner, or shall gild her grave.
The morrow's dawn! How brief the hours of night,
And yet he longs, like Watcher, for the light;
Though the short interval of gloom must bear
The eventful fruits of many a labouring year.

Nor blame ye, sternest patriots, if a care,
Softer, but not less pure, found entrance there.
How, in his country's weal, could be forgot
His queen, his Indra, and her doubtful lot?

The Sun his annual course thro' Heaven had burn'd
Since the high mission from afar return'd,
Their purpose baffled. On the mountain rude
The hall, his childhood's home, deserted stood;
The mountain blast rav'd careless thro' that hall,
The moss with gold distain'd its antique wall;
The bower, unprun'd, a deeper shelter gave,
And droop'd luxuriant o'er a recent grave.
No certain tidings could the neighbours show
Or whose that grave, or whose the living woe,
Or whither fled the mourner. But deceas'd,
Or with her gone, the venerable priest.
And some of visions spake, and voices dread
Heard when the storm-cloud wrapp'd the mountain's head,
And deem'd that Heaven's forbearance, weary grown
Of those whose worship differ'd from their own,
Had to the spirits of the Mount and Wild
Consign'd in either case perdition's child.

The watchful sentry's challenge, stern and low,
Breaks on his mood. That footstep he should know.

" What tidings, Theseus ?   Thy young footfall, aye,
Chimes to some anthem-peal of victory,
So oft announc'd of thee ? "

" My Prince, thy sword
Hath taught our lips one solitary word,—
Hath taught our step one measure firm and free,
'Twere marvel chim'd they aught but ' Victory.'
My warriors hold secure the eastern height :
I seek thy final mandate for the night."

" To whom consign'd thy post ? "

" To Sophron."

" Good.
A wary veteran, tho' of bearing rude,
Of halting speech, but ever-ready sword.
Secure thy post.   Recline thee on the sward,
My warrior,—we must watch the ebb and flow
Of war's strong tide ere yet our course we know."

Another challenge.   " Gyges audience craves."

" Welcome, brave Noble."

" Prince, my banner waves
High o'er the southern camp.   With morning light
18—2

The path, tho' steep, will serve, a foe in sight.
I seek thine orders."

    " Sit thee here."

        Appear'd
A herald posting from the western ward.
" What from the valiant Memnon ? "

        " Where the height
Bridges the torrent, bursting in its might
From the deep dell, his mountain legions keep
Good watch; secure each passage o'er the steep,
And on each verge the rocky deluge stor'd,
Its deaths reserving for thy signal word.
Inquires the chief, ' Or doth thy purpose stand,
Or for his guidance hast thou fresh command ? "

" Bear back our answer. Dion much approves
Brave Memnon's ardour for the land he loves.
Bid him his ground maintain 'gainst every foe
Would force an exit from the vale below.
But from without should foes his post assail,
Be't his, by well-feign'd weakness to inveigle

Their onward step, till thro' the gorge below
Press the new myriads on our prison'd foe:
Then let his country's wrongs his bosom warm,
And let her vengeance thunder from his arm.
Enough, good Courier, speed.   Hist, hear ye now
No distant murmur, as when breakers throw
Their wreathen spray on some far distant shore;
Or such as mountain pines at midnight pour
Down the rare gale?   Distinct that growing sound
From those which rising from the gulf profound,
Now startle, as if spoke beside us there
Some unseen spirit of the Flood or Air;
Now, distant floating in mid ether seem
Like phantom whispers of some shapeless dream."

Him answered Gyges: " Mid the mountains wild
Oft is the ear by Echo's spell beguil'd;
For Proteus' power the Nymph commandeth here,
And thousand tones fantastic cheat the ear.
The mountain huge hath voices of its own;
Deep heaves its bosom to the fateful groan,

Presage of coming woe: and accents rude
Oft scare the stillness of the solitude.
For of the spirits doom'd to dwell below,
Each sterner nature haunts the mountain brow;
And the vast caverns in its entrails min'd
Are throng'd with Genii, foes to human kind."

Thus Gyges spake. A silence long ensued,
Pursuing each his fancy's vagrant mood.
At length upon the breeze of night arose
A whisper small: the rock-deer's faint repose
It scarce had shaken; yet the ridgy crest
Of the dark mountain started from its rest
As at the clarion call. That rugged height,
Which gloom'd so peaceful in the hush of night,
Now gleams with starlit arms and plumes that wave
Mid the stern, deep-ton'd murmur of the brave.
Seem'd it enchantment's stroke had plum'd that height
With forest dense and all its deeds of night;
And o'er that forest the night-zephyr stole,
And woke to music deep its slumbering soul.

From crag to crag the low-breath'd murmur ran,
From rock to rock it leapt, from man to man,
Till, syllabled distinct, the busy sound
E'en at the Regent's ear an audience found.
Sinope first, then Indra's name, and then
The spellword " Victory."
      In the hostile glen
The wakeful sentry hears as 'twere the clang
Of demon wings that in mid-ether hang;
And, shuddering, closer draws his mantle round,
As the night-blast were chill'd by that drear sound.

The courier charg'd to scour that ridgy height,
And learn whence rose that murmur of the night,
Return'd at length. From height to height, he said,
From post to post, inquiring still, he'd sped.
Each guardian of the night had heard the sound
Progressing onward from the farthest bound
Of the arm'd ridge, its source to all unknown,
Until the last night-sentry's beat was won.
He, whilst with measur'd pace he wore away
The lingering night, and humm'd his martial lay,

Mark'd a young warrior from his sleep upstart,
Shouting the words deep grav'd on every heart,
" Sinope, Indra, Victory." The cry
Was echo'd by a comrade slumbering nigh,
And pass'd from lip to lip, till all that height
Thrill'd the wild cry, and gleam'd with flashing light
Of warrior steel.
 The portent Dion bless'd,
To his small band at needful hour addrest.
These o'er the heights in groups discursive strown,
Add future fields to fields already won.
So sped the hour; yet clos'd not ere once more
The mountain ridge a stir tumultuous bore,
Through which was heard, in fast-succeeding swell,
The challenge stern of wakeful sentinel,
And then swift hurrying steps. And through the night
A wild form burst upon the Regent's sight,
And panting, gasping as for life, fell low
At Dion's feet, with dust-degraded brow:
And whilst in silence, strangely boding, each
Expectant listed that strange herald's speech,

A vague, but dire presentiment of ill,
Each heart arrested with its sickening chill;
E'en Dion's spirit the contagion own'd.
" Whence, and from whom?" he ask'd. The herald groan'd,
But lifted not his head that glance to meet,
As in faint whisper answering, " From the fleet,
The fight, Sinope."
     Eloquent of woe
Those words, that accent, tremulous and low.
Apart the Regent sign'd him. " Now," he said,
" Detail thy tidings." But excess of dread,
Back'd by hard toil, the power of speech denied
To his parch'd throat. " Bring wine," the Regent cried,
" Recruit thy strength, renew thy heart, then show
What tidings falter in those notes of woe."

The summon'd menials, at the Prince's word,
Before the courier spread a warrior's board,
Alike the Regent's and rude soldier's cheer,
Coarse barley cakes, and flesh of mountain deer;

And, sparkling high as vernal fountains shine,
From golden flagon pour'd rich ruby wine,
Of minstrel lov'd, all potent to inspire
In minstrel heart the rapt heroic fire.
Untasted on the board the viands stand,
But grasps that goblet rich the herald's hand,
And clings his lip, like lover's, to the brim,
Where flashing fast the purple fire-gleams swim;
Then op'd his languid eye, his pallid cheek
Caught from the cup its rich empurpling streak,
The drooping form uprose in wonted pride:
" Now to thy tale of woe," the Regent cried.

" Our fleet at anchor off Amisus lay,
Rome's vast flotilla throng'd Sinope's bay.
The noble Chiron burn'd to tempt the fight;
But Tywold's galley lack'd that arm of might;
And Proceus, Mimas, Brastus, absent yet,
Strange hints of treachery circled through the
    fleet.
Distrust prevail'd, by counter rumours stay'd,
That Tywold brought strong succours to our aid.

Then sprang with morn the long-expected breeze,
Vulturnus,* ruffler of the curling seas.
With anchors weigh'd their oars our galleys ply,
Trim their white sails, and spread them to the sky;
Like dolphins, sporting mid the foam, they sweep,
Ploughing long furrows o'er the billowy deep.

"Rome's vast armada, anchor'd in the bay,
At mercy, long, of our light squadron lay.
Full on those towering castles of the wave
Their iron beaks the swift-wing'd galleys drave,
The grapnels cast, and whilst a steely shower
Darkens the sky, as when black tempests lour,
The crews intrepid scale each galley's side,
And o'er the bulwarks pour their battle tide;
Shouting their Indra's, their Prometheus' name,
Mid volleying blows and jets of rising flame;
And hurling fiercely from the shatter'd deck
Each foe, yet rampant o'er the blazing wreck.

---

* The North-west wind.

"Meanwhile the Roman fleet intact that lay
  Their cables slipp'd, and, rowing, clear'd the bay.
  Reform'd their broken line and backward bore,
  Sails fill'd, mail'd warriors manning each high prore.
  The oars in triple tiers their labours ply,
  The warriors shout, the strong-wing'd galleys fly.
  Cleft by the keel the writhing billows lie,
  Hissing like hydras in their agony.
  What may sustain the first terrific shock
  Of that dread phalanx? What its fury mock,
  So dense, so swift? Our light-arm'd galleys know,
  And turn intrepid to oppose the foe;
  So springs the leopard from his bowery haunt
  Full on the dire, gigantic elephant.

"I saw the coming foe. In shallop light
  I stood, with minstrel lay to cheer the fight.
  High tower'd their vasty prows. Each ample sail
  A cloud impregnate with destruction's gale:
  Shield link'd to shield, and crest surmounting crest,
  A dragon each, whom brazen scales invest.

The sun shone brightly o'er the rich display,
In golden blaze return'd his golden ray;
A golden blaze, through which in shimmering glance
Play'd keener fires from sabre, glaive, and lance.
The azure wave, first trampled into snow,
Grew black in shadow of each gloomy prow;
Then caught from arms and armour rang'd on high
The sunset glories of th' autumnal sky.

" Then met with crash that Heaven's blue concave rent
In mid career each hostile armament.
Those iron beaks, like vulture's rending, go
Deep to the bowels of each groaning foe.
The engines, giant-like, heave up on high
Huge rocks, and send the tempest through the sky.
The mail-arm'd warrior crushing where they light
Like insects stricken by the hailstorm's might;
And javelins rain a glittering, deadly shower,
And blazing torches their red mischief pour;
And where the boarders scale the galley side,
A blood-red torrent meets the ocean's tide.

Naught could the Roman galleys' shock sustain,
Our barks fell piecemeal, scatter'd o'er the main
Before their ponderous beaks. One crash, no more,
One yell of wild despair, and all is o'er.
Red roll the billows litter'd with the wreck,
And drowning forms, late guardians of the deck.

"Oh! brightly shone our warriors in that fight,
Skill, valour, struggling 'gainst o'erwhelming might.
Our light-wing'd barks evade the hostile prow,
And, tacking, midships strike th' unwieldy foe,
Assail him still with iterated shock,
But waste like waves their fury on a rock.
Borne down, o'erpower'd, their wrecks the billows strew;
The deep, remorseless, whelms each hapless crew.
I left them not, till hope had left the fight,
And our small remnant spread the sail in flight,
What time, downbearing mid the North Sea's foam,
White sails bore succour to the fleet of Rome;
Then hither hasted, night and day, to bear
These tidings dismal to my Prince's ear."

" And Chiron ? " said the Prince, " he should not be
Of those who live their country's shame to see ;
Chiron knew not the road to shameful flight."

" Nor knows it yet : he perish'd in the fight ;
Long strove to rally each retreating prow,
But, failing, steer'd his galley on the foe.
He doubtless perish'd. But the west wind's might
Uprose and bore my shallop from the fight."

" Bard of ignoble strain," the Prince replied,
" Liv'st thou to say, ' We fled, our hero died,
Our country wept ? ' What, could'st thou find no
    brand
In her dread cause to arm thy woman hand ?
Or, lost that cause, was there no hostile dart
To pierce and consecrate a patriot's heart ? "

Abash'd the minstrel shrunk. The Prince alone
Explores his thoughts and lists his heart's deep moan.
" Alas ! his noble country ! Was it so ?
Had war's first billow laid her promise low ?

How had she trod but now the curling sea,
How fair a thing, how sacred seem'd to be!
Old Ocean crouch'd, her fairy step to kiss,
And round her roar'd, intoxicate with bliss;
Or hush'd his waves, his tumult still'd, and press'd
Her beauteous image closer to his breast.
It seem'd as Heaven must note her wealth of charms,
And fence that marvel with celestial arms.

"O Heaven!" he cried, "let each his several share
Of retribution singly, separate bear,
But spare my country. Not on her impose
Our crimes, our follies, our deservèd woes.
O God of Battles! bar not in our path
The barrier hopeless of almighty wrath.
Give us privation, torture, woe to bear,
But leave us hearts to suffer and to dare.
And leave, blest Liberty, as ever, still
The guerdon sacred of th' all-daring will."

He said, and walk'd forth in his virtue's might,
Proof-arm'd by faith in Heaven to guard the right.

He met his chieftains with enkindled eye;
They read some great event. How might they spy
In that full tide of fire their glances meet
That stern resolve—disaster, and defeat?

The distant sound which scarce had scal'd that height
Now grew, and fill'd the boundless void of night:—
As when some river, flooded deep, yet pent
By mountain walls and winter's strong cement,
Its barrier sapp'd in deluge, thunders free,
And hurls th' uprooted valley to the sea,—
So that hoarse tumult. But a tide more dread
Dion in those continuous murmurs read:
Thy living waves, Arabia, Persia hurl'd
Swoln, with destruction, on a hapless world.

" Haste ye, my warriors, to your posts," he cried:
" Restrain awhile your followers' warlike pride;

But when above this mountain ridge ye see
Prometheus' banner floating far and free,
Then from your eyrie to the vale beneath
Rush like strong eagles to the feast of death.
All there be foes. But ye shall none assail,
Save him whose fortune threatens to prevail.
Example terrible our need demands—
Th' annihilation of these locust bands.
Not victory's self your country long can save ;
We, or our foes, must fill destruction's grave.
Prevails the Arab ? Rend his robber ranks.
The Scythian ? Thunder on the spoilers' flanks.
Spare not, till, minish'd, shatter'd, powerless, both,
With grounded arms they deprecate your wroth.
Think on your country's need, be keen, be true ;
Think, above all, on her deep faith in you."

Each kiss'd the hilt of his blue starlit brand
In deep devotion to his Chief's command :
Then sought his post. And Dion treads alone
The guarded circle of his mountain throne.

But swift events resistless thronging there
Divert the inroads of remorseless care.

Straight to his army of reserve beyond
The classic strand of wave-lash'd Trebizond,
Swift heralds speed, with mandate to prevent
Throughout that coast their Roman foe's descent;
With powers and clear instructions to complete
And send swift succours to the shatter'd fleet.
This done, dismiss'd the subject from his mind,
His undistracted powers he bent, to find
In present victory the means to meet
Each baneful consequence of late defeat.

He walk'd along the arm'd and ridgy height,
At times dim measuring the waste void of night.
'Gainst the starr'd sky the sentry's form arose:
All else was wrapt in torpor of repose.
"Children," cried Dion, "of a bleeding land,
Blest Freedom's small but consecrated band,

Sleep on secure; snatch, whiles ye may, the rest
Not always granted to the guileless breast.
Sleep in your innocence, your courage, sleep;
Heaven's host above, around you vigils keep.
Your Prince high honour deems it to partake
Their cares, to watch, to suffer for your sake.
On some, perchance, the morrow's eve shall close,
Lock'd in a sterner, less disturb'd repose.
Ye shall escape, at least, *one* harrowing woe—
Your country's loss, the triumph of your foe.
And for the remnant who survive th' affray,
To bless the Giver of another day,
With Heaven to aid, we'll choke the rising sigh
In thankful songs and shouts of victory."

Those sounds, portentous of approaching ill,
Now sudden ceas'd upon the midnight hill.
A pause, long, anxious, more appalling far
Than e'en that human deluge' distant jar,
Ensued. But Dion scarce resum'd his post,
When shouts of skirmish high to heaven were
    toss'd;

The distant clash of steel, the rallying cry,
The yells of warriors in death's agony,
Transfix'd or headlong hurrying to th' abyss.
O Night! dread mother of repose and bliss,
Sweet nurse of fairy dreams, must thou, too, know
Throughout thy solemn halls man's murder-yell of woe?

END OF CANTO X.

Canto XI.

THE SUCCOUR.

Part I.

Light o'er the Euxine's curling waves of blue,
With roebuck speed, the sportive galley flew
Straight to the beach, where billows love to play,
And cliffs Caucasian beetle o'er the spray.
Behind her track for many a rood they spring,
Dark-bosom'd wanderers of the snow-white wing:
Scatter'd they seem as by the tempest's might,
Rent the proud mast, and bulwark's shadowy height:
The very sail may scarce the blast delay,
That, whistling shrill, impatient glides away.

Yet joy seems common to the stately throng;
Burst from each hull wild peals of martial song,
And plashing waves and rustling winds unite
That choir to swell, with harmonizing might.
Still as in turn they near the billowy shore,
Loos'd each white sail to float above the prore;
Then furl'd and folded as the falcon's wing,
They stately glide, and fast in moorings swing;
Then yields the song to many a rough sea cry,
And echo gives to boisterous oaths reply;
As from each wave-rock'd galley pours the tide
Of life, dark streaming from her furrow'd side.
And now with stroke and flash of feather'd oar,
Shoot the trim shallops gaily to the shore.

High on that cliff the ancient Seer reclin'd,
His thin grey locks were scatter'd to the wind;
His eye far turn'd upon the rolling main.
Yet though his ear may catch the wild waves' plain,
No vision there may bless his eyesight dim,
No dancing wave is plum'd with light for him.

The waves roll on, the stately galleys glide,
But wave nor galliot streaks his visual tide.
There all is starless night, an ocean dread,
Sunless and breezeless, motionless and dead.

His grey dog still beside the Prophet lay,
Friend of his night, as follower of his day.
His own dim eyes now serve his master's need:
A light in darkness is a light indeed!

Foremost two warriors land. Their bearing high,
The stately march, calm brow, and flashing eye,
Token alike command: but differing wide
In form and mien. This strode in giant pride
The trembling Earth, like him whose arm of yore
Purg'd of each monstrous pest th' Argolic shore;
And that, for stature less observ'd than grace,
Whose slight frame well beseem'd his angel face;
Whose might not corporal, but the power confest
Of his high presence in each throbbing breast.

Such form thy maids, Athena, thrill'd to see,
When Phidias' touch th' imprison'd God set free.

Prompt at his voice the Prophet's brow was rais'd,
Intent that dim eye on the speaker gaz'd;
And tho' no traits his glance might there descry,
Joy lit his features as he made reply.
" Com'st thou, my son, with laurel-wreathen brow,
From that bold course, so seeming fraught with woe?
Oft would I weep that young, fair head laid low,
But not one tear from these dim eyes would flow.
Now thrills thy voice, like some long-buried strain
Lov'd of my youth, and calls that youth again.
And with my youth its promise fresh and bright
Of bliss unfolding to my country's sight.
What is thy spell, young chief, that each least tone
Of thine wields power long deem'd my country's own?
That speaking thou, my country's voice I hear?
That answering, starts the long-forgotten tear?
That eyes so dark have learned again to see
The vision'd past remould itself in thee?"

" Old Seer, forbear. The present need demands
Prompt, forward steps, steel'd hearts and ready
    hands.
Speak brief thy tidings. Life, death, hope require
Brief, ready accents, and a tongue of fire."

" No tidings late have claim'd mine anxious ear,
No herald's, wanderer's step hath reach'd me here:
But visions fearful of the heady fight
Have chain'd my senses, since the dawning light.
I saw our host embattled, few, but bold,
The heights which wall some sunless valley hold;
I saw the Scythian host beneath them strew'd
Countless as foam-globes of the ocean's flood.
I mark'd, that streaming thro' the tunnell'd side
Of that huge wall the Arab squadrons ride.
How then the demon of confusion rose
And mix'd in deadly strife our adverse foes.
From earliest dawn hath rag'd the bloody fight;
But now 'twas raging with unminish'd might.
Thrice had the Scythian, thrice the Arab host
In turn the battle won, the battle lost.

Still, as to either side the scale inclin'd,
Prometheus' standard floated on the wind:
And as it rose, the mountain's rocky side
Pour'd on the conqueror's flank its living tide.
And, equal, once again, the scales of fight,
Sinks that dread standard on the mountain height;
And, summon'd from their work of death, retires
The patriot band, as that dread sign expires.
But, as eve's shadows vest the mountain height,
Each foe withdraws his torn and shatter'd might;
Like cloudy hosts, when some strong wind divides
And piles their ridgy ranks on adverse sides.
Who lingers last? The grim Erectheus there
I mark, like panther in his corse-strown lair,
In carnage riot high: his vengeful mood
Unstill'd, unsated by that feast of blood:
His mighty arm untir'd: terrific, grim,
E'en in retreat war lends her gloom to him.
His armour black with gory stains imbued;
His sable steed bath'd saddle-deep in blood;
His sable plume unras'd of hostile brand;
The sword of ruin blazing in his hand;

As some black eagle from the carnage flies,
His strong wing dew'd with gore of sacrifice."

"Enough, enough. Brave Tywold, give command
Our crews to muster on the surf-sown strand.
Urgent the haste. The fateful spot I know,
Where Dion purpos'd to entoil the foe,
From hence not seven hours' march. The dawning light
Our band must usher to the field of fight."

Low Tywold bow'd, and, turning to depart,
That warrior stern held parley with his heart.
"Where Tywold's vaunted pride? Subdued to fill
A vassal's part, subserve a stripling's will?
For high command he deem'd his spirit fram'd;
An infant's voice the braggart mood hath tam'd;
Still deem'd a captain 'mong the free and brave,
A leader counted, but in truth a slave.
Yet stranger still, that in the shock of fight
All yield subservient to a stripling's might.

War's iron front, her practis'd skill and guile
Borne down, o'ermaster'd by a stripling's smile."

"My prince," the old man said, "I'll lead thee where
Thy steed for thee impatient snuffs the air.
Proud will he be thy noble weight to know,
Will bear thee fleetly on the robber foe."

He said, and tow'rd the cavern'd mountain strode,
Where Art or Chance had delv'd his rude abode.
Thence by an outlet, through the hard rock min'd,
Led his young guest a tortuous path and blind;
That, merging sudden into open day,
Startled young Calthas with its bright display:
A grassy valley open'd on the eye,
Wall'd in by cliffs whose summits kiss the sky;
Feather'd with tree and shrub of each soft hue,
May strike rich contrast with that heaven of blue.
Four streamlets gushing from the rocks around,
Thro' the green vale their coils of silver wound;
Meeting to bask in lakelet still and deep,
Where aspens quake and drooping willows weep;

And near whose marge with spire fantastic crown'd
A granite rock in lonely grandeur frown'd :
Like some vast minster, work of Titans grey—
Fane of old gods, whose rights have pass'd away.

The old man led to where that huge rock's side
Was upward cleft in tunnel high and wide ;
And, as by portal entering, onward strode
Halls, where with Twilight Silence held abode ;
Who, sudden scar'd by Echo from her reign,
Flew restless round, then settled grim again.
Thus wandering on, a chamber vast they won,
Where lights flash'd radiant as from noon-day sun—
Where gems of all rare form and all rich hue
Pendent in crystals stalactitic grew,
That dome immeasur'd clustering rich with dyes,
By Fancy imag'd but in Paradise.

Full in the central space where swarming shone
The hues that glorious vault shower'd richly down,
A war-horse, harness'd, stood. No form was there
With him the silence of that vault to share ;

Yet, all caparison'd for speed or flight,
He stood, his harness glistering with the light
Of matchless gems, that blaz'd and flash'd confest,
At each least movement of his noble crest.
He joyful neigh'd, as Calthas' step drew nigh—
Toss'd his proud head; fire flash'd from his dark eye.
So light of form, so faultless fram'd was he,
Young Calthas deem'd in that rare steed to see
No mortal thing, but spirit, dwelling lone,
In the bright bow of hues that round him shower'd and shone.

Exclaim'd the Seer: "He honours thee alone,
Last of his race, erst* sacred to the Sun.
A thousand years from mortal burden free,
His stainless race in vain have waited thee.
Fleet is his hoof, unmatch'd his bounding might,
He'll bear thee proudly to the chase or fight."

---

* " Τὰς ἐν Πιερίῃ θρέψ ἀργυρότοξος 'Απόλλων."—*Ilias*, B.

The good steed knelt young Calthas' weight to bear,
Then joyful rose, and, bounding, trod the air;
But at his rider's word his fires subdued,
And meek as lamb the prophet's step pursued.
He led thro' tunnell'd hill beyond the bound
Of that fair vale with mountains wall'd around.
Here spread the plain its velvet soft and green;
A temple here with twilight aisles is seen,
Whose arches gray, o'erlaid with lichen's gold,
Droop'd down th' ivy's mantling banner fold.

Rang'd on the sward in attitude of rest,
As waiting mandate to some high behest,
A lusty band of warriors strew the mead;
Each holds by slacken'd rein a harness'd steed.
At once they rise; their clanging armour sounds,
As each to saddle-seat impatient bounds:
Swift form'd in line, a gallant ridge appears
Of broad keen scimitars and taper spears.
Sable their steeds, the warriors' horse-hair crest,
Their harness black, and black the mail-lin'd vest;

Of burnish'd steel the massive helm alone,
And lance and blade in glancing sunbeams shone.
Silent and motionless the banner'd line,
Life spake not there in gesture, voice, or sign,
Till Calthas nearer drew: then, at a word
Falls the gay pennon'd lance and broad bright sword;
And each keen eye in reverence beams on him,
And trump and bugle peal the martial hymn;
And war-steeds champ the bit and scarce command
Their fires obedient to the curbing hand.

The old man sigh'd: "My son, behold thy guard,
Long for thy presence hold they watch and ward.
The hour ordain'd is come, full come, but we
Had fondly hop'd far other form to see.
But life and death, our country's need demand,
And Fate to thee assigns this chosen Band."

THE SUCCOUR.

PART II.

MEANWHILE, within the fatal valley's bound
The Arab host and Scythian strew'd the ground:
Some in the sleep exhausted nature gave,
And some in trance, whose cradle were the grave.
And many still whose tortuous wounds bequeath
Nor slumber's balm, nor opiate strong of death.
O'er each and all Night pour'd her haunted shade,
And hid the wreck Man's hateful lusts had made.

To council call'd by Ukhbur's summons brief,
Flock'd to their leader's flag each Arab chief.
Worn, shatter'd relics of a gallant Band,
In groups dejected round the Sheikh they stand.

No counsel they to his stern need afford:
Spent their whole aid, and foil'd that aid—the sword.
E'en Ukhbur's mind no last resource may know,
How force that pass, how triumph o'er a foe,
Whom the rude rocks bring forth his might to mar,
E'en when down beaten, yields the adverse war.
And whence those countless Horse? The mountain rude
Ne'er rear'd that dense, o'erwhelming multitude.
Had Jooj, Majooj,* outburst from prison den (18)
For their last triumph o'er the sons of Men?
Or Deev Sofaid, by Roostum quell'd in vain,
Brought his dire brood to waste Mankind again?

One crest, that sable plume of Death alone,
Had through the conflict held unwavering on:
One face had never swerv'd. In anxious mood
He sought Erectheus; and Erectheus stood
Sudden before him. Started, in despite
Of pride, the veteran from that brow of night:

---

* Gog and Magog.

For not as mortal tower'd, like mortal stood,
Mid forms of mightiest mould, the Man of Blood.

" Welcome, dread Prince! Thine arm hath sway'd the fight.
Let now thy wisdom prove our beacon-light.
Pent in this den, where famine holds domain,
Our swords alone may burst th' enthralling chain:
But thou hast mark'd, when fresh of heart and might,
The faithful host maintain'd unflinching fight;
How, when before our charge the foe went down,
And triumph would our righteous labour crown,
Earth's teeming womb a new-born host outpour'd,
And rag'd on flank and rear th' avenging sword.
Now, worn with toil, dishearten'd, wounded, slow,
What chance of triumph o'er this monstrous foe?
Yet morn must hear our shouts of victory rise,
Or garish gild our blood-stain'd obsequies."

" Fate cherish'd of thy creed! The Houri's charms
Boast ye not his rich meed who falls in arms?
Then welcome Night's brief reign; more welcome far
The fateful morrow and its doom of War."

"True; for the Soldier 'tis enough to know
Fate's mandate grav'd in mystery o'er his brow.
Higher the Captain's aims, and prouder be,
T' interpret each dark scroll in victory.
Thou know'st our need, our doubt: in brief, declare
Canst aid our counsels, our wide wreck repair?"

"Alike to me," Erectheus stern replied,
"All chances show. Death rolls o'er each his tide.
But to my aid and care ye've title good,
And something owe I for this feast of blood.
Of all the perils which beset you round,
The worst is doubt. Be some staunch warrior found
T' explore the hostile camp, their purpose know,
Whence those vast hordes, and why become our foe.
I mark'd, that on *their* flank, as on our own
When fortune smil'd, that hornet brood came down.
Their sport, perchance, by turns, for them we drain
The o'erwrought spirit and exhausted vein."

" Keen are thy words as thy good battle brand.
Which of you, Chiefs, would this emprise demand?
Can mouth the jargon of this barbarous horde?"

None answer'd. Fear o'erhung, like keen-edg'd sword,
Each awestruck turban'd head.
      Erectheus cried,
" Mine be the task, by danger dignified."
Then from his brow the crested helm remov'd,
Whose nodding plumes the Fiend of Darkness lov'd:
Donn'd a close Scythian cap, and, fold on fold,
Round his swart arms his cloak disguising roll'd;
Then strode into the gloom, and straight is gone.
Silence his egress mark'd; and each grim son
Of battle, vers'd in war's stern, deathful art,
Drew freer breath, and own'd a lighten'd heart.

Through the deep shadows of the night, amid
Vast hecatombs of carnage, partly hid
In that black gloom, and part reveal'd to sight,
As torch or watch-fire flash'd its feeble light,

O'er turf grown fat with gore, Erectheus sped,
Through ranks commixt, the dying and the dead.
The few words caught of that barbaric host
Bore sound familiar, for the Euxine's coast
In youth he'd wander'd o'er; in tent of felt,
With the poor fisher of Mœotis dwelt;
Back'd the wild steed that wanders unconfin'd,
And chas'd the thistle with the desert wind. (19)

'Twas hard, o'er plain thick strewn with wrecks of fight,
Where yet the war-steed urg'd his frantic flight
With shrilly neigh, where gloom confusion cross'd,
To pierce the precincts of that barbarous host.
Yet fires, half swath'd in smoke, flash frequent there,
And dark forms flitting intercept their glare;
And nearer still the hum confus'd is known
Of voices broken by the frequent moan;
Increasing ever, till the spot be found,
And paus'd to gaze with searching eye around.

Stern was that gaze, and stern and strange the sight,
From thence to where the mountain roots unite

With the deep vale. Outspread before him lay,
Of lurid smoke and watch-fire's blood-red ray,
A firmament inverted. Such may know
The realms unblest of everlasting woe.
At random strewn those fires, as space allow'd,
'Twixt carnage heaps and pools of purple blood.
And round them flitting, scarce in human guise,
The shapes uncouth distemper'd sleep supplies.
The hide of steed for mantle round them spread, (20)
The gray wolf's spoil as bonnet for the head,
Begash'd with frequent wound and grim'd with gore:
Thus satyrs foul appear, their drunken orgies o'er.

Here, o'er the carcase of a steed, that ne'er
To war or chase the desert child shall bear,
A dark form leans, and carves with glittering steel,
From the yet quivering haunch his reeking meal.
Here, basking in the watch-fire's ruddy ray,
Gorging, supine, a group of warriors lay,
And tore with gleaming fangs and reeking jaw
From blood-red steak the morsel rank and raw.

Broach'd on the shaft, ordain'd to deadly strife,
These broil the flesh must feed their lamp of life.
While some, more human, grateful aid repay,
Tend the good steed, his fiery thirst allay.
He, tether'd to the corse of friend or foe,
Repays the care with murmur'd neigh and low.
The shatter'd lance, the dazzled pennon's fold,
The tatter'd vest and turban sprent with gold,
Feed the red flame. E'en avarice' voice is vain,
Sole hope th' escape from that ensanguin'd plain.

Confusion all. Nor front, nor flank is here:
One tangled mass the quick and dead appear.
Where rests their Khaun no clue remains to show,
None heeds, none questions in that general woe.
Erectheus gaz'd. Unsated yet thine eye,
Proud chief? Thine ear appeas'd not with the cry,
Which from those writhing, tortur'd heaps doth rise,
Blaspheming Heaven with Hell's curs'd sacrifice?
Oh! not remorse that quivering lip can shake,
No pitying ray that stern brow's ice may break.

But shame at triumph for high Powers unmeet,
Lament o'er vengeance still so incomplete.

With step aye stumbling o'er the corse-strown plain,
Long had Erectheus sought the Khaun in vain.
At length an undule of the vale he near'd,
Whose summit dark with shadowy forms appear'd:
In crescent rank dispos'd, a silent band,
With eyes downcast and folden hands they stand—
Like granite statues group'd round Memnon's shrine,
Outliving those who fram'd and him they deem'd divine.

Reclin'd the centre of that silent ring
Sat Baidoo Khaun,* wide Scythia's desert king.
Cloaks rudely pil'd upbuilt his regal seat,
And the long spear stood planted at his feet,
Drooping with oxtails from Tibetan mountains, (21)
Whence Indus pours o'er Earth his icy fountains.
His strong, tough bow of horn beside him lay; (22)
His quiver, stor'd with arrows of Kathay;

---

* This name is not historical.

Few arms could teach that stubborn bow to yield,
Few cope with Baidoo Khaun in battle-field.
His war axe, rich inlaid, and battle brand,
And bossy shield lay strewn on either hand.
Bundles of Scythian shafts and spears supply
The flames that, fountain-like, gush'd up on high,
Gleam on the arms, subside in purpling fire
Mid the rich folds that form his wild attire,
And from Night's void the massive features bring,
And vasty outline of the Desert King.
Behind, his favourite steed, a dappl'd gray,
With drooping crest enjoy'd the genial ray,
Stretch'd o'er his head to take the proffer'd food,
The lov'd caress with whinnying murmur woo'd.

On the Khaun's cheek the watch-fire's ruddy light
Show'd traits accordant with a frame of might.
Erectheus read at one keen glance the mind
More form'd to rule than triumph o'er his kind;
Virtue and wisdom for the father's part,
A generous spirit and a dauntless heart;

But not keen instinct's levin-bolt of light,
Subduing all things by its master might.
O'er his broad brow and features' swarthy hue
Its shadow black a sable bonnet threw.
A single jewel there of price untold,
The Jigha* blaz'd, like beacon o'er the wold: (23)
Sole badge of sovereignty those shepherds know.
A chain of gold constrain'd the heavy flow
Of the rich sable cloak that swath'd him round,
Where, gleaming bright, a jewell'd glaive was bound.

Of one, attendant there, he made demand,—
" Hast summ'd the Leader of the Oozbeg band?"

" I have, O Khaun! The chieftain nought replies:
Seal'd are his lips and darkness shrouds his eyes."

" And him who rules Tanaïs' mighty horde?"

" He laid upon his eyes thy sovereign word;
But, faint from loss of blood the warrior lay,
And wide dissever'd from his own array."

---

* Jigha, a jewel representing a nodding cypress: the common pattern of shawls.

"A generous spirit in a frame of might:
  We mark'd his prowess in the lists of fight.
  What answer gives the Yem's uncultur'd lord?" (24)

"He roams, unheeding e'en his Khaun's dread word,
  On that sad shore where silence holds her reign,
  And thin ghosts flit and mandates all are vain.

"A boisterous heart, but brave. The black Kulpauk, (25)
  Hath he obey'd our hest?"
                           "Thy strong-wing'd hawk
  Another lure hath train'd. I saw him lie,
  Chain'd his strong wing; Death's hood o'er his proud
    eye."

"Peace to his rest. No mightier ever drew
  The blade of valour with a hand more true.
  My Kara Ogloo, I behold not him?"

"He stands before the presence," said a dim,
  Scarce earthly voice. "How tend my Lord's commands?"

"Bear swift our mandate to the scatter'd bands.
  But hold. Art equal to the task?"

"My Lord,
Strong is thy servant's heart."
"From horde to horde
Bear this our signet ring. Ere morning light,
Let each elect a leader for the fight:
Be 't his, the scatter'd ranks to form, combine,
That morning dawn not on a frontless line.
Thou and thy faithful horde the night-watch take,
And be thou wary, for thy monarch's sake."

He turn'd to go; but, staggering, fell to earth.
To stay his steps a friendly form rush'd forth.
Too late, alas! His dark, rude garment hides
Full twenty wounds, whence gush the vital tides.
Khaun of the Valiant, seek thou other hand
To bear the signet to thy scatter'd band.

Tears dimm'd the monarch's eye. "The lion-hearted,
The faithful, generous, wise—are all departed?
Too long in world so false Attaisir's son
Thy sojourn proves. Thy golden sands are run.

Thy subjects wait thee in the Kārā Koom,*
Whose sands are silence, whose black tent the tomb.
But who art thou?" he cried, encountering there
Of dire Erectheus' eye th' appalling glare.
" Speak! who?"
      Replied the chief: " E'en whom to know
Hath cost thy shatter'd ranks no measur'd woe;—
Who owes thee some amends."
        The Monarch's hand
Instinctive wander'd to his battle brand;
For stern defiance breath'd in every tone,
And the proud eye with vengeful lightnings shone.
Prompt spring the guards, around th' intruder close
In ring of levell'd spears and bended bows;
But awe restrain'd each arm uprais'd to smite,
Till the Khaun's mandate rose upon the night.

" Ho! harm him not! The fearless here be free,
 We love th' unflinching tongue, the never-trembling knee.

---

* Black Desert: literally, Black Sand. The tract between the Oxus and Caspian is so called.

Speak thy petition, Stranger, brief as bold:
Hard though it prove, 'tis half allow'd ere told."

" He fronts thee, Khaun, whom mortal never knew
For mortal boon to mortal power to sue.
We come to mark how bears the Desert lord
Reverse and ruin from the Moslem sword.
We come his views, his motives to demand;
What seek his armies in our trampled land?"

" He will not lack, the countless nations' lord.
But this rude speech! The harsh discourteous word
To him, whose nod the trembling nations own?"

" Peace, Monarch. One who values not thy frown
Confronts thee. One whose utter'd word could sever
Thee, and the homage of thy hordes, for ever."

" Hah! dost thou threaten?"

" Threats and boasts beseem
Boys', women's prattle; not the tongues of men.

Thy fate I show thee. If the Arab host
Thou'rt come to check, already art thou lost.
If some strange error blind thee, hope may grow
By timely counsel from thy present woe."

"There's promise in thy speech, how rude soe'er:
'Tis bold and suits *his* need, who all must dare.
Hither we march'd our vassal's pride to quell,
And leave waste sites for cities that rebel. (26)
We deem'd to meet a half-arm'd peasant crew,
Without or funds or science, faint and few:
Sudden, her womb relax'd the labouring Earth,
And horsemen gave by myriads at a birth.
No mountain squadrons these. The whole might show
As vision wild. But all too real the woe."

Erectheus mus'd: "Who lur'd thy horsemen, then,
Mid yon waste mountains to this deadly den?"

"The foe before us to the mountain fled.
Our onward path o'er Kawf's rude barrier led;

Our guides the mountain race. Long stray'd we
    here
In chase of foes still seen, but never near:
Deterr'd from scaling passes, where 'twas said
Hoar Winter still his snowy mantle spread.
Then forage fail'd. Our guide this vale made known
In pasture rich. We enter'd, were undone."

" Khaun, thou art grossly snar'd. The mountain snows
    Long since have fail'd. Mere pretext this of foes
To hold thee here, mid barren rocks and rude,
Till Famine thin thy countless multitude.
Those defiles past, spreads many a swelling plain,
Where horse may act, nor pasture seek in vain.
Here Famine reigns. The mountains space deny
To squadrons charging, as to hosts that fly.
And this dire den, a very pitfall set,
By skill superior for thy simple feet:
So guarded now by mountain spear and bow,
No rock, no shrub but screens a living foe.
One outlet rests. Thy path to life lies there:
'Tis guarded fast, must yield to thy despair."

" We will not stint.   But 'twixt us and the pass
   Our late opponents leaguer, mass on mass.
   Worn, minish'd now, what hope to rout a band,
   Who in our might defied us hand to hand?
   Break we their ranks—"
                    " *That* never shalt thou boast:
   If they resist thee, thou and thine are lost.
   But thou nor sought our enmity, nor we
   In this emprise deem'd aught of thine or thee.
   Common our foe, our peril: mutual aid
   Should crush, who both has equally betray'd.
   A master Spirit wields us at his lust,
   And, one with other, grinds our strength to dust.
   This must not be.   Dismount one horde t' assail
   The North, while we the Southern rampart scale:
   Ere morrow's dawn those ramparts must be won:
   Then westward bending, link our bands in one
   O'er the dark outline of this deathful den;
   That master'd, all is ours, and we are men.
   Our present need this mutual aid demands.
   That past, thy claim to empire o'er these lands
   Ourselves will answer."

"Soldierly and strong
Thy counsel sounds; tho' mystery shrouds thy tongue.
Who art thou, stranger? that we may, when free,
With rank and wealth make known our debt to
  thee."

"Hereafter mayst thou learn. For, fail we not
Our hosts to rescue from this fatal spot,
A soldier's boon we will of thee demand—
On thy good steed to meet us, hand to hand."

"We never shunn'd the warrior's greeting rude.
Since peace thou wilt not, take our gage of blood."

The monarch from his girdle drew and gave,
Sheath'd in pure gold, his jewel-hilted glaive.
Erectheus proffer'd in return a brand
Of huntsmen worn, choice work of Syrian hand.
Its surface clear as mirror'd lake, betraying
Beneath ten thousand veins of azure straying;
The hilt a mass of gems, so rich and bright,
The eye shrunk dazzled from their keen-ray'd light.

The monarch marvell'd at that kingly prize,
Perus'd the blue steel with admiring eyes,
Then tow'rd the donor turn'd in curious mood:
But there no longer stern Erectheus stood.

Long toil'd Erectheus o'er that fatal plain,
Ere reach'd the spot where Ukhbur held domain.
Brief he detail'd his tidings. Brief and stern
Replied the Arab: " Rather will we learn
Our necks to slavery's galling yoke to bow
Than league God's chosen host with Kawfur foe."

Grim smil'd Erectheus. " Righteous is the Host,
Who o'er their sires superior unction boast;
Kawfurs those sires. Fling back the life they gave,
Brook not their contact in the very grave.
Oh! shame to manhood. Those contend for fame,
For rank, lands, booty, vengeance, lust, or shame—
Whate'er their thirst, 'tis honestly avow'd;
Ye back your hellish lusts with name of God.
But choose your part. It recks not aught to me
If here your hosts ye sacrifice or free.

Alike the banquet of the wolf is spread:
If ye their feast, or foes whose blood ye shed,—
Kite, crow perchance, the flavour high allow
Of Moslem blood o'er blood of Kawfur foe.
Enough. Ye know your fate."

         He ceas'd, and Night
Receiv'd his step and clok'd him from their sight.

END OF CANTO XI.

Canto XII.

THE BATTLE.

PART I.

DAUGHTER of Rhea and the golden Sun,
Aurora, youthful in the World's decay,
Still strew'st thou roses o'er th' arena run
By great Hyperion's flaming wheels of day?
How is the mighty fallen! How past away
He who from Earth's embrace with Heaven arose!
Th' ethereal steeds an upstart hand obey,
Yet tread in reverence o'er each votive rose
Once strown in gladness; now, tribute of filial woes.

Orion lov'd thee with a warrior's love;
His monster-quelling arm thine arms enchain'd:
Blest in thy charms he envied not high Jove
His throne; and, gazing in those eyes, disdain'd
Heaven's peerless huntress, pure and unprofan'd.
Ay, when bereft of sight he turn'd on thee
His darken'd orbs, they sudden power regain'd;
Thy beauty set his prison'd vision free. (27)
Dark roll'd the sun; he found his light, bliss, heaven
    in thee.

O beauteous Queen of freshen'd hearts and flowers,
Smiling to bliss the soul-wrung tears of Night,
Waking to song the silence-haunted bowers,
Scaring grim phantoms by thy beauty's might,
Wooing all hearts to unalloy'd delight—
Ah! can it be that man thy charms will shun
To toy with furies in their den of Night,
When nectar may from thy pure lips be won,
When in thy heaven-born smile his basking soul may
    sun!

Oh! sad the sight and foul that waits thee now,
Queen of the blooming cheek, the sunny brow.
Ope not thy golden portals, go not forth;
Not Nature's bridal this, but Man's fell wrath.
Leave Night and Mystery undisturb'd to brood,
Nor break thou rashly on their solitude.

Morn slowly dawn'd upon the hellish scene,
On field with corses pil'd of steeds and men;
Slimy with gore and gay with turbans strew'd,
And banners torn and garments roll'd in blood.
And with her light awaking yet to wrath,
Nākā and horn their stirring peals gave forth.
Timbrel and shawm took up the stirring sound,
And huge kerreenas* scatter'd thunder round.
Here the Moowuzzin's sonorous voice is known
To prayer inviting: "God is God alone."
His minaret now the heap'd-up corses form,
Pulpit for him, as banquet for the worm.

---

* The largest war-trumpet of the Scythian.

Rous'd by those sounds throughout that vale of
   death,
Like sere leaves stirring in the Siroc's breath,
The living rise, forsake the dead, and form
In groups, like clouds that muster for the storm.
To Mukka's shrine the turban'd warriors bow,
Th' ensanguin'd dust pollutes each prostrate brow,
Mercy's dread Lord with mutter'd prayer t' implore,
O'er deeds that sicken e'en the Fiend of War.

The Scythians, grouping, seek—how oft in vain!—
Their chieftain's banner o'er that fatal plain.
Dishearten'd looks and faltering steps are there,
And scarce revenge can buoy them o'er despair.
That impulse dire to them is all unknown
Which spurs the Arab's flagging courage on :
Rapine and lust, indeed, their fires combine,
But claim no birthright of a source divine.
There, where the dead and dying thickest throng,
His mangled form the warrior trails along.
But late the foremost, where the mighty trod,
Scarce crawls he now upon the corse-strown sod ;

Whilst from those heaps full many a wretch in vain
Lifts the pale head, then helpless sinks again.
O'er all shall soon the strong-hoof'd charger speed,
And heedless trample on the quick and dead.

But mark yon dark, dense mass that moves along
Silent as death, uncheer'd of trump or song.
With spear and falchion arm'd and strong horn-bow,
They climb that height, they storm the watchful
    foe.
Stern is the greeting each to each affords:
Spears dint on corselets, swords encounter swords.
But numbers urg'd by strong despair prevail:
The mountain bands, few, thinn'd, outnumber'd, fail.
The sweeping torrent dark of life rolls on,
Westward the ridge invades, and ere the sun
Streams o'er that valley deep the pass is won.

Meanwhile the Arab host the outlet throng.
Strait, dark the pass, the tide of horsemen strong.
Death and despair in rear, and life in view,
That treacherous gorge they headlong hurry through,

Each urging other: 'till the slippery rock
Betrays one floundering steed with sudden shock,
And o'er his prostrate form, horse, rider go ;
For what may check that living torrent's flow ?
What but the tangled heaps now writhing there,
And choking Hope's last outlet from despair ?

The Scythian Bands, the Moslem rear that press'd,
Now throng'd, impatient of th' unwelcome rest.
Sternly Erectheus struggles to maintain
Order and peace: his efforts all are vain.
Ukhbur, insensate, wheels his squadrons round,
Their ranks arrays, and bids the Tukhba * sound.

Then high to Heaven the battle-cry was toss'd,
The " Ulla Ukhbur " of the Arab host,
Answer'd by louder challenge to the war,
The Scythian's madd'ning shout and wild hurrah :
As the strong Northern horse and Arab fleet
In mid career, like adverse tempests, meet;

* The battle-cry of Muhummedans.

Sweeping before their all-destroying breath
The leafless forest,* whose dire fruit is death.
And mingling dark Hyrcania's living sea (28)
With thy throng'd waves, white-turban'd Araby.
Then rose th' uprooted soil, and hid from sight
Forms dimly imag'd in the gray twilight:
But thro' the dusky canopy arose
The crash of meeting and conflicting foes,
The living torrent's fierce, impetuous jar,
The madd'ning shouts and tumult of the war;
And chiming deeply in a separate key,
The trampled Warrior's groan of agony.
Each hero, hanging on the mountain brow,
Drank in those sounds, commixt of wrath and woe,
With ear athirst. Impatient now of rest,
The struggling foot advanc'd; as oft repress'd,
Obedient to his Dion's high behest:
And the strong hand resign'd its deathful clasp,
And, as for life, the deep, broad chest did gasp;

---

* Namely, of lances.

And every nerve of sense to frenzy wound,
Hung the stern warrior victim to a sound.

Thus uproar wild, confusion dire had reign :
Ranks, mixt and broken, strew the deathful plain ;
Man grappling man, and steed with steed engag'd,
Disorder'd hate and senseless vengeance rag'd.
Ukhbur, Erectheus toil to recombine
The rent battalia and disorder'd line.
Wary the weight of Scythia's giant steed,
The Arab's lighter frame and fleeter speed ;
With Persian lances fill their central ranks,
With Arab sabres wide extend the flanks.
Wedg'd in a mass, the myriad steeds, as one
Champ the strong bit, impatient eye the sun.
While from their nostrils jets of vapour part
The smoke of fires which rally round the heart.

Then slack'd the bits, with one accord they launch
On the rude foe, like some vast avalanche,
Their ranks compacted. Not the Northern horse,
Strong tho' his frame, can bear th' impetuous force,—

THE BATTLE.

The might concentrate of the Persian host:
They reel, they waver, turn—the battle's lost.—
Not so;—more deathful in retreat than fight,
Each as he turns hath drawn a bow of might, (29)
A cloud of deaths conceals them from the sight.
Another rises, and another still:
The foremost Moslem ranks have own'd the thrill,
Headlong to earth mail'd steed and rider go :
The tide of war is broken in its flow :
And o'er the prostrate wreck tumultuous thrown
The middle ranks and rearward files go down.
But soon the valley's walls with curb of might,
Bring up that headlong, death-bequeathing flight.
There, sudden bay'd, the countless horsemen wheel :
They shout, they charge ! The Moslem squadrons reel,
Back in one dark swoll'n wave resurging far
O'er the whelm'd Persian rolls the tide of war.

Hark—hark ! on either wing the Tukhba loud,
As spurs the Arab on the frantic crowd :
Full on the rallying Scythian's flank he bears.
Well the bold Arab loves the shock of spears.

See how he bounds amid the tumult grim,
The waves of war be toys of sport for him.
His deep chest pants in transport of delight;
His wide red nostril snuffs the steam of fight:
Arch'd his proud crest; dark fire his eye inflames,
And the wild neigh his stormy joy proclaims.
O'erpower'd, opprest with this new tide of life,
The frantic Scythian scarce maintains the strife.
Fain would he flee; but whither urge his flight?
The Arab here, and there the mountain height;
And more than mountain cliff, or Arab dire,
Erectheus' brow of gloom and eye of fire.

So Slaughter loos'd her harpies of the war;
Her first-born Man quaff'd high his Brother's gore.
How may that barbarous host the Fiend atone,
How plead for mercy in a tongue unknown.
Swift speeds the work of Death. Oh! swift to woe
Man's step—to goodness and to blessing slow.
Deep, deep in gore his blade each Moslem dyes,
A Kawfur's blood his waft to Paradise.

Then Dion bade Prometheus' banner rise,
And spread its folds to long-expectant eyes.
High, far it floats. The mountain legions see,
They hail the signal of their liberty—
Prometheus' standard to the winds unfurl'd,
Joy to the brave and freedom to the world!
As the hoarse thunder, shouting, greets his bride,
So shout the patriots on the mountain side.
Like rocks by earthquake shaken from their throne,
From crag to crag they leap tumultuous down:
There, in the vale, shield join'd to shield, combine
In dense dark phalanx and compacted line.

Oh! 'tis a pride that deathless Band to see;
Their tread how firm, their glance how bold, how free!
Bright gleams the sun from helm and corselet thrown,
Many their frames, the soul that knits them one.
The strong spears bristle in a triple row,
Within their covert lurks the deadly bow.
So mid rude hosts th' illustrious phalanx shone—
Athena's heroes and her Xenophon.

Young Theseus marshals them. His falcon eye
Flashes high zeal, presages victory.
See how along the faultless line he flies,
And reaps the meed of their admiring eyes.
Hoar veterans smile as on their youthful might,
And the young own their beacon thro' the fight.
Hark, as they move, in swift but measur'd time,
The soul of joy o'erflows in music's chime.
Young Theseus' manly voice the burden bears,
The chorus swell they with the clang of spears:

Song.

"Ho! for the feast of fight;
 The board of Death is spread:
Here banquet all sons of might:
 There sleep the mighty dead!

"The red wine flows around—
 The sons of battle shout;
The reeling squadrons strew the ground,
 High swells the wassail rout!

"Strong is the wine of death.
　　Three beakers pledge we high :
Our beauteous queen, our free-born breath,
　　Our land—her liberty !"

Borne on the wings of freedom and of song,
They hurl their might in one swoll'n wave along.
Down on the pausing Arab's ranks they bear,
And lend brief succour to the Scythian spear.
Hemm'd in and yielding to his turban'd foe,
The frantic Scythian, like his own strong bow,
Recoiling hurls his pent-up powers of life
Back on the Arab, and renews the strife.

Through the wild tumult of the heady fight
The grim Erectheus spurr'd his steed of might.
The shatter'd ranks his dreadful course betray,
And carnage strews behind his murderous way.
Thus, all-destroying in his course, he found
The Scythian monarch dealing death around.

His mighty arm the turban'd Arabs own,
And the red field with headless corses strown.
Him he accosted:

"Khaun! Thy rage forego
On these, and turn thee on our common foe.
Thou know'st this gaze. At fitting hour again
'Twill meet thine eye, not idly, nor in vain.
Turn now thy glance upon our adverse flanks.
Know'st thou the foes that strew the Moslem ranks?
Not thine those bands; for late their brunt ye bore.
The mountain children riot in our gore.
The Arab chief, besotted by his lust,
To heaven ascribes it, heavenward turns his trust,
With eye fast clos'd. Thy chosen horse command
To wheel, encircle swift yon mountain band.
Let them not charge upon the serried spear;
Destruction lurks in deadliest ambush there;
But, distant rang'd, from every quarter pour
Their darts, o'erwhelming with the steely shower.
Yon northern height, ye've rescued from the foe:
Where man can climb, the foot of horse may go.

Thither your squadrons lead, dismounting scale:
Leave to the mad and dead this fatal vale."

Promptly the Khaun that counsel sage pursued,
Call'd forth his bravest from their toil of blood,
Their leaders prompted in the novel fight—
Then on the mountain phalanx hurl'd his might.
Around the patriot band his squadrons sweep,
As whirlpools gird some victim of the deep;
Twang the strong bows, the darts incessant hail,
Their deadly showers transpierce the warrior's mail.
In vain they charge. The foe, like desert wind,
Leaves as he flies his sting of death behind.
Thinn'd are their ranks. Like autumn leaves they fall,
When hoarse-voic'd thunders on the whirlwind call.

Meanwhile the Scythian bands that senseless fight
Successive quit to scale the mountain height.
The Moslem host, relieved, each shatter'd rank
Turn on the foe who triumphs on their flank.
Hemm'd in that patriot phalanx grimly stand,
O'ermatch'd, unyielding, still a dauntless band.

The bristling pikes their foeman's charge restrain,
From sling and bow dense deadly vollies rain,
But fast they fail. No mail of proof may bear
The storm of darts incessant beating there.
Still as they fall, the living close and show
A minish'd front, yet dreadful to the foe.
Dion beholds their need: from near and far
He summons succour to the failing war;
His chosen squadrons marshals, and assumes
His steely helm with all its nodding plumes.
Calls for his steed; that steed so bold and true,
Whose neigh was victory to the chosen few.

Mark where he moves in all his clashing arms;
War on his aspect sheds her madd'ning charms;—
The step that, curb'd to stately pace, can ill
Conceal youth's buoyant pulse and lightning thrill.
High, like the fleecy clouds, his war plumes rise,
His rich cuirass th' ethereal hue supplies.
The silver belt, gold-boss'd, that clasps his form
Like dread Orion's threatens wrath and storm;

Glisters the air around, like waves that span
The scaly volumes of Leviathan.
But would ye Heaven's imperial impress know?
Mark the calm, massive, all unwrinkled brow,
That eagle eye which fronts the sun's hot glare,
Imbibing fires transfus'd to lightning there.

A sudden joy his matchless band possess'd,
Three mighty shouts their boundless glee express'd.
Their ardor, long restrain'd, now gushes forth.
How near akin the warrior's joy and wrath!
They watch his eye, his step, already see
The victory won, their lov'd, lost country free!

Past the descent: the vale of Death is won;
Form'd the mail'd line and gleaming in the sun.
That bugle note, how well its cheer they know!
They sweep a tempest on the Scythian foe.
Before their charge horse, man, downstricken go;
Their country's wrongs give weight to each home blow,

Edge ev'ry sword. But chief, Prometheus' brand,
Flames like dread Azrael's sword in Dion's hand.
No temper'd blade may bear the lightning shock,
No quilted fold its downward impulse mock;
Like blight of death it moves thro' that dense band,
Promethean temper in Promethean hand.

So sway'd the fight; from early morn renew'd,
Nor yet appeas'd the slaughter-field with blood.
Though past the midway goal, and westward tending
Heaven's golden chariot now was homeward wending.
And Nature, fainting 'neath the Day-god's might,
Droop'd her worn head and panted for the Night.
So rag'd the fight. Where'er the patriots press'd,
The hostile ranks their matchless might confess'd.
But worn with toil, with slaughter wearied now,
Their nerveless arms scarce speed the deadly blow.

Around the phalanx Dion wheels his horse,
Now here, now there hews down th' encroaching
  force,

Points where the mountain crags a refuge show,
Then, charging, cleaves a passege thro' the foe:
They, staggering, follow in his dreadful wake.
Their furious foes charge in, their phalanx break,
Young Theseus falls; his followers yell. The sound
Reach'd Dion's ear: he wheel'd his charger round;
Spurr'd to the rescue; fell'd the foes that press'd
Their frantic steeds against the warrior's breast;
Then, stooping from his sell, with grasp of might
Upcaught and raised him from the field of fight.
From his wild steed the nearest Scythian beat,
And help'd young Theseus to the saddle seat.
Then, mid death's billows plunging, wav'd his brand,
And clove a path for his exhausted band.

THE BATTLE.

PART II.

MEANWHILE the Arabs on the south assail'd
The patriot bands, and numbers still prevail'd.
O'erwhelm'd with clouds of missiles, long they stood,
Bay'd on all hands and faint, but unsubdued.
'Twas not until, downbearing on their course,
The dread Erectheus led the Persian horse—
Five thousand bristling spears—that fear possess'd
The even temper of one patriot breast.
He halts the squadron. At his word arise
Dense clouds of missiles dark'ning all the skies;
And ere the ranks their shaken wedge repair,
The horse are in, their strong spears stabbing there.

In vain black Gyges labours to restore
The vantage lost, and seals it with his gore.
In vain, with succours hasting from afar,
Their Dion rends a passage through the war,
Too distant yet. The work of death goes on,
The broken foot are trampled and o'erthrown:
The battle's lost;—their very country's woe
Enhanc'd by triumph of their barbarous foe.

'Twas then upon the adverse mountain height,
Gush'd to mid heaven a jet of ruddy light—
A vasty pyramid of dazzling flame,
Which put the golden lord of day to shame.
Curling, it rose in spiral column twin'd,
Then stedfast settled, spite the mountain wind.
Firm as a spire of adamant it stood,
A spire surcharg'd with Heaven's electric flood.
At that dread signal, from the mountain height
Which bridges o'er the torrent's foaming might,
The Scythian host like mountain deer are driven,
Or like Night's watchers by the Sun of Heaven.

Hurl'd from the crags they headlong plunge below,
Those crags reverbing yells of wrath and woe.
Above them, brandishing his father's spear,
On his free rocks grim hangs the mountaineer.

The wondering Moslem stay'd his arm of might,
As flash'd that marvel on his dazzl'd sight,
Dropp'd from his grasp the rein and sabre dire,
And gaz'd bewilder'd on the mount of fire.
Not long his gaze. From yonder mountain crest
Rank following rank the patriot legions press'd,
And from the deathful gorge, the open'd pass,
Of mounted warriors pour'd a lengthening mass.
Deploying now, their squadrons, dense combin'd,
Pause like some storm cloud tarrying for the
    wind.
Along the ranks keen, fitful lightnings run,
As the blue war-blade greets the lurid Sun.
But dark, beside, as night the squadron's gloom ;
Sable the steed, the warrior's vest and plume.
Death marks the hue most grateful to his eyes,
And like a raven o'er the column flies.

Who leads that force? Mark well that form of might,
That blood-red plume, so fatal in the fight,
That eye and brow so stern, more dreaded far
By those he rules than all the plagues of war.
'Tis Tywold—name in war eclips'd by none,
Save Dion's fame. He leads them not alone.
Young Calthas' spirit—form, so frail and fair,
Their gaze absorbs, like angel lighted there.
He scann'd the field, the shatter'd phalanx knew,
And swift as falcon to the rescue flew.
His silver arms strange o'er that war-field show'd:
His plume, as sea-gull o'er a lake of blood.
Stern Tywold close upon his traces press'd,
Marshall'd the ranks, fulfill'd his least behest;
Like father watching o'er an only child,
That warrior grim on only Calthas smil'd.

Erectheus mark'd the downward hurrying storm.
Rais'd his fierce shout, drew up his giant form.
Call'd off his bands from triumph incomplete,
Then spurr'd his mighty steed his foe to meet.

Full on young Calthas urg'd his fiery course.
What mortal frame may live before that horse,
That rider's arm, terrific in its sway,
That fiery blade which mows whole ranks away.
Not thine, young chief! And thou, like shallop light
In brunt of huge trireme, hadst set in night,
But that thy steed of more than mortal strain
Eludes the shock, the blow that falls in vain;
And ere can wheel his coal-black charger round,
The mighty Tywold closes with a bound.

Oh! dread the sight when heroes meet in arms,
Then War her carnage hides, unfolds her charms:
When might with might, skill baffling skill, we see,
And not for blood the strife, but victory.
So Tywold strove: Eretheus' vengeful mood,
Was still athirst, insatiate yet of blood.
Now foil'd as ne'er before his passing might,
The fiend of vengeance nerv'd him for the fight.
Thrice as they clos'd, with shock resounding far,
Their conflict silenc'd e'en the pulse of war!

The pausing host its earthquake influence own,
And wounded warriors still the dying groan.
But, as again they clos'd, some distant bow
Launch'd its keen shaft, and Tywold's steed laid low.
And the dire blade, down thundering from above,
Shear'd the red crest, the massive helmet clove,
Plough'd deep his brow.   To Earth horse, rider roll'd:
Death clasp'd the hero in his fatal fold:
Yet ere o'ermaster'd quite, he rais'd on high
His shatter'd brow and strain'd the blood-quench'd eye,
And tow'rd young Calthas stretch'd his arm in vain,
Already fetter'd in the Tyrant's chain:
Then laps'd that mighty frame, the heart-throbs ceas'd,
Ere Love's pure flame its shatter'd fane releas'd.

What turmoil raves? what sounds the field affray,
As thro' dense woods some whirlwind held its way?
'Tis Dion rending through the host his path:
Tornado's rage were tame beside his wrath.
The crash of splinter'd spears and helmets riven,
And steeds o'erthrown, fills high the vault of heaven.

Hope, love, despair, he knows nor whence nor why,
Nerve his strong arm, lend terror to his eye.
The spears be reeds: as potsherd vain and frail,
Barb'd steed and rider panoplied in mail.
Fix'd on Erectheus' sable crest his gaze,
Hope, fear alike on him converge their rays;—
And straight as arrow from the Parthian bow,
His course of havoc tow'rd that mighty foe.

The turmoil wild reach'd grim Erectheus' ear,
He knew some ruler of the battle near,
Left Calthas in his blood and wheel'd him round,
And on the foeman urg'd his charger's bound:
But when he knew his rival's towering crest,
Delirious joy his vengeful soul possess'd.
Already there in hate's keen second sight
His foot is trampling on those plumes of white,
Effacing from the features' mould sublime
Each hateful vestige of Prometheus' line.
A shout of fiery joy his soul betray'd,
High pois'd he shook his all-destroying blade—

That blade which, forg'd in flames of wroth and woe,
Was temper'd keen in Stygian billows' flow.

As two tall cliffs, disparted by the roar
Of hoarse deep floods, from snowy realms that pour,
Together rush impell'd by earthquake's thrust,
While forests crash, and rocks are ground to dust,—
So o'er war's billows towering in their might,
Rush those dread foes to mix their souls in fight.
Their steeds, the raven black and hue of snow,
See each in other's form a mortal foe.
Like dragons fiercely to the charge they fly,
Snorts the wide nostril, flames the dark red eye,
Scarce felt the bit, the master-hand scarce own'd,
With pawing hoof and wounding teeth they bound.
And as they meet, those dreadful blades on high
Sweep fiery arcs which measure out the sky:
This the red hue imbib'd in realms of Night,
And that Truth's brand from armoury of Light;
As Comet dire and Morn's effulgent Star
Their spheres had left to wage portentous war.

That conflict fierce Earth's firm foundation shook,
The battling foes their strife of blood forsook,
Leant on the brand or spear each languid form,
And grouped like herds that watch the coming storm.
That mightiest strife inspires undreamt alarms,
And puts to shame their puny deeds in arms.

    Five times, ̗with shock that palsied Earth's strong frame
Down to the dismal realms of wroth and shame,
Those heroes met; as oft with frantic bound
Their steeds, ungovern'd, disappoint the wound;
And those keen swords, so fearful in their sway,
Innocuous clash or rend but plumes away;
Yet when they meet long tongues of fire outstart,
As from some cloud where lightnings whet the dart,
And the high clang fills heaven's affrighted bound,
As Ætna's caves Cyclopean blows resound.
But when at length their chargers' rage represt,
They hand to hand contend, and crest to crest,
Their perfect skill, their equal strength afford
No vantage pass to either deadly sword.

Wheeling as eagles in the starry sky,
In dizzy whirl their circling chargers fly;
Now meet, now part, the rear, the flank invade,
While flash by flash down whirrs the deadly blade.
No mail of proof avail'd in that stern fight:
The sword of Fire met there the sword of Light.
Had either fail'd the falling blow to ward,
Corselet and helm had vainly spread their guard.

To frenzy fir'd such equal might to know,
And meet it wielded by his mortal foe,
Erectheus rous'd his every nerve to life,
Resolv'd with one fierce blow to end the strife,—
With voice and rein his charger's mettle stirr'd—
Then with concentrate hate on Dion spurr'd.
A whirlpool's force, which sucks a navy down,
In his right arm, Hell's fury in his frown;
His steed, like some black billow from beneath
Upheav'd by earthquake o'er the sea of Death;
Like scythe of Fate his sword's huge segment show'd,
Or Death's red rainbow in a sky of blood,

As mustering all his soul he rose on high,
And launch'd the deathful weapon from the sky.

Prometheus' brand the blazing mischief stay'd,
But blow so fierce the stable guard o'ersway'd,
Cleft the high crest, the marble brow laid bare,
But, baulk'd its fury, paus'd reluctant there.
E'en as it fell, his war-steed Dion made
Rear high in air—then flash'd Prometheus' blade;—
No eye might view it. But behind it came,
And linger'd there, a pale, blue, liquid flame,
Like that seen o'er Oïleus' impious head
When Pallas' bolt his breast transfixing sped,
As high she caught him with a whirlwind shock,
And dash'd him mangled on the pointed rock.*
Th' infernal blade no more that edge withstood,
But sever'd fell, disgorging pools of blood.

Hurl'd from his war-sell on the field of fight,
Erectheus fell in his arrested might:

---

* "Illum exspirantem transfixo pectore flammas
Turbine corripuit, scopuloque infixit acuto."—*Æneid.*

The sullen clang his sable armour gave,
Succeeds a silence, settled as the grave.
None dare believe that battle-breaker low,
None dare approach to mark the stricken foe.
Hate and revenge absorbs their mightier dread,
His very victim half averts the head.

Prone lay Erectheus. Life not yet was past,
Tho' the red torrent now was ebbing fast.
Above, with drooping crest and weeping mane,
Stood his black steed, the terror of the plain.
The war, the chase, life's fortune, smile and frown,
That matchless courser with his lord had known:
And faithful most when all have fickle prov'd,
Still fondly lingers by the lord he lov'd.
And *have* all else forsac'en him? Doth his sight
But paint some phantom of Death's gathering might?
Or is *she* there, the lov'd, the lost, the lone,
Sole power his stern, relentless heart hath known.
How wan that cheek! How soul-crush'd that deep eye!
The battle's roar drowns not that heart-wrung cry,—

Despair's last sob. For all indeed is lost,
The seal is set, the die for ever cast.
Dark shadows grow upon his swimming sight,
And gloom within meets—blends with outer night.
Long stood that steed impatient of his rest,
His dark mane drooping o'er his master's breast,
With murmur'd neigh and pawing hoof in vain
Would rouse that heart shall never throb again!

Oh! not an instant Dion paused to scan
His foeman's fall. His eye wild-flashing ran
O'er that red plain. He starts. Extended there,
Where mighty Tywold makes his bloody lair,
A warrior lies: his plumes of white are strew'd
O'er the red turf: his corselet plash'd with blood,
His silver buckler cleft. Entranc'd he lay,
If life indeed hath not yet ebbed away.
Why trembles Dion? He, good sooth, knows not,
Yet quits his steed and hurries to the spot!
Bends o'er the seeming youth, his casque removes,
And sees—joy, rapture, misery!—her he loves.

THE BATTLE.

Yes! tis his Indra. Wonder, triumph, fear,
Distract his soul: for she he loves lies here,
Pale, in her faultless beauty; her large eye
Clos'd as the violet when the storm raves high.
He calls her name. He shouts it with the might
That oft hath turn'd the adverse host to flight.
She ope's her languid eye. In his strong arms
Uprais'd he bears her all-unconscious charms;—
His proud steed mounts. His warriors rally round,
Call'd by the spell of that thrice-honour'd sound.
He lifts his dreadful crest. His voice afar
Terrific shouts defiance to the war.
Leap the bold hearts of all his warriors high,
They know but triumph in that battle cry.
Their broken phalanx swiftly they reform,
Their shaken squadrons muster for the storm.
Full on the pausing Persian host he bears,
Rends their dense ranks and snaps their brittle
    spears.

In vain the Scythians, rallying, urge the fight;
Their monarch falls before his matchless might:

Dion to him and his vast host accords
Their lives in purchase of their render'd swords.
Then on the Arabs spurs. Stern Ukhbur still
Fought without hope, but with unswerving will.
His turban'd warriors, hope's last vestige lost,
Fought still, a minish'd yet a mighty host.
Forth from the patriot band a horseman press'd:
No corselet screen'd this mountain shepherd's breast.
A buckler bright upon his arm he bore,
And grasp'd a spear oft stain'd in sylvan war.
The Arab chief he met in full career,
And smote to earth with his transfixing spear.
" Die, stain to manhood, infant murderer, die!
Know'st thou the Shepherd thou didst late defy,
Jarthon, thy mountain guide, whose infant's blood
Thou wouldst have pour'd forth on the torrent's flood?
'Tis shame to smite so hoar a head as thine;
'Twere sin to leave thee, heaping crime on crime."
He said, and left him in his gore.

        And now,
Dion withheld his squadrons from the foe,

Their leader fall'n, destruction pressing hard,
He grace proclaims for each surrender'd sword.
The few stern zealots who that grace disdain
Hemm'd in, o'erpower'd, are trampled down and slain.

Then Dion spurr'd to reach a swelling height,
Whose verdant turf had 'scap'd the stains of fight;
His ardent followers, hither hasting, bring,
The cushion'd throne of Scythia's captive king:
Carpets, and furs, and rich brocades of gold,
In one vast pile together heap'd and roll'd,
A lofty seat upbuild. Alighting down,
He bears, instals her on her country's throne.
Unwinds the arms that still around him grow,
Salutes her queen, and, kneeling, bends the brow.
Confus'd, amaz'd, scarce waken'd from her trance,
She casts on him, on all, a wilder'd glance.
For truth so blissful credence cannot find,
Dire tumults threaten to divorce her mind.

Around, on either hand, the phalanx stood,
Begrim'd with dust, with wounds deform'd and blood;

In front the Horse, a deep, dense column frown'd,
But vest and armour token'd many a wound:
Deep silence long repress'd their anxious dread,
But, when their queen uprais'd her drooping head,
And round her gaz'd, while o'er her head the fire,
Lambent and pure, of her illustrious sire,
Descending play'd,—their joy, their triumph rose
In shouts, heart-withering to their vanquish'd foes:
"Indra, our queen, our queen!" Heav'n's concave vast
Round and around those thrilling thunders cast,—
While flash'd the blade and wav'd the pennon fold,
And the wide sea of plumes tumultuous roll'd;—
And war steeds, deeming other fields were nigh,
Toss'd their proud manes, like thunder-clouds, on high.

Strange was the Maiden's guise;—of silver fair,
With gold-emboss'd cuirass and gorget rare.
But, helm and gorget loos'd, down stream'd to view
Each long rich tress of hyacinthine hue,
Streaking her ermin'd robe and corselet bright,
And throat so pure, with hues of tenfold night.

Strange was that guise for beauteous maid I ween:
But each stern warrior gaz'd upon his queen,
His land's deliverer, and in her renew'd
The line of heroes of Promethean blood.
And who beheld the corselet's ruddy stains
Of life-blood trickling from her pure, sweet veins,
But treasur'd up the pledge mid memories dear,
Home's, Heaven's high claims, his very country's tear.

And now, long filing twixt a double row
Of levell'd pikes, the Vanquish'd wended slow.
Each as he pass'd, his weapon pil'd, and gave
A vassal's homage to the peerless Maid.
Princes and Nobles, Chiefs and Syuds* pure,
Kulpauk† and Turban penance like endure.
The arms up-pil'd four lofty pyramids show,
Of lance and sabre, battle-axe and bow.
Guards and videttes around the foe they post,
In number still a dense, o'erwhelming host.

---

* Syud, a descendant of the Muhummedan's Prophet.
† The cap of fur of the Scythian.

'Twas Summertide; o'ertoil'd, the Steeds of Day
Held thro' the clouds of eve their homeward way.
Yet paus'd on great Prometheus' land to see
His line restor'd, his long-lost country free.
The clouds up-pil'd in towers fantastic rise,
To youthful gaze an untrod paradise.
Full in the midst, from out his massive hold,
Apollo whelms the skies with molten gold.
That mighty flood, too bright when first it rose
For mortal eye, turns crimson as it flows,
And heaven's rich azure meeting, ebbs in waves
Of purple, varying as the clouds it laves—
Gold-coasted clouds that, like th' Hesperian isles,
Bask in the sunshine of the Day-god's smiles.

Bland was the air. Day's fervour all was done,
Soft sighs came floating from the westering sun.
A little cloud, slow flitting o'er the plain,
From moist wing flirted down the sparkling rain,
And at its bosom bore in sportive play
An infant rainbow from the God of Day.

But who the foreground shall depict, where stood
Those ardent warriors, breath'd from toil and blood ?
The level rays their warm, bright hues impart,
From helm and blade in dazzling pencils dart,
On waving plumes prismatic glories throw,
And banners teach to mate the show'ry bow.
But more than tints, ethereal beams display
Emotions stampt on every living trait:
The power by turns joy, rapture, wonder prove,
And fervid blessing and adoring love.

But Indra saw not, knew not of the sky,
Eve's growing shades or balm-distilling sigh;
The very throng array'd in glittering arms,
Entranc'd in wonder of her matchless charms.
The plaudits, blessings, shouts of triumph all
Unheeded rise, unnoted round her fall.
One form she sees, one eye, one glance alone,
Tho' her lov'd country round her breath'd and shone:
That form, that glance is Dion's. Pale he knelt,
With eye that ever fondly, raptly dwelt

On her lov'd face, with voice that murmuring found
To breathe her name, then bless the beauteous
    sound.
Oh! what to either years of suffering past,
Since here they meet in life, in peace at last!
There's not one woe their backward gaze may spy
But adds fresh blessing to the rapture nigh.

A herald comes. The op'ning crowd gives way.
What tidings bears he from Sinope's bay?
Dion alone half dreads his queen should know,
In this her mood o'erwrought, the tale of woe.
The herald speeds, his frame with toil o'erworn,
His gorgeous robes with briar and thicket torn;
His reeling steps denote unswerving speed,
But on his brow no woe can Dion read.
Scarce hath he paus'd obeisance low to make,
Ere from his lips the glowing tidings break:
"Rejoice, rejoice, my prince! the battle won!
Our fleet victorious! tyrant Rome's o'erthrown!
A hundred galleys scatter'd o'er the deep,
Three score and ten black Pontus' caverns keep:

And thrice a hundred, with the crews that mann'd,
Our fleet hath train'd in triumph to the strand.
Rejoice! rejoice!"

"How, what? Rash man, beware!
Falsehood were treason in thy sovereign's ear.
Another herald, who beheld the fight,
Reports Rome's triumph, our disastrous flight."

Then Indra spake: " Both tidings true have shown:
The day *was* lost. We rallied: it is won."

" Thou, Indra, gracious queen! Thou there expose,
As here, thy sacred life to murderous foes!
Oh, say not thus."

" Speak, herald!" Indra said,
" Declare how far'd the day, who won, who fled."

But speechless long the gazing herald stood,
By that rare beauty dazzled and subdued.
He heard her titled "queen." Hope, joy, amaze
At once within his troubled bosom blaze.
Scarce found he words at length:

"In full retreat,
Press'd by Rome's galleys, fled our shatter'd fleet,
In number, size, unequal long to brave
Those ponderous three-deck'd tyrants of the wave.
Sails hove in sight, down bearing from the north,
Pursued, pursuer their whole strength put forth,
Those in the hope—how faint!—of succour there,
These lest allies the promis'd booty share.
They grow in size, mast, spar and hull emerge,
Then the long oars that aye her progress urge.
They grow apace, they hurry down, and now
We hear the surge hoarse roar against each prow.
A gallant fleet, wedge-form'd, they hither fly,
Like white swans sailing in a summer sky.
The foremost, swiftest, mightiest of the line,
All eyes explore her keenly for a sign.
No flag appears; but on the poop we spy
A form that fills with light each gazer's eye—
A youthful warrior seem'd he; but *we* saw
Beauty and grace surpassing mortal law.
All wing'd for heaven beside the helm he stood,
And stretch'd his hand as 'twere to sway the flood.

Swift on the Roman fleet his galley goes,
And midships smites the mightiest of our foes.
Mid crash of meeting barks and arrowy storm
He stands serene, as one exempt from harm.
His followers well their several parts maintain,
And, wearing round, we tempt the fight again.
Of Rome's vast fleet a scatter'd remnant flee.
I sped with tidings of the victory."

Swift through the ranks that glorious notice spread:
" Rome's dire Armada, captur'd, sunk or fled,
  Their queen, their Indra, victrix then as now.
  Two crowns of oak to grace her conquering
      brow!"
Three veterans seam'd with scars, in warfare grey,
At Indra's feet the votive chaplets lay.
Her brow to crown is Dion's honour'd care;
Their joyous shouts rose blent with heartfelt prayer.
Tho' warriors they who shout the high award,
Yet patriots, too; her country's voice she heard:
Her country's voice, its blessing pure and warm,
Its freedom won, renew'd its every charm;—

24—2

Her Father's throne unsought to her restor'd,
And, crowning bliss, her heart's own chosen lord.
She rose to speak, her voice the utterance tried,
"My friends, my people"—there in sobs it died.
Passion's strong conflict all her soul alarms,
She trembles, totters,—falls, to Dion's arms.
Those arms around her wind, that voice so dear
Breathes her lov'd name, instils and whispers cheer.
Well hast thou found the haven of thy rest,
His bliss thou art, and in his blessing blest.
Thy strength in need, thy courage in despair,
Heaven's own vicegerent of thy heart is there.

So deep absorpt were both, the tumult loud,
That instant rising from the warrior crowd,
They heeded not. "The Seer, the Prophet, ho!
Give way. He comes with blessing on his brow."
Two milkwhite mules the Prophet's litter bear,
He cleaves the ranks, he nears the royal pair.
There lighting, staid his steps of reverend hands,
Confronting Indra's throne the Prophet stands.

Erect he stood. Against the evening sky
Reliev'd distinct those traits sublime and high.
Round his tall form the robe flow'd loose and fair,
The breeze blew back his white, far-floating hair;—
On Indra fixed that eye, so dim till now,
Which blazing fills with light th' o'erarching brow.
The box of gold unseal'd he first, and shed
The sacred unguent o'er the Maiden's head.
Then heavenward stretched his arms, the while elate
His breast seem'd swelling with the voice of Fate.

"Now close, thou dull, dim eye. Enough for thee
Thy queen, Prometheus' matchless child to see,
Thy country's wrongs aveng'd, her children's children free!
Yea, close, dim eye, nor deign on earth to gaze,
Nor ope till wak'd by heavenly hymns of praise.
Long, long and weary was thy night of gloom,
Prometheus' exile, his sad country's tomb.
But from his ashes see the phœnix soar,
The selfsame wings her godlike father bore,

Promethean majesty in form refin'd,
A soul as lofty, but a fate more kind.
I see the clouds with future blessings stor'd,
The deep for her his unsumm'd treasures hoard.
I see the rivers waft her peace and wealth,
I hear the breeze soft whisper promis'd health.
From Heaven above the dews ripe form'd distil,
While laughs the vale and shakes the wood-crown'd hill,
And woods and wilds in peaceful verdure drest
Bless her who governs—yea, who *shall* be blest.

" Hark to the wings of Spirits fluttering nigh :
Faint voices whisper from the starry sky.
These from her head avert each baleful ray
Of sun, moon, star : those call the Seer away.
Oh, then, farewell, sweet dream of every breast,
Young hope, thro' ages of thy land's unrest !
The long'd-for summons has gone forth, yet fain
Am I to see thee, bless thee once again.
Scarce Death itself the old man's prayer shall quell.
My country's glory, oh ! farewell—farewell ! "

His last look brighten'd on Prometheus' child,
His dying glance on Indra beam'd and smil'd,
His dying lips proclaim'd Heaven's high behest,
Prometheus' Land and peerless Daughter blest!

END OF CANTO XII.

Conclusion.

LIGHT of my lonely heart!—ah! whither fled,
My golden Sunbeam? Night broods deep around:
My harp-notes tremble mid the silence dread—
They wake dire phantoms with their bodeful sound.
    Thine ear they have not found:
Thine, for whose sake was fram'd the votive lay,
    Whose praise perchance had bound
Thy lover's temples with the proudest bay.—
Star of my desolate night! what murk cloud hides thy ray?

Fondly I'd hoped, with laurels hardly won,
To build my Bride a fair, unfading bower.
Alas! those wreaths, uncull'd, if e'er mine own,
Can now but serve her timeless grave to dower.
Then, wither—wither, bay and myrtle flower!
That brow is low ye should have twin'd around :
Still'd the sweet heart could once have felt your power ;—
The senseless marble only can be crown'd.
Wither, and rustling strew the bleak cold funeral ground!

NOTES.

NOTES.

Note 1, page 15.
*Can ever (more than senseless matter) prove
Curb'd in duration.*

So far greater in dignity and importance than the body did the soul appear to some of the ancient philosophers, that, dazzled by the consideration, they discredited the very existence of matter, accounting as delusion the evidence of the senses, and regarding mortal life as a peculiar trance of the soul. This, even now, is the doctrine of the Hindoo philosopher. With all its folly, it is surely more rational, more accordant with the experience of an intelligent being, than any material system that has boasted proselytes. Matter, even so far as we can trace it, is susceptible of an infinity of combinations, altering its character from gaseous to fluid; from fluid to solid; from opaque to transparent; from metal to earth; from earth to metal. Analogy warrants the supposition that the whole mass of our earth may be susceptible of transition to a gaseous form;—yea, to a gas so subtle as to be manifest to none of our senses. But no experiment justifies the supposition that any particle of it could, by the action of any known or natural agent, cease to exist. If, then, our baser portion—our material body—be incapable (so far as we know) of annihilation, who shall doubt the indestructibility of the soul? If such a doubt arise, it is in defiance of all analogy, and is not, therefore, reason, but a diseased effort of the mind to resist that reason which tends to faith, confidence, and peace.

Note 2, page 27.

I heard the mighty Mountain's distant groan.

The following is from Stewart's *Sketches of the Highlanders:*— "Previous to a tempest, some of the mountains of the Highlands emit a loud hollow noise, like the roar of distant thunder: and the louder this noise, the more furious will be the tempest, which it generally precedes from twelve to twenty-four hours. From this warning, when 'the spirit of the mountain shrieks,' the superstitious Highlanders presage many omens. Beindouran, in Glenorchy, near the confines of Perth and Argyle, emits this noise in the most striking manner. It is remarkable, that it is emitted only during storms of wind and rain. Before a fall of snow, however furious the tempest, the mountain (which is of a conical form and 3,500 feet high) is silent. In the same manner several of the great waterfalls of the Highland rivers and streams give signals of approaching tempests and of heavy falls of rain. Twenty or thirty hours previous to a storm, the great falls of the River Tummel, north of Shichallian, emit a loud noise, which is heard to the distance of several miles. The longer the course of the preceding dry weather, the louder and more similar to a continuous roll of distant thunder is the noise. Consequently, it is louder in summer than in winter. When the rain commences, the noise ceases. It forms an unerring barometer to neighbouring farmers. Why mountains and waterfalls in serene, dry weather emit such remarkable sounds, and are silent in tempests and rains, might form an interesting subject of physical inquiry."—Vol. i. p. 88, *note.*

Pilgrim, an Indian traveller, in his wanderings in the Himalaya, says: "During the two nights I rested at Kedar Nath (one of the sources of the Ganges), I was frequently awoke by rumbling sounds, like the report of very loud but distant thunder, although the entire firmament was cloudless. When I was residing a few days at Chini, in Kunnawur, I remarked the same phenomenon, which was of almost hourly occurrence in the magnificent pile of snowy mountains overhanging the Sutlej at that place. There, as well as at Kedar Nath, the noises were ascribed to the anger of the gods. In the Rocky Mountains of North America, it is attributed by the poor Indians to the thunders of the guardian genii over hidden treasure."

After mentioning that his first theory of these sounds ascribed them to the disruption of avalanches, he states that he has been led by comparison of the phenomena to attribute them rather to subterranean explosions, and to believe that the interior of the mountain is a hidden crater.

Pilgrim does not observe that these sounds in the Himalaya are followed by tempest. And, indeed, I imagine the sounds heard by him are of a class distinct from those mentioned by Stewart. But I prefer the theory of avalanches and disjected rocks to that of subterraneous explosions. There is no doubt that amid such a chaos of mountain peak and snow-clad precipice some disruption is occurring every hour during the summer months. Such disruptions, happening at the head of a glen or chasm, would be multiplied like the sound of the human breath in a trumpet, and would be carried to as great a distance as those mountain walls might extend in a tolerably direct line. That these are oftener heard by night than by day is attributable to the greater stillness of the air, and the greater attention of the senses, during the night season. But the fall of a mass of ice or of rock is perhaps as frequently the effect of recongelation as of thaw. Water in the act of congelation expands with enormous power, sufficient when confined to overthrow the poise of very large masses.

As for the sounds described by Stewart, that emitted by the mountain and that of the waterfall, they seem to me deducible from two distinct causes. Previous to a tempest, there is often a hush of the atmosphere, which enables very distant sounds to reach the ear: and the roar of a waterfall, at other times unheard, will then be audible.

But the sound from a mountain peak requires some additional explanation, for the sound must be generated ere it can be communicated. Now an important cause of the limited range of sound is the convexity and roughness of the earth's surface; sound travelling in right lines, unless it meet with some smooth conducting surface.

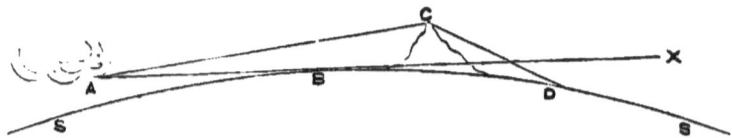

Suppose, then, the curve s s to represent the earth's surface, and that a thunderstorm is active at A, about 100 miles from D. The distant thunder might perhaps be heard at B; but much more distinctly at the summit C of the mountain Beindouran. But at D, it would be quite mute, even supposing no mountain to intervene; because the sound would pass in a right line to X, hundreds of yards above D. But the thunder peal striking the hollow side of the mountain peak at C, is there collected, and again dispersed in radiations both above and below, and in the stillness preceding a storm is distinctly audible at D, appearing to proceed from the mountain itself.

To be heard with best effect, the storm, the mountain summit, and the hearer should not be placed in the same line. Indeed, this could seldom long be the case, as the thunder-storm generally covers many square miles of the earth's surface.

Snow, if I recollect right, after the lapse of so many years, is seldom ushered in by thunder. And thunder is never known without a fall of rain from the cloud which utters it. Thunder-storms are generally most violent after long dryness of the atmosphere, when the electric fluid is isolated, and not carried off as fast as it accumulates, or is released, by watery particles in the air. And thus the sounds emitted or transmitted by mountains in Scotland are mute previous to snow-storms, and most remarkable when a heavy storm succeeds long dryness of atmosphere.

Note 3, page 48.

The awestruck peasant views that mighty form.

The following quotation is from Sir Robert Porter's *Travels in Persia*:—" Heathen traditions and classical writers affirm that Elborus was the huge and savage rock of Caucasus to which Prometheus was chained; and who but Æschylus has drawn the picture? There is still a tradition amongst the natives who reside in the valleys of Elborus that the bones of an enormous giant exposed there by Divine wrath are yet to be seen on its smaller summit. Indeed the story is so much matter of belief to the rude tribes of that quarter, that people are to be found who will swear to have seen the huge remains.

" Marvellous as the story is, it seemed so well attested that some time ago a Russian general officer thought he might make it the ground for penetrating farther into the mountains, and accordingly set forth, I am told, on his expedition, with a party of 200 men and a light field-piece, to ascertain the truth of so extraordinary a tale. However, the moment was not yet arrived for an European eye to behold this dead colossus; for scarcely had he penetrated any distance into the recesses of the mountain, when a tremendous avalanche rolled in fury down its side, and overwhelmed the whole party, excepting its leader and one or two soldiers. There was now no doubt among

the natives, that the intention of the expedition was to give charitable
sepulture to the unburied corse, and that the accident happened
in consequence of the vengeance of the Spirits of the Mountain, who
had the mysterious relics in charge; thus to show that the doom
of remaining to bleach for ever upon that unsheltered rock should
not be reversed."—Vol i. p. 129, 4to edition.

Note 4, page 54.

Beac'ning thine awful crest, proud peak of Demawend.

The principal summit of that range of mountains which, stretching
along the southern coast of the Caspian, is acknowledged as an inferior
chain of Caucasus, is called Demawend. The summit never loses
its snow. It is supposed to be haunted by a gigantic spectre: a
tradition very common in Persia, and attaching especially to the
chief summit of the main Caucasus, called Elboorz (Elbŏrus). To
those who have resided near mountains, it were needless to observe
that their apparent approach is indicative of a storm. I have often
used, to advantage, this barometer.

Note 5, page 69.

When at Elborus' base the pilgrim stood.

The mountains of Caucasus are called by the Persians *Kauf*, but
sometimes Elborus, and the principal summit bears the latter name.
Elborus, therefore, has the grave accent upon the second syllable, like
Pilŏrus. The second, in height, of the summits is called Kazibek.
These belong to the main range of Caucasus, overlooking the Euxine.
The third summit in celebrity, and probably in height, is Demawend,
south of the Caspian, in the subordinate range of Caucasus. The summit

to which Prometheus is traditionally reported to have been chained is Elbŏrus, overlooking the Euxine. It has two summits, and the lesser is said still to retain the gigantic skeleton. It is believed to be 18,000 feet above the sea's level. The base of Elbŏrus is said to be isolated by marshes. The latitude of Elbŏrus (the peak) is said to be 43° N., its longitude 43° 15′ E. The snow on the summit is perennial.

Shelley, in his *Prometheus*, fixes the summit on which he was tortured in the Indian Caucasus. This is contrary to Greek tradition, and was adopted by Shelley probably for the sake of poetic embellishment. It is, however, remarkable that traditions should exist to this day in the Sohant valley, at the southern foot of the Hindoo Koosh, or Indian Caucasus, supporting the licence of Shelley, by making that valley the abode of the Titans, the ruins of whose cities still exist, bearing the Titans' names. Although, however, there is no doubt that the Indian word *Dyta* is identical with the Greek word Τιτάν (Titan), yet the Indian and Greek names of Titans do not agree.—

GREEK TITANS.	LATIN.	INDIAN DYTES.
Uperioon	Sol	—
Kronos	Saturnius	Sthool Dyte.
Okeanos, or Amphitrite	—	Kahun Dyte.
Iapetos	—	—
Kottos	—	—
Briareos	—	—
Orion	—	—
Atlas	—	—
Epimetheus	—	—
Prometheus	—	—
Menœtius	—	Monama Dyte.
Titan	—	Kiri Chuk, a semi-Titan by a human mother.

Sthool Dyte, *quasi* Saturnius, may have given the Romans their name for Kronos.

The valley of Sohaut is highly classical ground to Sanscrit scholars. Not only did the Titans reign here, building cities, whose ruins remain with names unaltered; but hither also retired the five Pandoo Brothers and the Wife they shared between them—the beautiful Diroopdi—and took service under Raja Viraht, the ruins of whose palaces and stables are shown to this day. When Alexander the Great visited Sohaut, he or his officers* were shown the cavern in which Prometheus had been chained to feast the eagles. This is probably the large and remarkable cavern yet existing at an old site called after one of the Titans (St'hool Dyte) Dyte Kulli, or Titan's Fort. This valley is at present closed against research by the jealousy and hostility of the independent Pathans who occupy it, and who were undoubtedly there when the Macedonians invaded it, as is evinced by their bearing the same names. But their own want of such a government as can punish marauders of their own tribe must some day open to us this valley, which Ukhbur's armies invaded without success. It is the most interesting spot, to an antiquary, in Eastern Asia.

* Strabo says of the Macedonians (lib. v. p. 688): "'Ιόντες σπήλαιον ἐν τοῖς Παροπαμισσάδεις ἱερὸν, τούτῳ γὰρ ἐνεδείξατο Προμηθέως δεσμωτήριον καὶ δεῖρο ἀφῖγμενον τὸν Ἡρακλῆα ἐπὶ τὴν ἐλευθέρωσιν τοῦ Προμηθέως." —"Seeing a sacred cavern in the Paropamisas, they said Prometheus had been imprisoned there, and that Hercules had come thither to release Prometheus." Strabo very naturally supposed this to be an invention of Alexander's flatterers. But there is no doubt that the tradition existed in Alexander's day; and I believe that the more our knowledge increases, the more truthful will the Greek historians appear—that is, that they did not wilfully deceive, though they may sometimes receive fables as truth.

Note 6, page 70.

And now from Kazibek's twin peak of dread.

Mount Kazibek is the second in altitude of the summits of the Caucasus. Messrs. Englehardt and Parrot ascended to near the summit. The natives of the country hold it in superstitious reverence, calling it " Christe Zup," or the Hill of Christ, believing that the Virgin Mary dwelt there, and that a Roc still watches over the cradle of the infant Jesus. The guide pointed to a cross and monastery, in which he assured them the cradle lies, but refused to conduct the travellers farther. Dr. Parrot, however, reached the cross, which he found to be of porphyry, fixed upon a rocky mass of the porphyritic cliff. Near it was a low circular wall of loose stones, a considerable cairn of stones, and a rude pillar of porphyry. The monastery, as it is called, is a grotto excavated in the cliff, about 900 feet above the cross, and quite inaccessible from beneath. The portal of the cavern is in the midst of a space cleared with the chisel in the cliff. It is partly enclosed by two slabs of stone, resembling folding-doors. These are supported on each side by pillars, which, as well as the doors, glister like mica. This rock is at least 3,000 feet above the limit of perpetual congelation. Its height is 12.018 feet above the Euxine; and Dr. Parrot, although he could not reach the mountain summit, reckons it at 14,400 feet.

Note 7, page 78.

In whose compare hoar Saturn's ancient sway.

Old as may seem to us the reign of Saturn, the ancients went farther back in their theology, and deifying Chaos, Matter, the

Heavens, and the Earth, established gods whose origin was lost in eternity; but whose power was decayed, whose worship well nigh forgotten. Of these are Cœlus, Terra, Chaos, Night, &c.

Note 8, page 80.

While shapeless rocks to fair proportions grown
Round Ilium bind th' insuperable zone.

Apollo assisted Neptune in building the walls of Troy, and, as twanging the lute was easier than shouldering the hod, it may be supposed that it was preferred by Apollo to reduce the stones to order.

The wall of Troy was never overcome. Treachery did what might could not effect. One of the surest evidences of the antiquity of the *Iliad* is in the ignorance it betrays of even the rudest arts of attacking fortified places. Neither battering-ram, nor catapult, nor moving tower, nor secret mine, nor wall of circumvallation, seem then to have been known.

Note 9, page 86.

The bird of Jove, dim wheeling thro' the sky.

There is, I believe, more than one instance on record of the shouts of a multitude stunning birds as they flew overhead. They suit, however, the page of the poet better than that of the historian. They were credited, nevertheless, by Plutarch, who, in his "Life of Pompey" says, speaking of the Roman people when Roscius had proposed to them to give Pompey a colleague:—

"Incensed at the proposal, they set up such a shout, that a crow which was flying over the Forum was stunned by the force of it, and fell down among the crowd. Hence we may conclude that when birds fall on such occasions, it is not because the air is so divided with the shock as to leave a vacuum, but rather because the sound strikes them like a blow when it ascends with such force and produces so violent an agitation."—*Langhorne's Translation.*

If it really has occurred, it has been produced by syncope, the effect of sudden terror.

Note 10, page 121.
" *The Mount, the Sea of Light.*"

KOH-I-NOOR AND DERRIAU-I-NOOR.

When this note was first written the Koh-i-noor was known in Europe only by the description of travellers. It has since been exhibited to public gaze in London. Its sister, the Derriau-i-Noor, or Sea of Light, still belongs to the King of Persia. It is uncut, and is described as nearly hemispherical, or forming three parts of a sphere; its natural crust being partly or entirely polished off. It hung ever over the pillow of the late king, Fulleh Ali Shah, that his eyes might fall upon it first in waking. It was also the last mortal object which he gazed upon. It seems to contain about the same substance as the Koh-i-noor, though differing from it in shape. The latter, as a table diamond, weighed one ounce and two-fifths. But it then had no lustre, and it was difficult to believe it to be anything better than rock crystal, and much substance must have been lost in making it a brilliant.

Note 11, page 122.

*Which of their golden fruit despoil'd the trees
And gem-dropt fountains of th' Hesperides.*

This exploit is attributed to Hercules. What a world of conjecture has been built upon the ancient traditions relating to the Hesperides. There can be little doubt that they were nothing more than the oases of the Great Desert, which produce the finest dates in the world, and little else. These not being the fruit of Europe, and abounding in saccharine matter, before the general use of the sugar-cane, when honey and date sugar were the chief substitutes, would have been regarded with peculiar interest by the men of ancient Greece; whilst the inaccessibility of the oases would have given birth to all the exaggeration of fable. To this day, the date and the raisin supply Afghanistan with its native sugar, which is even extracted from the water-melon.

Note 12, page 142.

The Scythian spurr'd his wild, deep-chested steed.

Scythia is a name applying to all Tartary, and a large portion of what at present is Russia. The Scythian best known to the Greeks was the Kuzzauk (Cossack), who was then probably lord of all the steppe, as far as the Sea of Aral, which, indeed, is his present *habitat;* although he is tributary to the governments of Russia and of Khiva. The Parthian or Toorcumun seems to have held his present locality in the steppe intervening between Persia and the Caspian and the river Oxus. The horse of the Cossack is a sturdy galloway. That of the Toorcumun, the Oozbeg, and the Mogul, is the largest, and one of the finest breeds in Asia. Its great size and strength make it very valuable as a war-horse; and its powers of endurance are severely taxed by the Toorcumun in the predatory life he leads—for he must often ride a hundred miles without drawing rein. I do not mean that he gallops, or even canters, such distances; but the horse is heavily laden with its own and its master's food for several days—its own and its master's water and clothing—and has often to carry a captive in addition.

Note 13, page 169.

And Genii haunt each vasty chasm there.

Kawf, the Caucasus of the ancients, is, according to the Arabs, Persians, and Toorks, the especial residence of Djins, Peris, Ufreets, and other supernatural beings. It is here that Jooj and Majooj (Gog and Magog) and their gigantic host were imprisoned under the seal of Solomon;—the walls of Durbund, connecting the Caucasus with the Caspian, and built to prevent the inroads of the Scythians, having apparently led to the fable. So many wonders, however, have been invented and hoarded up regarding the Kawf, that the human mind is no longer contented with a material mountain under that title, but expects a prodigy, which exists no one knows where towards the rising sun.

Æschylus places the Caucasus upon the remotest confines of Scythia, while it is south-eastward of that region.

Note 14, page 186.

But thro' Earth's centre plunging to those seas
And isles where roam th' unblest Antipodes.

Were a tunnel perforated through the earth's centre to our antipodes, and were a heavy weight cast into it, it would not stop until it had almost reached the antipodes. There, its velocity being balanced gradually by the central attraction, it would pause, and gradually fall back to the centre, increasing in velocity until the centre were passed, and then, with ever abating speed, rushing almost to the point of outset. Thus would it vibrate to and fro between the antipodes, the length of the vibrations ever decreasing, until by degrees it settled in the earth's centre.

When first the sphericity of the earth was established by philosophy, many wild speculations arose amongst the ignorant regarding the antipodes, who were supposed to walk on their heads.

Note 15, page 221.

. . *and like that fiend which haunts the crest*
Of precipice, the fatal plunge suggest.

That desperate impulse which tempts the unpractised to leap headlong down a precipice, and to which, under peculiar circumstances, the steadiest brains may be liable, is supposed by barbarous nations to be the suggestion of a demon haunting the precipice's verge. It seems in reality to be a momentary distrust of the power of volition at the instant that the sense of danger rushes upon the mind. The horror of falling from such a dizzy height is too sensible. The will, which every hour of our lives preserves us from peril, is forgotten for the moment. We have used its force mechanically, without reflecting upon it, or troubling our heads to consider its nature or origin. It is an invisible power. The demand for its aid is frightfully visible, and we distrust that aid. In the confusion of our senses we mistake the dread of falling for the impulse to throw ourselves down.

This singular sensation is not confined to the brinks of precipices. It may be felt by the imaginative when the nerves are disordered, by weakness of the stomach, under every circumstance, moral and physical, with which dread intermingles; and many of the bravest have been tormented by mistaking the dread of cowardice for the weakness itself; whilst the dread of being suspected of crime has made many of the purest-minded appear guilty.

In all such confusions of the mind, arising from nervous exhaustion, it seems wiser to shun than to combat the suggestion—to forget, than to argue with it—to will that it *shall not* be, than to prove that it *ought* not to exist.

Note 16, page 234.

The moss-wreaths drooping from the pine-branch high.

In Alpine countries the lichens which overrun forest-trees often hang in festoons from the branches. In the mountains of Nepaul not only is the whole tree swathed in drooping moss, but long streamers of a white, parasitical plant hang here and there from the extremities of the branches, to the length of from six to twelve feet, like veils of the most delicate white gauze. Several varieties of fern also find root in the bark of the oak or pine, affording in their bright metallic green a vivid contrast with the almost sable velvet of the mosses.

Note 17, page 251.

. . . *from the hills*
Of Bankoo, rife of thousand fiery rills.

Bankoo, on the western coast of the Caspian, is still celebrated for its inflammable gases, which gush from every incision made into a particular circle of the hill. It is a spot much venerated by fire-worshippers (Ghubbees), and even by Hindoos, especially of the Punjaub, many of whom still retain the worship of fire, and resort to Bankoo as to a shrine.

Note 18, page 308.

Had Jooj, Majooj, outburst from prison den
For their last triumph o'er the sons of Men?

Jooj and Majooj are rendered by us Gog and Magog, and we probably owe our knowledge of the names to the Crusaders. The Koran, which was compiled by the son of a Jewess, retains many of the traditions of the Jews; and among them is numbered the great field Armageddon, when Jooj, Majooj, are to burst their prison caves in the Caucasus, and to threaten extermination to believers; which event is to usher in the Messiah as their conqueror.

Note 19, page 312.

And chas'd the thistle with the desert wind.

For an account of the gigantic thistle, in size a tree, growing upon the steppes north-east of the Caspian, see Kohl's most interesting account of Southern Russia. These thistles, when dry, are easily uprooted, and borne along by the strength of the wind with extraordinary speed, presenting a spectacle peculiar to those steppes.

Note 20, page 313.

The hide of steed for mantle round them spread.

The Kuzzauks (Cossacks), the least civilized of the Tartar tribes, were those best known to the ancients, as Skuthoi, or Scythians. The derivation of the name we cannot even conjecture.

The Kussauk, even to this day, has no dress but the hides, half-tanned, of his cattle. A little linen here and there finds its way from nations bordering upon his steppes, but this is appropriated by the women, who often have none. The use of bread in any form, of vegetables, or of fruit, is utterly unknown. It is probable that the Oozbegs, Kulmauks, and Moguls, were equally uncivilized some hundreds of years ago, though, from settling in towns and villages, they have since learned many of the arts of civilized life. The Kuzzauk claims a common origin with the Toorcumun, who is apparently the Parthian of antiquity. They are, however, very dissimilar in feature and character.

Note 21, page 315.

Drooping with oxtails from Tibetan mountains.

The yok, or Tibetan ox, is of dwarf dimensions, covered with shaggy hair like a bear. The tail is bushy, like a horse's, but is composed of hair of extreme delicacy, and of the purest white. This is the celebrated chowry. Its principal use is as a fly-flap, for which the delicacy of its hair especially fits it. Horsehair is apt to wound the eye. It is set in handles of beaten silver or gold, richly wrought, and no man of rank sits without two attendants armed with such chowries.

Officers of rank wear the oxtail at their saddles — a custom originating probably with the Tartar conquerors of Asia in the bleak steppes from which they came, but introduced by them into India as well as Turkey. The spears of noblemen are bearded with chowries instead of banners. The chowry can be purchased at from 4s. to 5l. each. The ox which furnishes it has, in addition to his long shaggy hair, an undergrowth of Pushm, or shawl-wool, with which Nature furnishes most animals in that region of deadly wind.

Note 22, page 315.

His strong, tough bow of horn beside him lay.

The bow of China is formed of two curved rods of buffalo horn firmly united at the grasp. When relaxed, it does not become straight, like a bow of Europe, but bends back into a rapid curve the reverse of that which it assumes when strung. When strung it resembles the bow with which painters arm Cupid. It is of two degrees of strength. The stronger cannot be drawn with the arms alone. The bowman lies upon his back, and turns the soles of his feet toward the mark; he places the soles of his feet against the grasp of the bow, where are loops to prevent them from slipping; the arrow, four feet in length, and headed with an ounce of lead, is then adjusted, and is drawn with both hands to the archer's breast, and thence released. The force is said to be very great, but the range I do not remember. The smaller bow is drawn as in Europe, excepting that the arrow is not drawn to the right ear, but to the chest, which is no doubt the reason why the Amazons, a Tartar race, extirpated the right pap, which otherwise must have been bruised by the hand in its recoil. This bow has been introduced into India and Persia by the Moguls, but in a modified form. At present, small strips of buffalo-horn are taken as the springy portion of the bow, and are firmly lashed upon a grasp of wood or centre, with thongs of the fresh entrail of the sheep dipped into boiling glue. Two sticks of mulberry wood are, in like manner, lashed on to the extremities of the horns, and into these notches are cut for the bowstring; the whole is then completely cased in a swathing of entrail dipped in glue, and is varnished over with coloured copal varnish.

Rudely as these bows are, generally constructed by the most clumsy workmen, they often possess a power which will enable them to vie with the long bow of England. And there is no doubt that such a bow, constructed by a skilful English bowman, might prove an admirable weapon, especially for horsemen, its length being little more than half that of an English bow. To this bow reed arrows are used, which it will send 220 yards. Its chief enemy is the excessive damp of the Indian rainy season, which softens the glue, and often causes the bow to warp.

That horn was the material of the bow of ancient Greece we have abundant evidence in the Iliad and Odyssey. The horn of the mountain goat seems to have been preferred. This was, perhaps, the Ibex, for the common mountain goat has a spiral horn. Homer thus describes the bow of Pandarus:—

> "Αὐτίκ' ἐσύλα τόξον ἔΰξοον, ἴξαλου αἰγὸς
> Ἀγρίου, ὅν ῥα ποτ' αὐτός ὕπο στερνοῖο τυχήσας,
> Πέτρης ἐκβαίνοντα δεδεγμένος ἐν προδοκῇσι
> Βέβλήκει πρὸς στῆθος· ὅ δ' ὕπτιος ἔμπεσε πέτρῃ.
> Τοῦ κέρα ἐκ κεφαλῆς ἑκκαίδεκα δῶρα πεφύκει.
> Καὶ τὰ μὲν ἀσκήσας κεραοξόος ἤραρε τέκτων.
> Πᾶν δ' εὖ λειήνας, χρυσείην ἐπέθηκε κορώνην."

"Instantly he stripped his polished bow, of the bounding wild goat, which he on a time had reached upon his belly, as descending from a rock it fell into his ambush; he wounded it in the breast, and it fell upon its back from the rock. The horns of its head grew to sixteen palms (64 inches), and them the horn artificer shaping adapted (together), and planing them throughout fitted golden tips."

It is manifest that this bow was made throughout of horn, excepting of course the grasp and the tips, being similar to the Chinese bow of the present day, excepting that the horn of the buffalo is used in China as in India.

Note 23, page 317.

The Jigha blaz'd like beacon o'er the wold.

In the Scythian kingdom of Khaurism, this is the sole symbol of royalty. It is intended to represent a cypress bent by the wind, and is formed of precious gems. It is the pattern so common upon Cashmere shawls: but so little like a cypress, as probably never to have been recognized as such by any European eye. It forms one of many state jewels in India and Persia, where probably the Moguls introduced it. It is worn on the turban or cap in front.

Note 24, page 318.

What answer gives the Yem's uncultur'd lord?

The Yem Djem, or Emba, forms at present the northern boundary of Khaurism and the southern boundary of Russia. At least down to the Yem the influence of Russia over the Kuzzauks of that Steppe is greater than that of Khivà, although the tribes claim independence.

Note 25, page 318.

The black Kulpauk.

The Kārā Kulpauk, or Black-hatted, are a tribe of Oozbegs, dwelling at present at Ghoonguraut, south of the Sea of Aral. The words Kārā, black; Auk, white; Yuhohi, good; and Yummun, bad—are of great significance among a people of shepherds, who have few words and fewer ideas. In this tribe a singular custom at present prevails. When a stranger approaches, the young women of the tribe challenge him to wrestle. The conqueror has, for the time, complete power over the person of the conquered. It is said that the women are rarely thrown, and that they cruelly abuse their advantage when conquerors. This report, whatever its truth, is generally believed in that country.

Note 26, page 322.

And leave waste sites for cities that rebel.

The desolation occasioned by Chungiz Khaun and Timoor in Central Asia, by the wholesale slaughter of both sexes and of all ages, in cold blood, without pretext or provocation, is scarcely to be credited by any who has not actually visited the once populous countries which those monsters reduced to the condition of deserts. To cut the throats of 50,000 men, women, and children, in cold blood, after their surrender on promise of mercy, was an ordinary act of Chungiz. Centuries have since elapsed, but the countries he desolated have never recovered.

Note 27, page 330.

Ay, when bereft of sight he turn'd on thee
His darken'd orbs, they sudden power regain'd ;
Thy beauty set his prison'd vision free.

When, by the treachery of Œnopion, Orion's eyes had been deprived of sight, Orion ascertained by inquiry the aspect of the east and the hour dawn, and turning his sightless orbs to the spot where his beloved was rising, her beauty restored his lost sight.

Note 28, page 335.

And mingling dark Hyrcania's living sea.

Although Herodotus had early recorded that the Caspian is a lake, dissevered from the ocean, succeeding generations took up the belief that it is a gulf of the Indian Sea, and it was for a thousand years known as the Hyrcanian Gulf. Even Alexander, who had passed between it and the Indian Ocean, strangely persisted in thinking it a gulf of that flood.

Note 29, page 337.

Not so ;—more deathful in retreat than fight,
Each as he turns hath drawn a bow of might.

The Toorcumun, who is probably the descendant, and certainly the successor, of the Parthian, differs from the latter very little in manners and habits. He has exchanged the bow for the matchlock, which has gone far to abate his terrors as an enemy. For his poverty, and the backwardness of the country in the arts, causes him to be ill-armed in comparison with his neighbours, and he cannot afford to expend in the practice of the matchlock enough gunpowder to become an expert marksman ; whereas his forefathers, by constant practice with the bow, rivalled all their neighbours. The Toorcumun is a bad shot, and is chiefly formidable by the great endurance of his horse, which enables him to make astonishing marches and unexpected attacks, and to cut off supplies, where their loss is destruction.

THE END.

LONDON:
PRINTED BY SMITH, ELDER AND CO.,
LITTLE GREEN ARBOUR COURT, OLD BAILEY, E.C.

65, *Cornhill, London,*
March, 1861.

NEW AND STANDARD WORKS

PUBLISHED BY

SMITH, ELDER AND CO.

IN THE PRESS.

Framley Parsonage.
By Anthony Trollope,
Author of "Barchester Towers," &c. Illustrated by J. E. Millais, R.A.
Three Vols. Post 8vo. Price 21s., cloth. (*Just Ready.*)

Household Medicine;
Describing Diseases, their Nature, Causes, and Symptoms, with the most approved Methods of Treatment, the Properties and Uses of Remedies.
By John Gardner, M.D.
8vo, with numerous Illustrations.

Japan, the Amoor and the Pacific.
A Voyage of Circumnavigation in the Imperial Russian Corvette "Rynda," in 1858–59–60.
By Henry Arthur Tilley.
8vo. With illustrations.

Ragged London.
By John Hollingshead. In One Vol.

The Book of Good Counsels:
Being an Abridged Translation of the Sanscrit Classic, the "Hitopadesa."
By Edwin Arnold, M.A., Oxon.
Author of "Education in India," &c. With Illustrations by Harrison Weir.
Crown 8vo.

Philo-Socrates.
Part I. "Among the Boys."
By William Ellis.
Price 1s. (*Just Ready*.)

The History of England;
From the Earliest Period to the Death of William the Conqueror.
By J. A. St. John, Esq.
In Two Vols. 8vo.

⁎ The author has availed himself of the valuable information on important points of English History afforded by the chronicles published by direction of the Master of the Rolls.

Life of Mahomet.
By William Muir.
Vols. III. and IV.

A New Novel.
By the Author of "Cousin Stella."
In Three Vols.

JUST PUBLISHED.

The Tragedy of Life.
By John H. Brenten.
In Two Vols.

Education in Oxford:
Its Method, its Aids, and its Rewards.
By James E. Thorold Rogers, M.A.
Post 8vo, price 6s. cloth.

Agnes Tremorne.
By I. Blagden.
In Two Vols. (*Now Ready*.)

Scripture Lands in connection with their History:
With an Appendix: and Extracts from a Journal kept during an Eastern Tour in 1856-57.
By the Rev. G. S. Drew,
Author of "Scripture Studies," &c.
Post 8vo, with a Map, price 10s. 6d. cloth.

The Conduct of Life.
By Ralph Waldo Emerson,
Author of "Essays," "Representative Men," &c. Post 8vo, price 6s. cloth.
⁎ Also a Cheap Edition, price 1s., cloth.

Egypt in its Biblical Relations.
By the Rev. J. Foulkes Jones.
Post 8vo, price 7s. 6d. cloth.

Turkish Life and Character.
By Walter Thornbury.
Author of "Life in Spain," &c. &c.
Two Vols., with Eight Tinted Illustrations, price 21s. cloth.

Shakspere and his Birthplace.
By John R. Wise.
With 22 Illustrations by W. J. Linton. Crown 8vo. Printed on Toned Paper, and handsomely bound in ornamental cloth, gilt edges, price 7s. 6d.

Legends from Fairy Land.
By Holme Lee.
Author of "Against Wind and Tide," "Sylvan Holt's Daughter."
Fcap 8vo, with Eight Illustrations by H. Sanderson, price 3s. 6d. cloth.

Bermuda:
Its History, Geology, Climate, Products, Agriculture, &c. &c.
By Theodore L. Godet, M.D.
Post 8vo, price 9s. cloth.

Tea Planting in the Himalaya.
By A. T. McGowan.
8vo, with Frontispiece, price 5s. cloth.

HISTORY AND BIOGRAPHY.

History of the Venetian Republic:
Her Rise, her Greatness, and her Civilization.
By W. Carew Hazlitt.
Complete in 4 vols. 8vo, with Illustrations, price 2l. 16s., cloth.
*** Volumes III. and IV. may be had separately.

Life of Schleiermacher,
As unfolded in his Autobiography and Letters.
Translated from the German by Frederica Rowan.
Two vols., post 8vo, with Portrait. Price One Guinea, cloth.

The Autobiography of Leigh Hunt.
Revised by Himself, with additional Chapters by his Eldest Son.
One vol., post 8vo, with a Portrait engraved on Steel from an Original Drawing. Price 7s. 6d. cloth.

The Life of Charlotte Brontë (Currer Bell).
By Mrs. Gaskell.
Fourth Edition, revised, one vol., with a Portrait of Miss Brontë and a View of Haworth Parsonage. Price 7s. 6d.; morocco elegant, 14s.

The Life of Edmond Malone

(Editor of Shakspeare); with Selections from his MS. Anecdotes.

By Sir James Prior,

Author of the "Life of Edmund Burke," "Life of Oliver Goldsmith."

Demy 8vo, with Portrait, price 14s. cloth.

Robert Owen and his Social Philosophy.

By William Lucas Sargant, Author of "Social Innovators and their Schemes."

1 vol., post 8vo. 10s. 6d. cloth.

Shelley Memorials.

Edited by Lady Shelley.

Second Edition. In one vol., post 8vo. Price 7s. 6d. cloth.

VOYAGES AND TRAVELS.

A Visit to the Philippine Isles in 1858–59.

By Sir John Bowring,

Governor of Hong Kong, and H.M.'s Plenipotentiary in China.

Demy 8vo, with numerous Illustrations, price 18s. cloth.

Heathen and Holy Lands;

Or, Sunny Days on the Salween, Nile, and Jordan.

By Captain J. P. Briggs, Bengal Army.

Post 8vo, price 12s. cloth.

Narrative of the Mission to Ava.

By Captain Henry Yule, Bengal Engineers.

Imperial 8vo, with Twenty-four Plates (Twelve coloured), Fifty Woodcuts, and Four Maps. Elegantly bound in cloth, with gilt edges, price 2l. 12s. 6d.

Through Norway with a Knapsack.

By W. M. Williams.

With Six Coloured Views. Second Edition, post 8vo, price 12s. cloth.

Voyage to Japan,

Kamtschatka, Siberia, Tartary, and the Coast of China, in H.M.S. Barracouta.

By J. M. Tronson, R.N.

8vo, with Charts and Views. 18s. cloth.

To Cuba and Back.

By R. H. Dana,

Author of "Two Years before the Mast," &c.

Post 8vo, price 7s. cloth.

Life and Liberty in America.

By Dr. C. Mackay.

Second Edition, 2 vols., post 8vo, with Ten Tinted Illustrations, price 21s.

Smith, Elder and Co., 65, Cornhill, London.

WORKS OF MR. RUSKIN.

Modern Painters.

Now complete in five vols., Imperial 8vo, with 84 Engravings on Steel, and 216 on Wood, chiefly from Drawings by the Author. With Index to the whole Work. Price 8*l.* 6*s.* 6*d.*, in cloth.

EACH VOLUME MAY BE HAD SEPARATELY.

Vol. I., 6th Edition. OF GENERAL PRINCIPLES AND OF TRUTH. Price 18*s.* cloth.

Vol. II., 4th Edition. OF THE IMAGINATIVE AND THEORETIC FACULTIES. Price 10*s.* 6*d.* cloth.

Vol. III. OF MANY THINGS. With Eighteen Illustrations drawn by the Author, and engraved on Steel. Price 38*s.* cloth.

Vol. IV. ON MOUNTAIN BEAUTY. With Thirty-five Illustrations engraved on Steel, and 116 Woodcuts, drawn by the Author. Price 2*l.* 10*s.* cloth.

Vol. V. OF LEAF BEAUTY; OF CLOUD BEAUTY; OF IDEAS OF RELATION. With Thirty-six Engravings on Steel, and 100 on Wood. Price 2*l.* 10*s.* With Index to the five volumes.

The Stones of Venice.

Complete in Three Volumes, Imperial 8vo, with Fifty-three Plates and numerous Woodcuts, drawn by the Author. Price 5*l.* 15*s.* 6*d.* cloth.

EACH VOLUME MAY BE HAD SEPARATELY.

Vol. I. The FOUNDATIONS, with 21 Plates. Price 2*l.* 2*s.* 2nd Edition.

Vol. II. THE SEA STORIES, with 20 Plates. Price 2*l.* 2*s.*

Vol. III. THE FALL, with 12 Plates. Price 1*l.* 11*s.* 6*d.*

The Seven Lamps of Architecture.

Second Edition, with Fourteen Plates drawn by the Author. Imp. 8vo. Price 1*l.* 1*s.* cloth.

Lectures on Architecture and Painting.

With Fourteen Cuts, drawn by the Author. Second Edition, crown 8vo. Price 8*s.* 6*d.* cloth.

The Two Paths:

Being Lectures on Art, and its relation to Manufactures and Decoration. One vol., crown 8vo, with Two Steel Engravings. Price 7*s.* 6*d.* cloth.

The Elements of Drawing.

Sixth Thousand, crown 8vo, with Illustrations drawn by the Author. Price 7*s.* 6*d.* cloth.

The Elements of Perspective.

With 80 Diagrams, crown 8vo. Price 3*s.* 6*d.* cloth.

The Political Economy of Art

Price 2*s.* 6*d.* cloth.

RELIGIOUS.

Sermons:
By the late Rev. Fred. W. Robertson,
Incumbent of Trinity Chapel, Brighton.

FIRST SERIES.—Eighth Edition, post 8vo. Price 9s. cloth.
SECOND SERIES.—Seventh Edition. Price 9s. cloth.
THIRD SERIES.—Fifth Edition, post 8vo, with Portrait. Price 9s. cloth.

Expositions of St. Paul's Epistles to the Corinthians.
By the late Rev. Fred. W. Robertson.
Second Edition. One thick Volume, post 8vo. Price 10s. 6d. cloth.

Lectures and Addresses.
By the late Rev. Fred. W. Robertson.
Post 8vo. Price 7s. 6d. cloth.

Sermons:
Preached at Lincoln's Inn Chapel.
By the Rev. F. D. Maurice, M.A.

FIRST SERIES, 2 vols., post 8vo, price 21s. cloth.
SECOND SERIES, 2 vols., post 8vo, price 21s. cloth.
THIRD SERIES, 2 vols., post 8vo, price 21s. cloth.

The Province of Reason;
A Reply to Mr. Mansell's Bampton Lecture.
By John Young, LL.D., Edin.,
Author of "The Mystery; or, Evil and God." Post 8vo. Price 6s. cloth.

"Is it not Written?"
Being the Testimony of Scripture against the Errors of Romanism.
By the Rev. Edward S. Pryce.
Post 8vo. Price 6s. cloth.

Historic Notes
On the Old and New Testament.
By Samuel Sharpe.
3rd and Revised Edition. 8vo. 7s. cl.

Tauler's Life and Sermons.
Translated by Miss Susanna Winkworth.
With Preface by Rev. C. KINGSLEY. Small 4to, printed on Tinted Paper, and bound in Antique Style, with red edges, suitable for a Present. Price 7s. 6d.

Quakerism, Past and Present:
Being an Inquiry into the Causes of its Decline.
By John S. Rowntree.
Post 8vo. Price 5s. cloth.

*** This Essay gained the First Prize of One Hundred Guineas offered for the best Essay on the subject.

Women of Christianity
Exemplary for Piety and Charity.
By Julia Kavanagh.
Post 8vo, with Portraits. Price 5s. in embossed cloth.

Smith, Elder and Co., 65, Cornhill, London.

WORKS ON INDIA AND THE EAST.

Christianity in India.
By *John William Kaye.*
8vo. Price 16s. cloth.

The Sanitary Condition of Indian Jails.
By *Joseph Ewart, M.D.,*
Bengal Medical Service.
With Plans, 8vo. Price 16s. cloth.

District Duties during the Revolt
In the North-West Provinces of India.
By *H. Dundas Robertson,*
Bengal Civil Service.
Post 8vo, with a Map. Price 9s. cloth.

Campaigning Experiences
In Rajpootana and Central India during the Suppression of the Mutiny in 1857-8.
By *Mrs. Henry Duberly,*
Author of "A Journal kept during the Russian War."
Post 8vo, with Map. Price 10s. 6d. cloth.

Narrative of the Mutinies in Oude.
By *Captain G. Hutchinson,*
Military Secretary, Oude.
Published by Authority. Post 8vo. Price 10s. cloth.

A Lady's Escape from Gwalior
During the Mutinies of 1857.
By *Mrs. Coopland.*
Post 8vo. Price 10s. 6d.

The Crisis in the Punjab.
By *Frederick H. Cooper, Esq.,*
C.S., Umritsir.
Post 8vo, with Map. Price 7s. 6d. cloth.

Views and Opinions of Gen. Jacob, C.B.
Edited by *Captain Lewis Pelly.*
Demy 8vo. Price 12s. cloth.

The Theory of Caste,
By *B. A. Irving.*
8vo. 5s. cloth.

Papers of the late Lord Metcalfe.
By *John William Kaye.*
Demy 8vo. Price 16s. cloth.

British Rule in India.
By *Harriet Martineau.*
Sixth Thousand. Price 2s. 6d. cloth.

The English in India:
Being the Early History of the Factory at Surat, of Bombay.
By *Philip Anderson, A.M.*
Second Edition, 8vo. Price 14s. cloth.

Life in Ancient India.
By *Mrs. Spier.*
With Sixty Illustrations by G. SCHARF.
8vo. Price 15s., elegantly bound in cloth, gilt edges.

The Parsees:
Their History, Religion, Manners, and Customs.
By Dosabhoy Framjee.
Post 8vo. Price 10s. cloth.

Tiger Shooting in India.
By Lieutenant William Rice,
25th Bombay N.I.
Super-royal 8vo. With Twelve Plates in Chromo-lithography. 10s. 6d. cloth.

The Vital Statistics
Of the European and Native Armies in India.
By Joseph Ewart, M.D.
Bengal Medical Service.
Demy 8vo. Price 9s. cloth.

The Bhilsa Topes;
Or, Buddhist Monuments of Central India.
By Major Cunningham.
One vol. 8vo, with Thirty-three Plates.
Price 30s. cloth.

The Chinese and their Rebellions.
By Thomas Taylor Meadows.
One thick volume, 8vo, with Maps.
Price 18s. cloth.

Hong Kong to Manilla.
By Henry T. Ellis, R.N.
Post 8vo, with Fourteen Illustrations.
Price 12s. cloth.

Land Tax of India.
According to the Moohummudan Law.
By N. B. E. Baillie, Esq.
8vo. Price 6s. cloth.

The Defence of Lucknow.
By Captain Thomas F. Wilson,
13th Bengal N.I.
Assistant Adjutant-General.
Sixth Thousand. With Plan. Small post 8vo. Price 2s. 6d.

Eight Months' Campaign
Against the Bengal Sepoys during the Mutiny, 1857.
By Colonel George Bourchier, C.B.
Bengal Horse Artillery.
With Plans. Post 8vo. Price 7s. 6d. cloth.

The Commerce of India with Europe,
And its Political Effects.
By B. A. Irving, Esq.
Post 8vo. Price 7s. 6d. cloth.

Moohummudan Law of Sale.
By N. B. E. Baillie, Esq.
8vo. Price 14s. cloth.

Moohummudan Law of Inheritance.
By N. B. E. Baillie, Esq.
8vo. Price 8s. cloth.

The Cauvery, Kistnah, and Godavery:
Being a Report on the Works constructed on those Rivers, for the Irrigation of Provinces in the Presidency of Madras.
By R. Baird Smith, F.G.S.,
Lieut.-Col. Bengal Engineers, &c. &c.
Demy 8vo, with 19 Plans. 28s. cloth.

MISCELLANEOUS.

Social Innovators and their Schemes.
By William Lucas Sargant.
Post 8vo. Price 10s. 6d. cloth.

Ethica ;
Or, Characteristics of Men, Manners, and Books.
By Arthur Lloyd Windsor.
Demy 8vo. Price 12s. cloth.

Slavery Doomed ;
Or, the Contest between Free and Slave Labour in the United States.
By Frederick Milns Edge.
Post 8vo. Price 6s. cloth.

Life of Lord Metcalfe.
By John William Kaye.
New Edition, in Two Vols., post 8vo, with Portrait. Price 12s. cloth.

Life of Sir John Malcolm, G.C.B.
By John William Kaye.
Two Vols. 8vo, with Portrait.
Price 36s. cloth.

The Autobiography of Lutfullah.
A Mohamedan Gentleman ; with an Account of his Visit to England.
Edited by E. B. Eastwick, Esq.
Third Edition, small post 8vo.
Price 5s. cloth.

The Life of Mahomet.
And History of Islam to the Era of the Hegira.
By W. Muir, Esq., Bengal C.S.
Vols. 1 and 2. 8vo. Price 32s. cloth.

Annals of British Legislation :
A Classified Summary of Parliamentary Papers.
Edited by Leone Levi.
The yearly issue consists of 1,000 pages, super-royal 8vo, and the Subscription is Two Guineas, payable in advance. The Forty-ninth Part is just issued, completing the Fourth Year's Issue. Vols. I. to VIII. may now be had. Price 8l. 8s. cloth.

A Handbook of Average.
With a Chapter on Arbitration.
By Manley Hopkins.
Second Edition, Revised and brought down to the present time.
8vo. Price 15s. cloth ; 17s. 6d. half-bound law calf.

Manual of the Mercantile Law
Of Great Britain and Ireland.
By Leone Levi, Esq.
8vo. Price 12s. cloth.

Commercial Law of the World.
By Leone Levi.
Two vols. royal 4to. Price 6l. cloth.

Gunnery in 1858 :
A Treatise on Rifles, Cannon, and Sporting Arms.
By William Greener,
Author of "The Gun."
Demy 8vo, with Illustrations.
Price 14s. cloth.

On the Strength of Nations.
By Andrew Bisset, M.A.
Post 8vo. Price 9s. cloth.

Sea Officer's Manual.
By Captain Alfred Parish.
Second Edition. Small post 8vo
Price 5s. cloth.

Victoria,
And the Australian Gold Mines in 1857.
By William Westgarth.
Post 8vo, with Maps. 10s. 6d. cloth.

New Zealand and its Colonization.
By William Swainson, Esq.
Demy 8vo. Price 14s. cloth.

The Education of the Human Race.
Now first Translated from the German of Lessing.
Fcap. 8vo, antique cloth. Price 4s.

Germany and the Tyrol.
By Sir John Forbes.
Post 8vo, with Map and View.
Price 10s. 6d. cloth.

Life in Spain.
By Walter Thornbury.
Two Vols. post 8vo, with Eight Tinted Illustrations, price 21s.

Life in Tuscany.
By Mabel Sharman Crawford.
With Two Views, post 8vo.
Price 10s. 6d. cloth.

Captivity of Russian Princesses in the Caucasus.
Translated from the Russian by H. S. Edwards.
With an authentic Portrait of Shamil, a Plan of his House, and a Map.
Post 8vo, price 10s. 6d. cloth.

The Life of J. Deacon Hume.
By the Rev. Charles Badham.
Post 8vo. Price 9s. cloth.

Results of Astronomical Observations
Made at the Cape of Good Hope.
By Sir John Herschel.
4to, with Plates. Price 4l. 4s. cloth.

Geological Observations
On Coral Reefs, Volcanic Islands, and on South America.
By Charles Darwin, Esq.
With Maps, Plates and Woodcuts.
Price 10s. 6d. cloth.

On the Treatment of the Insane.
By John Conolly, M.D.
Demy 8vo. Price 14s. cloth.

Visit to Salt Lake.
Being a Journey across the Plains to the Mormon Settlements at Utah.
By William Chandless.
Post 8vo, with a Map. 2s. 6d. cloth.

The Red River Settlement.
By Alexander Ross.
One vol. post 8vo. Price 5s. cloth.

Fur Hunters of the West.
By Alexander Ross.
Two vols. post 8vo, with Map and Plate. Price 10s. 6d. cloth.

The Columbia River.
By Alexander Ross.
Post 8vo. Price 2s. 6d. cloth.

Hints for Investing Money.
By *Francis Playford.*
Second Edition, post 8vo.   2s. 6d. cloth.

Men, Women, and Books.
By *Leigh Hunt.*
Two vols.   Price 10s. cloth.

Table Talk. *By Leigh Hunt.*
Price 3s. 6d. cloth.

True Law of Population.
By *Thomas Doubleday.*
Third Edition, 8vo.   Price 6s. cloth.

England and her Soldiers.
By *Harriet Martineau.*
With Three Plates of Illustrative Diagrams. 1 vol. crown 8vo, price 9s. cloth.

Grammar and Dictionary of the Malay Language.
By *John Crawfurd, Esq.*
Two vols. 8vo.   Price 36s. cloth.

Turkish Campaign in Asia.
By *Charles Duncan, Esq.*
Post 8vo.   Price 2s. 6d. cloth.

Poetics:
An Essay on Poetry.
By *E. S. Dallas.*
Post 8vo.   Price 2s. 6d. cloth.

Juvenile Delinquency.
The Prize Essays.
By *M. Hill and C. F. Cornwallis.*
Post 8vo.   Price 6s. cloth.

The Militiaman.
With Two Etchings, by JOHN LEECH.
Post 8vo.   Price 9s. cloth.

The Endowed Schools of Ireland.
By *Harriet Martineau.*
8vo.   Price 3s. 6d. cloth boards.

European Revolutions of 1848.
By *E. S. Cayley, Esq.*
Crown 8vo.   Price 6s. cloth.

The Court of Henry VIII.:
Being a Selection of the Despatches of Sebastian Giustinian, Venetian Ambassador, 1515-1519.
Translated by Rawdon Brown.
Two vols. crown 8vo.   Price 21s. cloth.

Traits and Stories of Anglo-Indian Life.
By *Captain Addison.*
With Eight Illustrations.   2s. 6d. cloth.

Infanticide in India.
By *Dr. John Wilson.*
Demy 8vo.   Price 12s.

Indian Exchange Tables.
By *J. H. Roberts.*
8vo.   Second Edition, enlarged.
Price 10s. 6d. cloth.

The Turkish Interpreter:
A Grammar of the Turkish Language.
By *Major Boyd.*
8vo.   Price 12s.

Russo-Turkish Campaigns of 1828-9.
By *Colonel Chesney,*
R.A., D.C.L., F.R.S.
Third Edition.   Post 8vo, with Maps.
Price 12s. cloth.

Military Forces and Institutions of Great Britain.
By H. Byerly Thompson.
8vo. Price 5s. cloth.

Wit and Humour.
By Leigh Hunt.
Price 5s. cloth.

Jar of Honey from Hybla.
By Leigh Hunt.
Price 5s. cloth.

Manual of Therapeutics.
By E. J. Waring, M.D.
Fcap 8vo. Price 12s. 6d. cloth.

Zoology of South Africa.
By Dr. Andrew Smith.
Royal 4to, cloth, with Coloured Plates.
MAMMALIA ... £3
AVES ... 7
REPTILIA ... 5
PISCES ... 2
INVERTEBRATE ... 1

THE Botany of the Himalaya.
By Dr. Forbes Royle.
Two vols. roy. 4to, cloth, with Coloured Plates. Reduced to 5l. 5s.

Memorandums in Ireland.
By Sir John Forbes.
Two vols. post 8vo. Price 1l. 1s. cloth.

The Oxford Museum.
By H. W. Acland, M.D., and J. Ruskin, A.M.
Post 8vo, with Three Illustrations. Price 2s. 6d. cloth.

Life of Sir Robert Peel.
By Thomas Doubleday.
Two vols. 8vo. Price 18s. cloth.

The Argentine Provinces.
By William McCann, Esq.
Two vols. post 8vo, with Illustrations. Price 24s. cloth.

Travels in Assam.
By Major John Butler.
One vol. 8vo, with Plates. 12s. cloth.

Woman in France.
By Julia Kavanagh.
Two vols. post 8vo, with Portraits. Price 12s. cloth.

The Novitiate;
Or, the Jesuit in Training.
By Andrew Steinmetz.
Third Edition, post 8vo. 2s. 6d. cloth.

Signs of the Times;
Or, The Dangers to Religious Liberty in the Present Day.
By Chevalier Bunsen.
Translated by Miss S. WINKWORTH.
One vol. 8vo. Price 5s. cloth.

Principles of Agriculture;
Especially Tropical.
By B. Lovell Phillips, M.D.
Demy 8vo. Price 7s. 6d. cloth.

William Burke the Author of Junius.
By Jelinger C. Symons.
Square. Price 3s. 6d. cl.

National Songs and Legends of Roumania.
Translated by E. C. Grenville Murray, Esq.
With Music, crown 8vo. Price 2s. 6d.

FICTION.

Lavinia.
By the Author of "Doctor Antonio," "Lorenzo Benoni," &c.
Three Vols.

The Wortlebank Diary:
With Stories from Kathie Brande's Portfolio.
By Holme Lee,
Author of "Against Wind and Tide," "Sylvan Holt's Daughter," &c.
Three Vols.

Over the Cliffs.
By Mrs. Chanter,
Author of "Ferny Combes." 2 vols.

Scarsdale;
Or, Life on the Lancashire and Yorkshire Border Thirty Years ago.
3 Vols.

Esmond.
By W. M. Thackeray.
A New Edition, being the third, in 1 vol. crown 8vo. Price 6s. cloth.

Herbert Chauncey:
A Man more Sinned against than Sinning.
By Sir Arthur Hallam Elton, Bart.,
Author of "Below the Surface."
In 3 vols.

Transformation;
Or, the Romance of Monte Beni.
By Nathaniel Hawthorne,
Author of the "Scarlet Letter," &c.
In 3 vols.

The Firstborn.
By the Author of "My Lady."
Three volumes.

Netley Hall;
or, the Wife's Sister.
Foolscap 8vo. 6s., cloth.

Confidences.
By the Author of "Rita."

Cousin Stella;
Or, Conflict.
By the Author of "Violet Bank."
Three volumes.

Phantastes:
A Faerie Romance for Men and Women.
By George Macdonald.
Post 8vo. Price 10s. 6d. cloth.

Against Wind and Tide.
By Holme Lee,
Author of "Sylvan Holt's Daughter."
Three volumes.

Greymore:
A Story of Country Life.
Three volumes.

The Cousins' Courtship.
By John R. Wise.
Two vols.

The Fool of Quality.
By Henry Brooke.
New and Revised Edition, with Biographical Preface by the Rev. Chas. Kingsley, Rector of Eversley.
Two vols., post 8vo, with Portrait of the Author, price 21s.

Trust for Trust.
By A. J. Barrowcliffe,
Author of "Amberhill."
Three volumes.

Ellen Raymond;
Or, Ups and Downs.
By Mrs. Vidal,
Author of "Tales for the Bush," &c.
Three volumes.

New and Standard Works published by

CHEAP SERIES OF POPULAR WORKS.

Transformation.
By *Nathaniel Hawthorne*.
Price 2s. 6d. cloth.

The Autobiography of Leigh Hunt.
Price 2s. 6d. cloth.

WORKS OF THE BRONTË SISTERS.
Price 2s. 6d. each vol.

By *Currer Bell*.
The Professor.
To which are added the POEMS of Currer, Ellis, and Acton Bell. Now first collected.

Jane Eyre.
Shirley.
Villette.

Wuthering Heights and Agnes Grey.
By *Ellis and Acton Bell*.
With Memoir by CURRER BELL.

The Tenant of Wildfell Hall.
By *Acton Bell*.

Life of Charlotte Brontë (Currer Bell),
By *Mrs. Gaskell*.

Lectures on the English Humourists
Of the Eighteenth Century.
By *W. M. Thackeray*,
Author of "Vanity Fair," "Esmond," "The Virginians," &c.
Price 2s. 6d. cloth.

The Town.
By *Leigh Hunt*.
With Forty-five Engravings.
Price 2s. 6d. cloth.

Kathie Brande:
The Fireside History of a Quiet Life.
By *Holme Lee*,
Author of "Sylvan Holt's Daughter."
Price 2s. 6d. cloth.

Below the Surface.
By *Sir A. H. Elton, Bart., M.P.*
Price 2s. 6d. cloth.

British India.
By *Harriet Martineau*.
Price 2s. 6d. cloth.

Italian Campaigns of General Bonaparte.
By *George Hooper*.
With a Map. Price 2s. 6d. cloth.

Deerbrook.
By *Harriet Martineau*.
Price 2s. 6d. cloth.

Tales of the Colonies.
By *Charles Rowcroft*. 2s. 6d. cloth.

A Lost Love.
By *Ashford Owen*. 2s. cloth.

Romantic Tales
(Including "Avillion")
By *the Author of "John Halifax, Gentleman."* 2s. 6d. cloth.

Domestic Stories.
By *the same Author*. 2s. 6d. cloth.

After Dark.
By *Wilkie Collins*. 2s. 6d. cloth.

School for Fathers.
By *Talbot Gwynne*. 2s. cloth.

Paul Ferroll.
Fourth Edition. Price 2s. cloth.

Smith, Elder and Co. 65, Cornhill, London.

JUVENILE AND EDUCATIONAL.

The Parents' Cabinet
Of Amusement and Instruction for Young Persons.
New Edition, revised, in Twelve Shilling Volumes, with numerous Illustrations.

⁎ The work is now complete in 4 vols. extra cloth, gilt edges, at 3s. 6d. each; or in 6 vols. extra cloth, gilt edges, at 2s. 6d. each.
Every volume is complete in itself, and sold separately.

By the Author of "Round the Fire," &c.

I.
Round the Fire:
Six Stories for Young Readers.
Square 16mo, with Four Illustrations. Price 2s. 6d. cloth.

II.
Unica:
A Story for a Sunday Afternoon.
With Four Illustrations. 2s. 6d. cloth.

III.
Old Gingerbread and the Schoolboys.
With Four Coloured Plates. 2s. 6d. cl.

IV.
Willie's Birthday:
Showing how a Little Boy did what he Liked, and how he Enjoyed it.
With Four Illustrations. 2s. cloth.

V.
Willie's Rest:
A Sunday Story.
With Four Illustrations. 2s. cloth.

VI.
Uncle Jack, the Fault Killer.
With Four Illustrations. 2s. 6d. cloth.

Legends from Fairy Land.
By Holme Lee,
Author of "Kathie Brande," "Sylvan Holt's Daughter," &c.
With Eight Illustrations. 3s. 6d. cloth.

The King of the Golden River;
Or, the Black Brothers.
By John Ruskin, M.A.
Third Edition, with 22 Illustrations by Richard Doyle. Price 2s. 6d.

Elementary Works on Social Economy.
By William Ellis.
Uniform in foolscap 8vo, half-bound.
I.—OUTLINES OF SOCIAL ECONOMY. 1s. 6d.
II.—PROGRESSIVE LESSONS IN SOCIAL SCIENCE. 2s.
III.—INTRODUCTION TO THE SOCIAL SCIENCES. 2s.
IV.—OUTLINES OF THE UNDERSTANDING. 2s.
V.—WHAT AM I? WHERE AM I? WHAT OUGHT I TO DO? &c. 1s. sewed.

Religion in Common Life.
By William Ellis.
Post 8vo. Price 7s. 6d. cloth.

Books for the Blind.
Printed in raised Roman letters, at the Glasgow Asylum.

Rhymes for Little Ones.
With 16 Illustrations. 1s. 6d. cloth.

Stories from the Parlour Printing Press.
By the Authors of the "Parent's Cabinet."
Fcap 8vo. Price 2s. cloth.

Juvenile Miscellany.
Six Engravings. Price 2s. 6d. cloth.

RECENT POETRY.

Prometheus' Daughter:
A Poem.
By Col. James Abbott.
Crown 8vo.

Christ's Company and other Poems.
By Richard Watson Dixon, M.A.
Fcap 8vo, price 5s. cloth.

Sybil, and other Poems.
By John Lyttelton.
Fcap 8vo, price 4s. cloth.

Memories of Merton.
By John Bruce Norton.
Fcap 8vo. Price 5s. cloth.

Stanzas.
By Archibald York.
Fcap 8vo. Price 2s. 6d. cloth.

Hannibal; a Drama.
Fcap 8vo. Price 5s. cloth.

A Man's Heart: a Poem.
By Dr. Charles Mackay.
Post 8vo. Price 5s. cloth.

Edwin and Ethelburga:
A Drama.
By Frederick W. Wyon.
Fcap 8vo. Price 4s. cloth.

Shelley; and other Poems.
By John Alfred Langford.
Fcap 8vo. Price 5s. cloth.

Magdalene: a Poem.
Fcap 8vo. Price 1s.

Homely Ballads
For the Working Man's Fireside.
By Mary Sewell.
Ninth Thousand. Post 8vo. Cloth, 1s.

Stories in Verse for the Street and Lane:
By Mrs. Sewell.
Post 8vo. Cloth, price 1s.

THE CORNHILL MAGAZINE.
Edited by W. M. Thackeray.
Price One Shilling Monthly, with Illustrations.
A NEW STORY, BY MR. THACKERAY,
ENTITLED
"THE ADVENTURES OF PHILIP ON HIS WAY THROUGH THE WORLD,
SHOWING WHO ROBBED HIM, WHO HELPED HIM, AND WHO PASSED HIM BY;"
To be continued throughout Sixteen Numbers, commenced on the First of January.

VOLUMES I. and II., each containing 768 pages of Letterpress, with 12 Illustrations, 40 Vignettes and Diagrams, and a Chart, is now ready, handsomely bound in Embossed Cloth. Price 7s. 6d.

For the convenience of Subscribers, the Embossed CLOTH COVER for the Volume will be sold separately, price One Shilling.

READING COVERS for separate Numbers have also been prepared, price Sixpence in plain Cloth, or One Shilling and Sixpence in French Morocco.

London: Printed by SMITH, ELDER and Co., Little Green Arbour Court, Old Bailey, E.C.

www.ingramcontent.com/pod-product-compliance
Lightning Source LLC
Chambersburg PA
CBHW051733300426
44115CB00007B/550